The Spatial Structure of Development

Westview Replica Editions

This book is a Westview Replica Edition. The concept of
Replica Editions is a response to the crisis in academic and
informational publishing. Library budgets for books have been
severely curtailed; economic pressures on the university presses
and the few private publishing companies primarily interested in
scholarly manuscripts have severely limited the capacity of the
industry to properly serve the academic and research communities.
Many manuscripts dealing with important subjects, often representing the highest level of scholarship, are today not economically viable publishing projects. Or, if they are accepted for
publication, they are often subject to lead times ranging from
one to three years. Scholars are understandably frustrated when
they realize that their first-class research cannot be published
within a reasonable time frame, if at all.

Westview Replica Editions are our practical solution to the
problem. The concept is simple. We accept a manuscript in camera-
ready form and move it immediately into the production process.
The responsibility for textual and copy editing lies with the
author or sponsoring organization. If necessary we will advise
the author on proper preparation of footnotes and bibliography.
We prefer that the manuscript be typed according to our speci-
fications, though it may be acceptable as typed for a dissertation or prepared in some other clearly organized and readable
way. The end result is a book produced by lithography and bound
in hard covers. Initial edition sizes range from 500 to 800
copies, and a number of recent Replicas are already in second
printings. We include among Westview Replica Editions only works
of outstanding scholarly quality or of great informational value,
and we will continue to exercise our usual editorial standards
and quality control.

The Spatial Structure of Development:
A Study of Kenya
edited by R. A. Obudho and D. R. F. Taylor

In this examination of the complex correlations between spatial relationships and development planning in international, national, regional, and local contexts, the authors contend that an understanding of a country's or region's spatial linkages is essential to any attempt to solve its problems of growth. They provide basic data, not easily accessible elsewhere, from which emerges a general framework for spatial planning in Africa.

A central theme of the book is that the urbanization process in Africa is substantially different from that experienced in the developed countries. The authors articulate the nature of the interpenetration of modern and traditional forces that will shape future development in Africa and suggest new approaches and methods for understanding and formulating development strategies and goals.

R. A. Obudho is planning analyst for Johnson & Johnson Worldwide and coadjunct lecturer in urban studies, Rutgers University. Dr. Obudho has published numerous books and articles on the spatial aspects of urbanization and development planning.
D. R. F. Taylor, professor of geography and international affairs at Carleton University, served for five years as education officer with the government of Kenya, during which time he also conducted field research.

The Spatial Structure of Development: A Study of Kenya

edited by R. A. Obudho and D. R. F. Taylor

Westview Press **/** Boulder, Colorado

A Westview Replica Edition

Published in 1979 in the United States of America by
    Westview Press, Inc.
    5500 Central Avenue
    Boulder, Colorado 80301
    Frederick A. Praeger, Publisher

Library of Congress Catalog Card Number: 79-5183
ISBN: 0-89158- 597-4

Printed and bound in the United States of America

In memory of
Samson Mugo Kimani

This book is dedicated to the memory of a colleague
and friend, Dr. Samson Mugo Kimani. Samson Kimani
was essentially a gentle and sensitive man with a
deep respect and concern for other people. His
untimely death cut short a promising career as a
teacher and scholar. At the time of his death he
was a Senior Lecturer and Head of the Department of
Geography, Kenyatta University College. Working
closely with Samson in a field research environment
was a rewarding experience. He showed a degree of
patience and understanding in difficult research
situations which was exemplary. To his research in
Murang'a he brought a personal awareness and commitment to rural people which enhanced the work in a
way which few others could have done. It is hoped
that this book will keep alive some of the concerns
and approaches which Samson engendered.

Contents

ix

Tables

Table

Figures

Figure

Preface

    The purpose of this book is to examine the role
of space in the development process in Kenya. In
comparison with writings on other aspects of development this is a topic which has received relatively
little attention. Although the book is focused on
Kenya as a case study it clearly has much wider theoretical and policy implications. Johnson, an economic
historian was a pioneer in this field with his
Organization of Space in Developing Countries published in 1970. The work of Soja, The Geography of
Modernization in Kenya (1968) and that of Riddell,
The Spatial Dynamics of Modernization in Sierra
Leone (1970) were also keynote pieces in the geography of modernization in Africa.
    Since 1970 however a great deal of research and
rethinking has taken place on the role of space in
the development process and the debate on this topic
is clearly evident in the chapters of this book. The
underlying issues of spatial equality and inequality
are present in almost every chapter especially in
those by Taylor, Ominde and Soja who has radically
revised his earlier views. In addition to the general
issues of spatial development the various chapters
deal with urban space, rural space, spatial interaction, and the diffusion of innovation and in each
case are contributions from authors involved with
basic field research in Kenya.
    The chapter on the location and function of
shopping centers in Nairobi is the work of the late
Kenyan geographer Samson Kimani to whom this book is
dedicated. Samson's death at a relatively early age
was a great loss to Kenyan geography. He was very
much a proponent of the "new geography" in Kenya and
the desire to commemorate his contribution to the
discipline has been a strong moving force in putting
together this book. Royalties derived from this
volume will go to Samson's family.

Acknowledgements

This volume could not have been produced without
the enthusiastic support and unrelenting patience of
the contributors without which the production of this
volume would not have been possible. Their efforts
have been tireless and they have produced some fine
pieces of scholarship. To them we must express our
special thanks. We hope that what we have assembled
here will be a contribution to the further understanding of the spatial structure of development especially in Kenya.

Organization, research and editorial assistance
has been given by a number of people and our thanks
go to all of them. The editors would like to express
special thanks to the following individuals for their
invaluable support: for organization Margie Babash
and Beverly Braxton, for research and administration
Barbara George, for the illustrations Christine Earl,
and for the final editing, preparation and typing of
the manuscript Phyllis Kingston.

All these individuals are, however, absolved of
guilt by association for any inaccuracies that still
remain in our volume.

R.A.O.
D.R.F.T.
New Brunswick, N.J., U.S.A. and Ottawa, Canada
June 1979

1. Spatial Aspects of the Development Process

D. R. F. Taylor

The role of space in the development process in Africa and in other parts of the third world was largely neglected in development literature until 1970 when Johnson's important contribution The Organization of Space in Developing Nations[1] appeared. This is perhaps not too surprising given that regional science, a major subject area in which spatial aspects of development are considered, did not gain prominence until after the Second World War. In addition substantial concern with the concept of "development" and development planning in the third world context did not manifest itself until about 1950.

In 1979, however, it is no longer necessary to make a case for the importance of space in the development process in the third world. The vital importance of both spatial structure and spatial process is now generally accepted by most development theorists although the implementation of spatial approaches to development planning is lagging.

There are perhaps real advantages to the late emergence of spatial planning in developing nations because it is becoming increasingly clear that existing spatial planning theory and practice require considerable review and modification to achieve the goals of successful development. This chapter will concern itself with some major issues facing those concerned with the role of space in the development process, and will examine these issues in the Kenyan context.

Space and Development

The role of space in the development process cannot be discussed without considering the basic question of development itself. Spatial development

1

theory and practice cannot be divorced from questions such as what kind of development and development for whom?

In recent years, there have been some fundamental changes in the field of development thinking. Some of these have been paraphrased in a recent article by Dudley Seers entitled "The New Meaning of Development".[2] He points out that disillusionment with the neo-classical paradigm of development and its emphasis on growth led, by the end of the 1960s, to a redefinition of the term development: "... growth was in itself insufficient, indeed perhaps socially damaging: a country was not enjoying 'development' unless in addition inequality, unemployment and poverty were declining."[3]

As attitudes began to change a new paradigm, summed up by Singer's phrase "redistribution with growth" emerged. This paradigm has a strong emphasis on satisfying basic needs and reducing inequality in the rural areas.

Seers claims, however, that there is "an air of unreality" about this approach as governments, despite policy rhetoric, have done little to change distribution. This perceived lack of action by governments is interpreted in different ways. "The basic assumption of the development profession is that they need technical help to do so. Radical critics, on the other hand, pointing to political interest rather than technical capacity, have repeatedly posed quite a simple question in one form or another: why should those with economic and political power give it away as these policies require, especially to the rural poor. The implication drawn by some is that social progress will be indefinitely prevented by a homogeneous ruling class until it is in due course overthrown in a revolution."[4]

In Seer's view, elites seem determined to pursue styles of consumption far beyond the reach of the majority of their fellow citizens and he argues that "The inertia of consumption and productive patterns was obviously in part attributable to external links. True independence was not merely one of the intrinsic objectives, but also a condition (though insufficient in itself of course) for achieving the rest."[5] In Seer's view, "The time is indeed ripe for another critical look at the meaning of development ... The essential element to add — as is being widely recognized — is self reliance."[6]

Seers suggests that a paradigm with a self-reliant component is likely to be more acceptable

2

than redistribution with growth to elites because
"... such a programme may appeal to what seems in
many countries to be a stronger force than social
conscience — nationalism."[7] He also suggests that
moves toward self-reliance are likely to become
cumulative whereas redistribution policies often run
into barriers. The paradigm is a new one and Seers
admits that "We do not yet understand much about
what self-reliance implies for development strategies"[8], and calls for a study of greater independence
with redistribution with growth which to him is the
essence of a new strategy.
Self reliance is not seen as autarchy —

> Of course, an emphasis on reducing dependence
> does not mean aiming at autarchy. How far it
> is desirable, or even possible to go in that
> direction, depends upon a country's size,
> location and natural resources; on its cultural
> homogeneity and the depth of its traditions; on
> the extent to which its economy needs imported
> inputs to satisfy consumption patterns which
> have to be taken — at least in the short term —
> as political minima. The key to a development
> strategy of the type suggested is not to break
> all links, which would almost anywhere be
> socially damaging and politically unworkable,
> but to adopt a selective approach to external
> influences of all types."[9]

Seers argues that such a strategy is applicable
to all countries and argues for the " ... explicit
endorsement of nationalism, including our own —
which ceases to be an 'obstacle' to development and
becomes instead part of the very essence of it."[10]
He is, however, not particularly optimistic that his
concepts will gain quick general acceptance: "In any
case, the cultural lag before this new definition is
accepted is likely to be particularly long. Besides
challenging a political alliance, which is not ineffective, and powerful commercial interests, it
threatens the comfortable academic ghetto of development studies ... ".[11]
What are the implications of all of this for
spatial development? It is useful to quote Seers
again:

> Cultural lags protect paradigms long after they
> have lost relevance. The neo-classical growth
> paradigm has been remarkably tenacious — in
> fact it still survives in places. It has suited

3

so many interests. It has been highly
acceptable to governments that want to slur
over internal, ethnic or social problems ...
It has generated almost endless academic
research projects and stimulated theorists to
construct elaborate models. It has not been
fundamentally unacceptable to economic modern-
izers across a broad political spectrum, including Marxists as well as members of the Chicago
school. Above all, as a paradigm it is very
simple."[12]

Two basic points emerge in relation to spatial
development: firstly, the neo-classical growth
paradigm is very much alive and well in many developing nations and secondly, existing spatial development theory is almost exclusively based on that
paradigm. The latter point is particularly significant because, if it is valid, then spatial planning
theory as it currently stands has little to offer to
governments who wish to adopt a development strategy
different from the neo-classical growth paradigm.
As the new development paradigms outlined earlier
have been formulated, there has been little corresponding emergence of spatial development theory.
Seers talks of "cultural lags" in the acceptance of
new definitions of development. There is an even
greater lag in the response of spatial theorists and
planners to these definitions. Seers is advocating
the acceptance of a new paradigm from the "redistribution with growth" model whereas spatial development
theory and practice have not yet responded effectively to the substantial changes which led to the
rejection of the earlier neo-classical growth model.
    New directions in theory and practice are, how-
ever, beginning to emerge.[13] Stöhr and Tödtling[14]
have presented some interesting anti-theses to
current spatial development doctrine. The authors
argue convincingly that the conceptual basis of
current development practice are: heavy reliance on
neo-classical economics; a strong concentration on
large-scale vertically organized institution-based
processes to the neglect of non-market and informal
processes; and a strong emphasis on economic process
to the exclusion of processes of a social and political nature. The empirical evidence they consider
suggests that the overall result of existing policies
has been a widening rather than a narrowing of disparities, and that growth centre/hinterland spread
effects have generally been small and limited in geographical extent. The evidence from the case studies

4

they examine leads them to conclude that in the context of policies for broad spatial development it is difficult to justify growth center policies for lagging areas. The evidence suggests that there is a lack of spread effects downward through the urban hierarchy or from a growth center to a broader hinterland. Increase of income in rural areas and lower order centers gives rise to income multipliers in higher order centers but the process does not work in reverse.

They suggest, as an addition to existing policies, a policy of "selective spatial closure" in certain conditions, which in essence is a policy of greater regional self reliance with a more explicit concern for non-economic variables. The authors argue:

> If strategies of selective spatial closure were adopted as explicit components of regional development policy, coherent sets of such policy instruments adapted to the specific conditions of the respective country or region would have to be elaborated and subjected to empirical testing. Only empirical tests will show whether such a strategy is better able than current regional development practice to contribute to established objectives of spatial equity. [15]

Stöhr and Palme, in a later paper dealing explicitly with developing nations,[16] argue for a strategy of regional "selective self reliance". Stöhr and Palme's approach is gradualist rather than revolutionary but has considerable relevance to the new development paradigm outlined by Seers.

Friedmann and Douglass have also explicitly recognized the problems and have suggested a new direction for policy. They identify the linkage between the neo-classical growth paradigm and regional development theory and practice clearly:

> The last few years have seen a reaching out for new paradigms of planning for development. The old paradigm is no longer compelling in its logic. The underlying idea was that human happiness and sense of well-being could flow, more or less spontaneously, from the relentless pursuit of economic growth; that economic growth would most readily result from rapid industrialization; that rapid industrialization would be accommodated most efficiently in a few metropolitan centres from where its benefits would 'spread'

5

to the rest of the national territory; that
planning for growth, industrialization, and
urbanization could be accomplished only through
coordinated central planning; and that coordinated central planning was a technical task that
would be solved through complex econometric
modelling joined to sophisticated administrative
technique.

Spatial planners tried to find a place for themselves within this scheme. Their principal
contribution to development planning was the
notion of growth poles and growth centres ...

In both its nonspatial and spatial dimensions,
however, this paradigm has come under fire. On
the one hand, it is argued that the paradigm
has failed to bring about the results expected
from it. On the other hand, the last few years
seem to be signalling the transition of the
international economy to a new state of affairs
which suggests that the unmodified pursuit of
the old paradigm would be, to put it bluntly,
suicidal.

As a consequence of this double criticism, the
contours of a possible new paradigm are beginning to emerge. Its primary objective is no
longer economic growth but social development,
with focus on specific human needs. According
to this paradigm, development must be fitted to
ecological constraints; priority attention (in
agrarian economies) must be given to rural
development; and planning for rural development
must be decentralized, participatory, and deeply
immersed in the particulars of local settings.
Planning, therefore, will have to be based on
qualitative judgements, as much as quantitative
techniques, and its style will have to be
transactive. [17]

Friedmann and Douglass surveyed regional development experiences in Asia and found that in few
cases were the central goals being met. They argued
that "The urgency of the present situation calls for
heightened political commitment to an inward-looking
and rurally-based strategy of national development.[18]
Their suggestion was a policy of "agropolitan development" using the agropolis, or "city-in-the-field",
as the center of largely self-reliant regions of
50,000 to 150,000 people.

6

These ideas have been picked up and expanded
upon by Lo and Salih[19] in the Asian context and
research is now underway to operationalize the new
agropolitan approach. As a first step, Lo and Salih
have presented spatial models of Asian countries
within the world system. They identify three dualis-
tic relationships: between North and South, urban
and rural, and formal and informal in both rural and
urban areas.

> The three dualistic relationships — North-South,
> urban-rural and formal-informal   all related
> and integrated in a complex manner which differs
> from country to country depending on the prevail-
> ing conditions related to resources, technology,
> demography and development ideology — are the
> context in which economic growth and development
> proceed. Within the general set of dependent
> dualistic structures and relationships, however,
> there is a need for further clarification
> before specific development conditions and
> opportunities can be outlined. [20]

The authors see development ideology as vital,
arguing that the choice is between a self-reliant
model and a free market model. In addition to this
the combination of natural resource availability and
technology is important.
Having described the external dependency structures and their influence on the three dualities
identified, the authors go on to consider the internal factors influencing rural-urban distortions and
distinguish a four-fold typology of regional structures. This framework is being used as the basis
of regional policy formulation in Asia.[21]
Friedmann and Weaver[22] provide a direct challenge to one of the dominant themes of existing
spatial theory and practice, namely that the
functional integration of national space is necessary if development is to occur. Weaver puts the
argument very bluntly indeed:

> My basic theme is that continued functional
> integration of the space economy, with its
> attendant territorial division of labor and
> polarization of economic and political power,
> is a major cause of such problems as urban
> congestion, regional inequalities, rural
> poverty and political rebellion. Despite the
> conventions of inherited regional development
> theory, and the emphasis of recent neo-Marxist

criticism, I will argue for the political
benefits of <u>territorial development</u> through
<u>selective regional closure.</u> [23]

Stöhr and Taylor[24] have drawn together a comprehensive set of studies where the issues outlined
above and those of "development from above" or
"development from below" are fully debated and
discussed but although the evidence suggests that,
with the notable exception of China, both regional
and interpersonal disparities are increasing, there
is no general agreement either on causes or on
solutions. The "development from below" school is
gaining in strength but is still viewed with
considerable skepticism by both neo-classicists and
neo-Marxists alike. Neo-classicists like Hansen
argue that existing spatial development strategies
have not failed but have simply not been properly
implemented nor given sufficient time to work. Some
disparity, he argues, is inevitable in the early
stages of development but this will disappear over
time. What is clear, however, from the evidence
available, is that if Hansen, Williamson and others
are right, then the time period required for disparities to lessen is much longer than was originally
anticipated. Modification of existing spatial development approaches has been suggested to remedy their
more obvious deficiencies, including a greater degree
of local participation and direct rather than indirect
policies to reduce disparities. These have been well
summarized by Rondinelli and Ruddle[25] whose proposed
strategy can be described as spatial integration from
below. These authors do not question the value of
integration for development, simply the way in which
integration can be achieved.
    Marxists and neo-Marxists also question any
strategy which does not involve the state in a dominant central planning role, and argue that existing
inequalities in centrally-planned economies where
these are admitted, will disappear over time as true
Communism is achieved. It is interesting that in the
latter 19th and earlier 20th centuries there was
considerable debate between Marxist and Anarchist
theoreticians on the role of local communities as
opposed to the State which has many similarities to
the issues being raised today.
    As well as the socio-political and economic
arguments relating to spatial development, there has
also been the emergence of an increased awareness of
ecological and environmental factors. Concern for
the impact on the environment of development strategies

and for an explicit consideration of the role of the
environment as a central variable affecting strategies has reemerged as indicated by the writings of
authors such as Sachs.[26]
    It is clear that a considerable degree of serious
reformulation of spatial planning theory is underway
and that this is likely to result in new policies. A
new synthesis involving the integration of socio-poli-
tical, economic and ecological elements is required
but as yet this has not been achieved. Unless new
policies are formulated and presented in a form which
will permit policy makers to implement them then it
is clear that no change can take place regardless of
the political will to do this. This is a major
challenge facing spatial theorists and planners today.
    For example, Seers says of his self-reliant
strategy,

        ... we do not yet understand much about what
        self reliance implies for development strategies
        but some of the economic aspects are obvious
        enough. They include reducing dependence on
        imported necessities, especially basic foods,
        petroleum and its products, capital equipment
        and expertise. This would involve changing
        consumption patterns as well as increasing the
        relevant productive capacity. Redistribution
        of income would help but policies would also be
        needed to change living styles at given income
        levels — using taxes, price policies, advertis-
        ing, and perhaps rationing. In many countries,
        self reliance would also involve increasing
        national ownership and control, especially of
        subsoil assets, and improving national
        capacity for negotiating with transnational
        corporations.

        There are other implications as well, especially
        in cultural policy. These are more country-
        specific, but as a general rule, let us say that
        'development' now implies, inter alia, reducing
        cultural dependence on one or more of the great
        powers. [27]

    If a self-reliant strategy based on greater
independence with redistribution and growth is
adopted, what theory and practice would spatial
planners suggest to ensure its effective implementation? We are fairly sure that existing "center-down"
approaches are inappropriate but what have we to put
in their place? We have the skeleton of emerging

"bottom-up" strategies but we still are required to provide the skeleton with substantial flesh.

Clearly developmental ideology and opportunities vary widely from country to country and each country must decide for itself the model which best fits its own economic, social, political, historical and ecological situation, but however development is defined, it must in my view, have real meaning to the vast majority of the poor in developing nations, the bulk of whom live in the rural areas. Spatial planners often lose sight of the fact that "place poverty" and "people poverty" are not synonymous and that the removal of spatial disparity does not necessarily lead to the removal of interpersonal disparity. Reductions in regional disparity can in some instances actually intensify interpersonal disparity as Gilbert and Goodman have so ably demonstrated.[28]

Spatial Structure and Process in Kenya

There are a number of different ways in which the development of spatial structure and process in Kenya can be interpreted. Soja in the Geography of Modernization of Kenya[29] presents what is still a major analytical approach which implicitly suggests that progress is equivalent to "modernization" which he defines and measures as being related to:

1. The development of a transportation network, partly in terms of the multiplication of routes but more importantly in increased traffic along these routes

2. The expansion of communication and information media as shown by their distributional pattern and the intensity of their use

3. Increased urbanization and the growth of an integrated urban system, including growth of rural-urban interaction

4. A breaking down of traditional ethnic compartmentalization

5. The emergence of an exchange of money economy as opposed to subsistence activities

6. The development of education, both on a per capita basis as well as in total numbers reaching particular levels of education

10

7. The extent of participation in non-parochial forms of organization and activity (e.g., political parties, national elections, trade unions, and other forms of voluntary associations)

8. Geographic proximity to and interaction with the most modernized sectors of society, particularly the core area(s) acting as the major concentrator, adapter, and distributor of the forces of modernization

9. The degree of physical or geographic mobility, both internally and beyond the given state-area or its subunit. [30]

Although Soja himself has now radically revised his views,[31] Kenya's spatial planning policies since independence in 1963 have continued to stress both modernization and integration as outlined above. Spatial planning is almost a textbook example of what Friedmann and Douglass describe as "the old paradigm".

Spatial planning in Kenya has to be considered within the political and ideological context in which it is found. Despite a nominal commitment to "African socialism" Kenya is clearly " ... a country relying on the forces of capitalism, productive efficiency and trade."[32] The influence of big business and finance is strong as are the links with metropolitan centers in Europe and North America. It might be argued that the existing spatial planning approach is well suited to the continuation of this pattern.

The internal political history of Kenya since independence should also be considered. A major task after independence was the building of national unity. "Tribalism" was seen as an evil, and as a barrier to national progress. "Tribes" often had clearly-defined territorial units and consequently decentralized planning on a regional or territorial base was seen by many as politically dangerous in that it might foster disintegration. The party in power, the Kenya African National Union (KANU) has a slogan "Umoja" (unity), in direct opposition to its chief opponent at the time of independence, the Kenya African Democratic Union, which campaigned under the slogan "Majimbo" (regionalism). KANU came to dominate Kenyan politics and increasingly centralized all political and economic power. The 1960s saw constant erosion of the political power of the regions by the center. Even today, the term "regional planning" is

11

rarely used, the terms "rural" or "district" planning being substituted. These political constraints seriously limit effective spatial planning of a decentralized type.

The Government of Kenya has identified its developmental aims in the current Development Plan for the country[33] and these include economic growth, reduction of disparity especially between urban and rural areas, employment creation, and social justice. These basic aims have remained similar since independence although the emphasis has changed with rural development now being seen as central.

In spatial development terms the "centre-down", urban-based, outward-looking model continues to dominate in Kenya and the political appeal of this to the present government is strong. When this is allied to the economic benefits of promised "trickle-down" over time, its appeal increases and politicians can rationalize their political policies in terms of "sound and objective" spatial development theory. Both growth pole policies and the creation of a new and more efficient urban hierarchy are explicit components of Kenya's strategy.

Many authors have been critical of spatial planning in Kenya and Acquaah-Harrison comments, "Often the assessments ignore the realities of politics and national development and they tend to offend political decisionmakers, chief planners and administrators. This is probably one of the reasons why chief decisionmakers ignore research and the evaluation of programmes."[34]

It can, however, be argued that Kenya's spatial development cannot be understood unless the dualities and contradictions which exist are explicitly recognized. Despite the fact that such analysis may not be particularly palatable to some politicians it is clear that many of the Government of Kenya's stated aims are in conflict and spatial planning has failed to take explicit notice of this. Eastwell comments,

> ... there will tend to be a basic conflict between the Government of Kenya's current policies of increasing total economic growth, allowing unchecked population growth, forcing people to go 'back to the land', and attempting to reduce urban-rural income disparities. [35]

Eastwell attributes these basic conflicts to ecological constraints but they could equally well be explained in ideological terms. There are many authors such as Leys,[36] Soja and Weaver,[37] and others who argue

12

that current strategies in Kenya can only lead to increasing disparity over time.

Figure 1 is a spatial model of the Kenyan economy extending previous work[38] to give an analytical framework comparable with that developed by Lo and Salih and described earlier. The three dualities are that between North and South, that between urban and rural, and that between formal and informal, in both rural and urban subsystems. Three structural characteristics and eight transformation processes are identified.

As a development ideology, the Kenyan Government has clearly chosen a free market model with continuing integration of Kenya into the international economy. A major structural characteristic is, therefore, what Lo and Salih call a relatively open domestic market. In the Kenyan case, there are very strong North-South linkages — a continuation of Kenya's colonial heritage.

The resource base is almost entirely agricultural, there being no minerals of great significance. Kenya has excellent conditions for arable agriculture but only in limited quantities. Over 80 percent of the land is unsuitable for arable agriculture, and with one of the highest rates of population increase in the world (3.4 percent per annum), the availability of good agricultural land is already a constraint. The resource base could therefore be described as adequate, but in dynamic terms this will become increasingly less so as population increases. In Eastwell's opinion, " ... Kenya's agricultural resource base is insufficient to provide a rising standard of living for the country's projected population increase ..."[39]

In terms of the third structural variable identified by Lo and Salih — technology — Kenya can clearly be classified as having relatively low technology.

Kenya has some of the structural characteristics of Lo and Salih's Model I described as Resource Rich Open Dependent Economies, except that untapped arable land and natural resources are not available. In this respect, Kenya is beginning to approach one of the major structural characteristics of Model II, the Low Per-Capita Resource Semi-Open Economy, i.e. low per-capita resource availability. In structural terms, therefore, Kenya is somewhere between Models I and II as identified by Lo and Salih.

Eight transformation processes are identified in Figure 1. Kenya, like so many other African countries, was a colony and this has been a major factor in determining and structuring all three of the dualities described earlier. Colonialization led to alienation

13

FIGURE 1.1

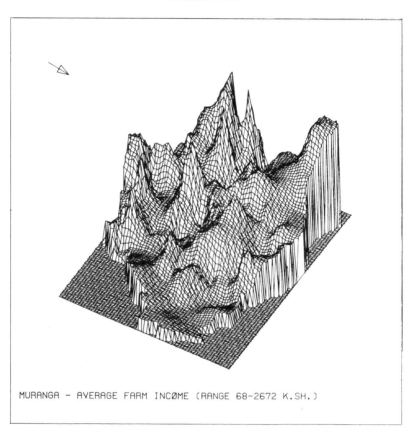

MURANGA - AVERAGE FARM INCØME (RANGE 68-2672 K.SH.)

of land by European interests mainly in the form of
farms and estates. There was considerable direct
European settlement.

Given the population density at the time (around
1900 A.D.) it could be argued that there was under-
utilized arable land available, but as population
densities increased, competition for available arable
land — a scarce and largely fixed resource —
increased. It should be noted however that much of
the land alienated to Europeans was far from being
"empty" and much of the better land was either tempo-
rarily abandoned due to a series of ecological disasters, or part of the migratory territory of pastoral
peoples. The land question was a critical factor in
the independence struggle in Kenya and continues to
be vital to an understanding of Kenya today. Independence in 1963 led to a breakup of parts of the former
"White Highlands" into settlement schemes but a substantial portion of the land is still in the form of
coffee or tea estates under the control of large
companies, many of which are subsidiaries of foreign-
based transnational corporations.

European settlement was accompanied by investment in and development of the commercial crop sector
especially crops such as coffee and tea. This led to
the second transformation process identified on **Figure 1.1** — resource-based primary product export.
This process continues today although there has been
an increasing involvement of African smallholders in
the process so that more than half of current agricultural exports such as coffee now come from farms of
ten hectares or less.

The third transformation process identified in
Figure 1 is foreign investment in import-substituting
modern industry. There has also been investment in
agricultural processing industries for export and
although the involvement of domestic capital is increasing rapidly Kenyan industry is still largely
foreign-controlled.[40] Modern industry has in several
instances led to the destruction of small-scale,
labor-intensive traditional industries such as soap
making and shoe making.[41]

These transformation processes led to the emergence of dualities in both the urban and rural sectors which are continuing and becoming more intensive.
The former colonial government concentrated almost
exclusively, in its rural development investments, on
the rural formal sector, especially in the White Highlands. Political independence has modified but not
substantially altered this process, although more
attention is being paid to the former "African Reserve"

15

areas. Land consolidation in these areas, a process
by which scattered fragments of land are brought together with a legal title being issued to an individual, was started in the 1950s by the colonial government. This policy has been continued by the independent Government of Kenya which has tended to concentrate its efforts on the "progressive" farmers
brought into being largely as a result of land consolidation, the selective introduction of cash crops
and related policies. The new political elite has
also been active in buying land in the former White
Highlands. Some land was transferred into high
density settlement schemes but many of the farms
ended up in the hands, not of the landless, but of
an emerging bureaucratic and political Kenyan
African elite.[42] It could be argued that land ownership has become increasingly more restrictive over
time — the process of land consolidation and the
buying of land by the elite cancelling out the gains
made by the takeover of sections of the White Highlands and the establishment of settlement schemes
for small farmers who were previously landless.
With land being a scarce resource, and population
increasing, the problem is clearly a serious one.

In the urban areas colonial policies made little
provision for African involvement. The towns were
seen largely as "European islands" and the colonial
period was marked by periodic destruction of the
"shanty towns" which grew up around the major city
of Nairobi. The ILO mission[43] documented the processes which have led to the increasing disparity
between the urban formal and urban informal sectors
and indicated that the policies of the independent
Government of Kenya towards the informal sector,
although more enlightened in some respects than
those of the former colonial government, were still
somewhat repressive. Recently there have been
changes and the urban informal sector is now receiv-
ing more positive attention.

Although these transformation processes (identified as 4 and 5 on Figure 1) led to increasing disparity in both the urban and rural subsystems, the
disparities were different in absolute terms. The
urban formal sector became increasingly more prosperous than its rural counterpart and the urban informal
sector, despite its difficulties, was seen by many
Kenyans as offering better prospects than landless-
ness and unemployment in the rural informal sector.
Increasing rural-urban disparity is seen as a major
factor in causing the sixth transformation process
identified in Figure 1 — excessive rural-urban

migration. Migration has taken place into both the
formal and informal sectors but in scale the migration from the rural informal to the urban informal
has been many times that of migration to the formal
sector.

Processes 7 and 8 on the diagram give an indication of some additional linkages between formal and
informal sectors in both urban and rural subsystems
and these lead to some redistribution and reduction
of disparity. There are also such relationships
between the urban formal and both the rural formal
and informal sectors.

Kinship-based economic remittances and return
and circular migration are important processes.
These occur in both the rural formal and informal
sectors and are an important redistribution and
"spread" mechanism about which relatively little is
known. There are difficulties in measurement
involved but it is clear that substantial amounts of
capital generated in urban areas (possibly as high
as twenty-five percent of total wages for example)
find their way into rural areas by these routes.[44]
Migration studies have shown that circular migration
of both a long-term and short-term nature may be
much more common than has previously been realized,
leading to transference of ideas and experience as
well as resources. Without such processes rural-
urban disparity would be even greater than it is at
present. The extent to which disparity is increasing
or decreasing and whether these are long or short-
term trends is a critical question.

The Impact of Kenya's Spatial Development Strategies

Kenya is a country which, since independence,
has sustained rates of growth in the gross domestic
product that have few equals among developing countries, although growth has recently slowed down.
Several studies have suggested however that growth
has been accompanied by widening income disparities
between regions in the country. The bulk of Kenya's
people live in rural areas and it is in those areas
that the impact of development strategies is most
critical. A recent study of the small farm sector
by Davis[45] using cash crop data makes the following
observations:

> An analysis of the geographic redistribution of
> income attributable to these programmes is
> related to the widening of gross income differ-
> entials and the emergence of a large lagging

17

region by 1970. What this analysis suggests is
that the widening of income differentials among
small-farming districts may be associated with
an emphasis on growth objectives in the overall
development strategy. That the pattern of
development has contributed to a narrowing of
the overall inequality between core and periphery, relative to what it might have been
without these programmes, is also evident. The
widening of income differentials within the
periphery, however, suggests the importance of
calibrating redistribution from growth models
to cope explicitly with the problem of inequalities that emerge within the periphery in the
course of development. Distribution aspects
within the periphery must be identified as a
major policy concern in future development
efforts.[46]

Davis points out that between 1954 and 1972,
"... the small-farm sector has absorbed a population
increase of 4.4 million people and achieved an overall per capita gain in gross revenue, in current
prices, from 42 Kenya shillings to 111 Kenya shillings, an average annual rate of increase of 5.5
percent."[47] He argues that the outward-facing
approach with the production and export bias has
been largely successful — "However, redistribution
of gross farm revenue associated with developments
in the small-farm sector has affected the differentials among producing districts. These effects are
the 'unplanned' consequences of an otherwise successful development programme."[48]
      The large region which Davis has identified as
lagging is around the shores of Lake Victoria. This
region has lost ground relatively between 1960 and
1970. Other districts have gained according to
Davis' figures and one of these is Murang'a which
in 1960/61 was eleventh of the small-farming districts with a per-capita gross farm revenue of 17.9
Kenya shillings (average of all districts 27.1
Kenya shillings) whereas by 1969/70 it had risen to
fifth place with a per-capita gross farm revenue of
92.5 Kenya shillings (average 56.3 Kenya shillings).
      Apparently Murang'a District is a success story
for the center-down, outward looking model of development followed by Kenya, and the need is to ensure
that the lagging regions of Kenya catch up. If this
is the case then there is evidence to support the
efficacy of this model in bringing positive change
to rural areas.

A closer examination of the situation within
the District, as revealed by an empirical study by
Kimani and Taylor,[49] however, reveals a very different picture. **Table** 1.1 shows **the distribution of**
income of a random sample of 5,142 farmers from all
over the District and whereas some farmers have
clearly done extremely well from the cash crop export
base approach, a much larger number have not. Over
25 percent of the farms surveyed report no cash
income and a further 32 percent are in the lowest
income category. Davis suggests that the gross
revenue differentials present between different
rural regions are permanent rather than transient
features of the economy, given the differential impact and application of the export base model. If
the inequitable distribution of income in Murang'a
is also present in other regions, and there is no
reason to suspect otherwise, then in the lagging
regions the absolute and the relative inequalities
are likely to be larger. In Kenya, only a small
group of farmers in the formal sector are benefiting
from rapid economic growth which seems to be having
little direct impact on a much larger group of poor
farmers. It is also worth noting that these inequities are among farmers who own land — a limited
commodity in Kenya as was shown earlier. In the
rural parts of Central Province for example, only
10 percent of the total population are registered
landowners. The situation of the landless in the
rural areas must be much worse. Harwitz recently
concluded that

> ... extreme poverty is the only description for
> the economic state of some 15 percent of Kenya's
> rural population. 48 percent of the total (or
> about 825,000 families) appear to occupy a
> slightly higher stratum that might be described
> as 'minimum subsistence'.[50]

The situation also has serious implications for rural
employment. If relatively few farmers are generating
cash income of reasonable proportions then the availability of wage employment for the landless is bound
to be limited. Some spread effects indubitably take
place although these are difficult to measure but
the data available suggest that the richer farmers
do not purchase inputs locally but from the major
towns. The savings generated also tend to find their
way into urban rather than rural areas.
The spatial distribution of farm income shown **in**
Figure 1.2 is also of great interest. This computer-

19

TABLE 1.1
Annual Farm Income - Murang'a District, Kenya

Income (Kenya Shillings)	No. of Farms	Percentage	Cumulative Percentage
None	1,321	25.7	25.7
1 - 500	1,637	31.8	57.5
501 - 1,000	831	16.2	73.7
1,001 - 1,500	396	7.7	81.4
1,501 - 2,000	263	5.1	86.5
2,001 - 2,500	179	3.5	90.0
2,501 - 3,000	105	2.0	92.0
3,001 - 3,500	79	1.5	93.5
3,501 - 4,000	54	1.1	94.6
4,001 - 4,500	57	1.1	95.7
4,501 - 5,000	39	0.8	96.5
5,001 - 5,500	25	0.5	97.0
5,501 - 6,000	27	0.5	97.5
6,001 - 6,500	16	0.3	97.8
6,501 - 7,000	20	0.4	98.2
7,001 - 7,500	11	0.2	98.4
7,501 - 8,000	10	0.2	98.6
8,001 - 8,500	12	0.2	98.8
8,501 - 9,000	8	0.2	99.0
9,001 - 9,500	7	0.1	99.1
9,501 -10,000	12	0.2	99.3
10,001 and over	33	0.6	99.9
Total	5,142		

FIGURE 1.2

SPATIAL MODEL OF THE KENYAN ECONOMY

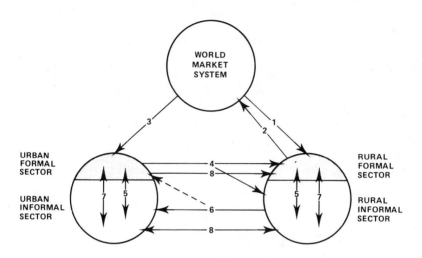

TRANSFORMATION PROCESSES

1 Foreign investment in resource and commercial crop sectors: land alienation

2 Resource-based primary product export

3 Foreign investment in import substituting industry

4 Investment in rural development

5 Increasing disparities between formal and informal sectors

6 Excessive rural-urban migration

7 Patron-client relationships

8 Kinship-based economic remittances; return and circular migration

STRUCTURAL CHARACTERISTICS

A/ Relatively open domestic markets

B/ Adequate resource endowments but limited availability of good arable land

C/ Relatively low technology

21

produced diagram has been rotated so that the view
is from the town of Thika, a successful industrial
growth pole right on the borders of Murang'a. Thika
is one of the intermediate-sized towns to which
industry has been decentralized in Kenya (Thika is
held out as a successful example of industrial decentralization). According to the center-down paradigm,
the town should have beneficial spread effects on its
rural hinterland. The result of nearly two decades
of the impact of this industrial growth pole appears
quite clear: in income terms at least, it appears
to have had exactly the opposite effect from that
planned. The income surface in Figure 2 should
decline from the foreground to the background if the
center-down paradigm is working — clearly the opposite is the case. Either the theory of spread effects from growth poles is wrong or the implementation is at fault.

Conclusions

The evidence available from Kenya suggests that
the strategy has resulted in economic growth but
that the benefits of this growth have clearly accrued
more to urban areas than rural. Disparities between
cities like Nairobi and the rural areas have widened.
The evidence also shows that disparities among rural
areas have increased and that a large lagging region
around Lake Victoria has emerged. It has been
suggested that these regional disparities are likely
to persist. There is also clear evidence that, even
in rural regions which have been relatively successful in development terms, there are substantial interpersonal disparities and that the direct benefits of
growth have gone to only a few farmers.
Since independence in 1963, however, the quality
of life for many Kenyans is much improved over what
it was in colonial times in both relative and absolute terms. The number of Kenyans involved in the
favored formal sector in both rural and urban areas
is however small, and with the recent slowdown in
growth these sectors are unlikely to be able to incorporate large numbers of new recruits. The rural
formal sector is limited by the scarcity of arable
land, even if the other conditions necessary to
support an increase in the number of "progressive"
farmers were favorable. In the urban formal sector
there is already open unemployment of serious
proportions.
The evidence suggests that the current spatial
strategies are not leading to the achievement of the

goals set for them by the Kenya Government and people.
The center-down, outward-looking strategy has not yet
succeeded in reducing disparity, and the evidence
suggests that the policies adopted have clearly
contributed to its increase both in regional and
interpersonal terms. Although it can be argued that
fifteen years is a relatively short time period in
which to judge the success or failure of a strategy
and that over the long term disparity will decrease,
there is no evidence to support this view in the
Kenyan case, nor is there evidence to support
Davis'[51] contention that without such policies rural-
urban disparities would be much wider. There is evidence to show that a small group of "progressive
farmers" have benefited considerably and the disparity between those individuals and people in the
formal sector of urban areas has decreased. The
great bulk of rural people have however seen disparities widen in a relative though not necessarily an
absolute sense.

As a minimum the existing strategy requires substantial modification. The type of modification required involves, in my view, the application of a
more self-reliant, bottom-up approach and a change
in the focus of Kenya's strategies. In this process,
the informal sector at all levels will probably be
critically important. Spatial planning in Kenya
would come closer to achieving the aims set for it
by concentrating on understanding and developing
space so that primacy is given to the needs of the
informal sector in both urban and rural areas rather
than to the "modernized" formal sector as is the case
at present.

In spatial planning terms it is suggested that
if disparities are to be reduced then direct priority
attention must be given to the peripheral rural subsystem, especially the informal sector of that subsystem, and that an important part of such a strategy
would be the creation of agrourban, small-scale
development centers at the lower orders of the urban
hierarchy. The term development centers is chosen
deliberately to indicate that these small urban
places must provide both for themselves and their
associated rural hinterlands a range of innovative
cultural, social, employment,trade and service
functions. Concentration on the rural subsystem is
necessary in most developing nations today, especially
those like Kenya where over 80 percent of the total
population live in rural areas. Policies of spatial
change must be concentrated in the rural periphery
because in human terms that is the "core" of the

nation. Development centers can be used to alter
the dysfunctional spatial structures currently.exis-
ting which, as many authors have pointed out, are
reflective more of an extractive colonial era and
are little suited to the stated aims of independent
African governments. The approach used rejects the
false dichotomy between urban and rural development
and views the problem as one of interaction between
subsystems which are part of a larger systemic
whole. However, as indicated in Figure 1, the two-
sector model where urban equals "modernized" and
rural equals "traditional" is also rejected as both
simplistic and misleading. What is advocated is a
"centralizing upward" or "bottom-up" approach
emphasizing the beneficial linkages currently existing between the rural and urban informal sectors,
the restructuring of unfavorable linkages, and the
relative neglect of the urban, and to a lesser
extent the rural, formal sectors. The approach
suggested, which has been more fully outlined elsewhere,[52] can be seen as giving more direct attention
to the rural areas and in a sense is a form of selective spatial closure of the informal subsystems from
the formal. It advocates the creation of different
linkages from those that exist at present with a substantial reduction of the present dominance of the
urban-controlled formal sectors. This would require
an alteration of the terms of trade and other relationships in favor of the rural areas. The approach
implies, by the relative neglect of the formal sectors in both subsystems, a weakening of the current
north-south relationship but not its eradication.
    Such an approach is not without its problems.
The creation of small development centers will not
in itself improve the situation of rural peoples
unless these centers are used to deliberately alter
existing relationships which means that their creation must be accompanied by policy changes favoring
the mass of the rural poor. The political likelihood of a radical change in political thinking in
Kenya is not great and Kenya is unlikely to abandon
its present development ideology. The basic question
of why those currently benefiting from the existing
structures would be prepared to see these changed
therefore remains. Without the political will no
change is likely to take place.
    Given current political realities there are
clearly limitations to the degree of change which
can take place without revolution. One can take the
view that Kenya's leaders are not seriously interested in change or alternately that they are and that

the lack of success so far in reducing disparity is
due to the inadequacy of the approach used. Existing evidence would support either view. The Kenyan
experience however clearly supports the contention
that existing approaches to spatial development are
inadequate and that the revisions called for by
authors like Stöhr, Friedmann, Weaver, Douglass, Lo
and Salih, and others, are long overdue. It is true
that without the political will change is unlikely;
it is equally true that if alternate theory and
practice are not available change is unlikely even
if the political will is present. If the theories
of the "development from below" school can be comple-
mented by sound practice then, given the political
will, the 1980s may see some radical new approaches
to spatial development in the third world and an
increase in the quality of life of all people which
is the ultimate goal of development.

NOTES

        1.   E.A.J. Johnson, The Organization of Space
in Developing Countries (Cambridge: Harvard
University Press, 1970).
        2.   D. Seers, "The New Meaning of Development",
International Development Review, Vol. XIX, 3,
1977/3, pp. 2-7.
        3.   Op. cit., p. 3.
        4.   Op. cit., p. 4.
        5.   Op. cit., p. 5.
        6.   Loc. cit.
        7.   Op. cit., p. 6.
        8.   Op. cit., p. 5.
        9.   Op. cit., p. 6.
       10.   Op. cit., p. 7.
       11.   Loc. cit.
       12.   Op. cit., pp. 3-4.
       13.   For a good survey of the literature see the
bibliography compiled by D. Slater, Radical Approaches
to the Urban and Regional Analysis of Peripheral
Capitalist Social Formations (Amsterdam, Center for
Latin American Research and Documentation, November
1976).
       14.   W. Stöhr, F. Tödtling, "Spatial Equity —
Some Anti-Theses to Current Regional Development
Doctrine", Paper read to the IGU Commission on Regional Aspects of Development (Dushambe, USSR, July 1976).

       15.   Op. cit., p. 21.

16. W. Stöhr, H. Palme, "Centre-Periphery Development Alternatives and their Applicability to Rural Areas in Developing Countries", Paper read to the joint ASA/LASA meetings (Houston, Texas, September 1977).

17. J. Friedmann, M. Douglass, "Agropolitan Development: Towards a New Strategy for Regional Planning in Asia", in UNCRD, Growth Pole Strategy and Regional Development Planning in Asia (Nagoya, Japan), pp. 333-334.

18. Op. cit., p. 335.

19. F.C. Lo, K. Salih, "Rural Urban Relations and Regional Development Planning", paper read to the third biennial meeting, Association of Development Research and Training Institutes of Asia and the Pacific (Goa, India, September 1977).

20. Op. cit.,

21. F.C. Lo, K. Salih, M. Douglass, Uneven Development, Rural-Urban Transformation and Regional Development Alternatives in Asia (Nagoya, Japan: UNCRD, 1978), p. 93

22. J. Friedmann, C.Weaver, Territory and Function: The Evolution of Regional Planning (London: Edward Arnold, 1979).

23. C. Weaver, "Regional Theory and Regionalism: Towards Rethinking the Regional Question", Comparative Urbanisation Studies, School of Architecture and Urban Planning (Los Angeles: University of California, 1978), p. 2.

24. W. Stöhr, D.R.F. Taylor, Development from Above or Below? A Radical Reappraisal of Spatial Planning in Developing Countries (London: Wiley, forthcoming).

25. D.A. Rondinelli, K. Ruddle, Urbanisation and Rural Development, Praeger (New York: 1978).

26. I. Sachs, Environment and Development — A New Rationale for Domestic Policy Formulation and International Cooperation Strategies, Environment Canada and CIDA (Ottawa, 1977).

27. D. Seers, Op. cit., p. 9.

28. A.G. Gilbert, D.E. Goodman, "Regional Income Disparities and Economic Development: A Critique" in A.G. Gilbert (ed.) Development Planning and Spatial Structure (London: Wiley, 1976).

29. E.W. Soja, The Geography of Modernization in Kenya (Syracuse: Syracuse University Press, 1978.

30. Op. cit., p. 4.

31. See Chapter   in this volume.

32. J.A.N. Eastwell, "Kenya 2000: A Study of Increasing Population Pressure in a Developing Country: Planning Possibilities in an Ecologic-Economic Perspective" (M.Sc. thesis, University of Toronto, 1973, p.74.

26

33. Republic of Kenya, Development Plan 1974-1978, (Nairobi: Government Printer, 1974).

34. R. Acquaah-Harrison, Rural Urban Disparities: Spatial Dimensions of Development Strategies, (Toronto: 1975), p. 37.

35. J.A.N. Eastwell, Op. cit., p. 146.

36. C. Leys, Underdevelopment in Kenya (Berkley: UCLA Press, 1974).

37. E.W. Soja, C. Weaver, "Urbanisation and Underdevelopment in East Africa" in B.J.L. Berry, Urbanisation and Counter Urbanisation (New York: Sage, 1978).

38. D.R.F. Taylor, "Spatial Organization and Rural Development" in Fry, M.G. (ed.), Freedom and Change: Essays in Honour of Lester B. Pearson, (Toronto: McClelland and Stewart, 1975), "Growth Centres and Rural Development in Africa" in Kuklinski, A.R. (ed.), Regional Development and Planning: International Perspectives, (Leiden: Sithoff, 1975), and "Regional Studies, Social Systems and Regional Policy in Africa: An Appraisal", (Krakow: August 1977), Paper read to the European Regional Science Congress.

39. Eastwell, Op. cit., p. (i).

40. National Christian Council of Kenya, Who Controls Industry in Kenya (Nairobi: 1968).

41. S. Langdon, "Multi-National Corporations, Taste Transfer and Underdevelopment: A Case Study from Kenya,"Review of African Political Economy, No.2, 1975, pp. 12-35.

42. C. Leys, Underdevelopment in Kenya: The Political Economy of Neo-Colonialism (Berkeley:1974).

43. International Labour Organization, Employment, Incomes and Equality: A Strategy for Improving Productive Employment in Kenya (Geneva: 1972)

44. G.E. Johnson & W.E. Whitelaw, "Urban-Rural Income Transfers in Kenya: An Estimated Remittances Function", Economic Development and Cultural Exchange, Vol. 22, No.3, 1974, pp. 473-79.

45. J.T. Davis, "Development of the Small-Farm Sector in Kenya, 1954-72", The Canadian Geographer, Vol. XXL, 1, Spring 1977, pp.32-58.

46. Op. cit., pp. 33-34.

47. Op. cit., p. 41.

48. Loc. cit.

49. S.M. Kimani, D.R.F. Taylor, Growth Centres and Rural Development in Kenya (Thika,Kenya: 1973)

50. M. Harwitz, "On Improving the Lot of the Poorest: Economic Plans in Kenya", African Studies Review, Vol. XXI, No.3, 1978, p. 69.

51. J.T. Davis, Op. cit.

52. D.R.F. Taylor, Op. cit.

2. The Geography of Modernization— A Radical Reappraisal

Edward W. Soja

In 1964, in a lecture given at the London School of Economics I tried to convey some of the excitement and insight being generated by what came to be called the "quantitative revolution" in American geography. I remember the naive joy with which I described the wonders of multi-variate analysis, the intricacies of nearest neighbor theory, and the almost aesthetic pleasures of mapping residuals from regression! I also recall the very clear pattern of responses I received, ranging from polite yawns and angry mutterings to the secret smiles of agreement and the enthusiastic expressions of intellectual brotherhood.

Once again I am excited with what some might call the zeal of a convert and wish, perhaps naively, to share my ideas about geography and geographical analysis. I am concerned with trying to focus and apply a newfound (but by no means new) perspective to the analysis of African development and to suggest the need for a significant reorientation of existing research interests and issues. In doing so I may incur the criticism of those who have gone much further than I — and the anger and boredom of those who have not tried.

But there the resemblances end. What is argued here represents a major transformation in my own thinking and a somewhat uncomfortable reevaluation of what I and a few other geographers working in Africa have accomplished over the past decade and a half. The central point is relatively straightforward and uncomplicated. It is that most geographical studies of development — and in particular that cluster of studies usually referred to as the "geography of modernization" — have been characterized by an uncritical and naive adoption of development models and ideologies which seriously misrepresent the

socioeconomic processes operating in the Third World.
As a result, a substantial if not total reinterpreta-
tion and reorientation in the geographical analysis
of development is necessary, not only because of
political or ideological reasons but also because of
ingrained errors of logic, insensitivity to empirical
events, and narrowness of analytical vision.

I would like to amplify these assertions in
three ways. First, I will outline briefly the evolution of my own personal thinking about geography,
development, and Africa because such a personal and
subjective view is, I think, necessary. Second, I
will explore some illustrative examples of widely
known approaches and models of development geography
which demand reevaluation if not complete dismissal.
And finally I will try to illustrate the critical
issues raised earlier with some empirical observations on the geography of underdevelopment in East
Africa.

My personal interest in the geographical analysis
of African development crystallized at a time when
most African states had just received their independence and when American geography was experiencing
major changes in its orientation and emphasis.

Nationbuilding on the one hand, and the development of geographical theory on the other, were the
vital contemporary issues. As a young geographer, it
was only natural to seek some link between the two
and from this search emerged my early work on the
geography of modernization in Kenya.[1] My objectives
were ambitious but entirely appropriate to the mood
of the times: I was going to help to revive regional
geography with a new cohesive focus on a new scientific toolkit, and to demonstrate to the other social
sciences the crucial importance of the spatial dimension and spatial analysis. With the creative contributions of Peter Gould, Barry Riddell, and others
there arose a distinctive research cluster in African
geography and a new vocabulary of modernization
surfaces, diffusion processes and development filtering through the urban hierarchy. There was an early
flush of good feeling about the accomplishments of
these studies, especially when they were sensitive to
the history and culture of the region examined. The
only critics heard at first were those appalled on
principle with the application of statistical analysis to their beloved Africa and most of these
critics were easily ignored.

A new set of critics arose soon afterwards, but
the geographers of modernization were by then ready
to take on all comers. This new criticism had two
components, one of which hinted at some ideological

29

issues (including our allegedly naive Western ethno-
centrism, urban bias, insensitivity to the political
realities of the Third World, Pollyanna-like optimism,
etc.) while the other tended to be essentially methodological. Too much emphasis was placed, they argued,
on the macroscale. The real problems were at the
microlevel, with rural populations, with man-environment relations, with the grass roots. What did the
poor Ghanaian farmer care about modernization surfaces
especially when that cascading wave of development
never seemed to surge very far in his direction?
Why all this fuss about post offices and telephone
calls when thousands could no longer feed their
families an adequate diet?

Much of the argument over these criticisms
revolved around the relative merits of the "macro-"
versus the "micro-" approach — and nearly all
involved eventually agreed that both were necessary
and complementary. Indeed, it became fairly clear
that the "macro" — or spatial systems — approach
and the "micro" — or man-environment ecosystems
approach had become the two dominant modes of contemporary geographical analysis, in many ways the geographer's equivalent of macro- and microeconomics.[2]
Another issue, however, involved the simple fact that
little real development was taking place in the Third
World, indeed that basic social inequalities were
increasing while most of the geography of modernization studies seemed to suggest an inexorable if slow
march toward balanced growth and development. In
response to this basic empirical fact there began to
emerge a new macrogeographical model of development
which attempted to address itself to these empirical
facts. The new model was forged largely out of the
work of usch people as Brian Berry and John Friedmann,
whose general theory of polarized development introduced a crucial bump on the development curve.[3]
Increasing primacy, increasing regional income inequalities, increasing political instability all were
shown to be expected patterns during the early phases
of development. They would reach a boiling point
midway along the curve and in the resolution of the
conflicts and crises thus generated would come the
eventual transformation to high levels of development and regional equality.

This conflict resolution — during which urban
and regional planning would play a key role — did
not automatically propel countries towards high
standards of living and social justice. Indeed,
much would depend on the guidance of sensitive
spatial planners armed with the tools of growth pole
theory, locational economics, transportation network

models and economic forecasting. A high premium was
therefore placed on the practical role of geographer-
planners, who began to travel the global paths of
advisor and government consultant heretofore monopo-
lized by economists and engineers. I will discuss
some of the problems involved in this new geographical model of development later, but I must first deal
with still another wave of criticism which has reached
full steam over the past several years and which has
had the most powerful effect on my own work.

In an article which has just recently appeared
but which I had written in 1970,[4] I attempted to syn-
thesize some of the new approaches to the geographical study of development and to achieve a greater
sensitivity to contemporary political issues in
Africa. As a synthesis which clarified and defended
the geography of modernization approach, it seemed
quite satisfactory and appeared to meet most of the
criticisms noted earlier. But it did not dampen one
group of critics, a growing community of radical geographers and Marxists who not only summarily dismissed
the geography of modernization but dismissed Friedmann, Berry, growth pole theory and practically every
thing else I had felt comfortable with as well. My
first impulse was to meet this comprehensive attack
with all the academic tactics I had been taught:
Ignore them, they will go away ... attack them as in-
competent and uncomprehending ... finally, show how
any valid criticism was already accounted for in the
original work if only it had been read properly. I
even toyed with the idea of tacking on the prefix
"under" every time I used the word development, to
demonstrate the weakness of the radical critique.

In an effort to "know mine enemy", however, I
began to dig more deeply into a literature I had
formerly and regretfully been just casually aware
of — the writings of Gunder Frank and Furtado on
underdevelopment and dependency, the writings of Marx
and Lenin on capitalism and imperialism, the works of
Samir Amin, Walter Rodney, and a few others on Africa—
and began suddenly to understand better the sources
and nature of the criticism being made. To cut short
this personal history, let me simply state that the
experience was a shattering one. To the inveterate
synthesizer adept at incorporating each new model and
each new point of view as they came along, here was
something which could not simply be thrown into the
pot to be digested into a new chapter or used to re-
pair or patch up some weak spot here and there. The
very foundations of the development model I had pur-
sued were pulled out from under me and for a long

period of time, I could only look back regretfully at the ruins.

Rather than continue this autobiographical exercise (I probably would have called it a paradigm shift five years ago!) let me move on to discuss a few very basic notions which in their essential undeniability demand the full attention and contemplation of all development-oriented geographers. First there is the simple proposition that there exists a process of underdevelopment, that is a process of societal change associated with the creation of social, economic, political and spatial structures which inherently leads to a dependency upon foreign interests and powerful external influence over local decision-making. These structures revolve around a system of unequal exchange between population groups or classes and between different locations in space and tend to promote the continuation of substantial poverty, social and spatial inequality, and subordination to the interests of western capital. Thus, underdevelopment is not just a condition but a dynamic process of societal change. A related proposition is that what we have conventionally called "development" is inextricably linked to the underdevelopment process. We need not argue that the development of advanced capitalist countries today has been wholly based upon the drainage of resources from the Third World, simply that the spread of capitalism has been associated in time and space with the creation of an integrated world economy in which there is an unequal distribution of power. Accepting a division between dominant and dependent regions, between global core and periphery, it seems perfectly logical to expect that significant net benefits have accumulated among the most powerful populations because of their stronger competitive positions. High levels of material development are thus at least partially explained by the underdevelopment of the Third World.

These observations are not simply a means of soothing liberal guilt over the sins of colonialism. Nor can they be comfortably incorporated within the liberal-reformist model of international development. They are the starting points for a radically different approach to the analysis of development. To illustrate, let me contrast this approach with the conventional diffusionist model of development which has overwhelmingly dominated western social science (and geography in particular).

The development model implicit within most western studies of development can be broadly outlined as follows: Certain areas of the world,

because of felicitous local conditions (ranging from
abundant physical resources and strategic geographical location to the Protestant ethic and high levels
of innate inventiveness) were able to pioneer the
modern development process. And from these core
areas, "modernization" — largely in the form of the
Industrial Revolution — spread unevenly outward
much like the Agricultural Revolution thousands of
years earlier. Where local conditions were most
propitious, adoption was quickest and deepest and
often associated with new innovative contributions.
Somehow, the factory system and industrial technology,
modern science and medicine, achievement motivation
and the nation-state, diffused in much the same way
as wheat, rice, and bananas! This perspective logically carried along with it a number of correlative
assumptions.
    It was possible, for example, to array all the
countries and societies in the world along with a
simple continuum according to how much diffusion had
actually occurred within them, as if each unit were
a separate system linked only tangentially to the
rest of the world. Relative position along the continuum was then explainable almost entirely in terms
of internal conditions, such as lack of sufficient
natural resources, an inhospitable physical environment, archaic social systems, resistant traditional
cultures and religions, and inappropriate psychologi-
cal attitudes. What was needed to rid these countries
of backwardness was to encourage the diffusion process
by "preparing" the country more effectively to receive
and accept external injections of development, demo-
cracy, and modernity.
    It was this process of preparation that justi-
fied the selection of variables used in the construction of modernization surfaces. Of course, the existence of a post office or the construction of a road
or an increasing number of telephone calls did not
automatically make people modern and economically
developed. But they were clearly important enabling
mechanisms which were associated, statistically at
least, with a high likelihood that an area was being
prepared to receive its dose of diffusing modernity.
Even if they were not always the best indicators of
modernization, they were available and relatively
reliable. And furthermore, using a whole batch of
them was clearly better than depending on some sim-
pler index such as per capita income. There was
continuing debate and argument over the selection of
variables and the various statistical manipulations
applied to them,but the debate was almost always

within the context of the conventional development model.

Stripped of much of its polemical content, the radical model posed a very different picture of the past four hundred years of industrial modernization and demanded a major change in the spatial analysis of development which went well beyond the choice of index variables. There has indeed been a kind of diffusion process, but one in which most of the world became progressively integrated into a single, global economic system with a dominant core region and a dependent global periphery. The prevailing influence within this system has been some form of capitalist resource exploitation through which an elite center (defined in terms of class and region) was able to concentrate enormous material wealth by combining the efficient accumulation of resources from the periphery with indigenous societal transformation (made possible in part by the nature of core-periphery relations). The cumulative impact of this process has been an increasing gap between rich and poor classes and rich and poor regions at the global scale and, in a nested hierarchical fashion reminiscent of classical central place theory, at progressively lower scales intranationally, regionally, and between city and hinterland.

In other words, the predominant process affecting the Third World was thus not so much the diffusion of development as it was the diffusion of underdevelopment. There were improvements in living standards in many areas, but these improvements were invariably associated with the creation of social, economic, political and spatial structures designed to maintain continuing conditions of dependency upon western capital and control over decision-making. Within such a structure, international trade and capital flow were based less upon the equal exchange and competitive advantage which underlay conventional international trade theory than upon a system of unequal exchange and a form of comparative advantage defined according to differential power and resource control. The Third World or whatever one chooses to call the dependent periphery of international capitalism was and is an inevitable byproduct of the growth and spread of capitalism itself. It survives not because of some evil conspiracy of neocolonialists or multinational gnomes or because of imperfections in the free market system but because it is an essential and inherent part of a capitalist world economy.

What are the implications of this radical perspective for existing approaches to development

34

geography? First of all, it must be accepted that all the equilibrium end-states and "happy endings" which underlie nearly all geographical models of development, from the city-size distribution and regional incomes inequality models of Berry, Williamson, and El-Shaks, to the transport network model of Taaffe, Morrill, and Gould, to nearly all the geography of modernization studies, can never be attained in Third World countries as long as they remain integrated within the global capitalist system or cannot find other, more underdeveloped countries to exploit. Analytical geography has been built upon the assumption of a world of isolated states occupied by individualistic and egalitarian societies driven primarily by the desire to reduce the energy costs of distance. This may be convenient and even useful as a contrived laboratory to examine certain spatial relationships unencumbered by the complexity of the real world. Key problems arise, however, when the analytical geographer attempts to understand why the real world persistently refuses to conform to the neat geometries and equilibrium-bound trajectories of the laboratory models.

What becomes clear is that analytical geography must move beyond simple homage to the distortions caused by agglomeration economies or resource localization; beyond the persuasive logic of "satisficing" behavior and risk avoidance (two of the most fashionable recent attempts to rationalize social inequality in space); beyond the residuals of imperfect probability or locational uniqueness of market imperfections to seek explanation for the spatial organization of society in the structure of social relations and the historical evolution of contemporary political and economic systems. Geographical analysis of development must become more openly normative and grounded in social process and social reality as they relate interdependently with spatial organization and behavior. Ironically enough, when this occurs, it is likely that the capitalist mode of production will be found to be more responsible than anything else for the emergence and maintenance of observed departures from our geographical models of society — particularly those with projected happy endings!

In many ways, these observations parallel very closely David Harvey's argument about the necessity to combine the sociological and spatial imaginations, to view human society as the product of an essentially dialectical relationship between social process and spatial form.[5] Geographers have vigorously argued for many years that social science models have consistently ignored the spatial dimension, yet they

have accomplished little more than producing spatial
models which ignore social process.

What is being called for then is a more comprehensive and grounded approach to the study of development, one in which the sensitive interaction between social process and spatial organization is analysed historically and in terms of concrete social
relations. Within this context, some of the old spatial models can prove useful, but attention must shift
away from more rigorous explanation of equilibrium
conditions to an empirical analysis of the social
and spatial forces which create and sustain dis-
equilibrium in the form of increasing regional inequalities, overblown primate cities bursting with
people but not with jobs, persistent rural poverty,
and unequal terms of trade. David Harvey's work,
Social Justice and the City, demonstrated effectively
how the social and spatial structure of the urban
system is shaped by a number of hidden forces which
redistribute income in favor of the already wealthy
classes. Essentially the same set of mechanisms engrained in the structure of international capitalism
has been shaping the social geography of development
at the national and global scales for hundreds of
years. More than anything else, it has been the
failure to treat these mechanisms directly, to ascertain their geographical expression rather than blindly
projecting the expectations of conventional western
geographical and economic models, that reduces the
literature on the geography of modernization to little
more than an interesting experiment in cleverly
described graphics.

These general points can be illustrated by an
examination of urbanization and underdevelopment in
East Africa.[6] It is my belief that contemporary urbanization in East Africa cannot be understood apart
from the more pervasive process of underdevelopment.
The nature, causes, and directions of urban growth
are so tightly entwined with the larger underdevelopment process that to attempt a more conventional descriptive analysis of population growth rates, employment figures, city-size distributions, and intraurban
land use changes divorced from this interpretive perspective would seem both misleading and tunnel-
visioned.

Several distinctive features make East Africa an
unusually attractive case study in comparative Third
World urbanization and an exceptionally clear illus-
tration of the imprint of underdevelopment on emerging urban patterns. East Africa, for example, forms
a central part of the least-urbanized major region in

the world, the eastern flank of Africa from Ethiopia
to Mozambique. Furthermore, although its percentage
rates of urban growth are high, the proportion of its
total population which remains rural has been declining much less rapidly than the rest of Africa and
indeed most of the rest of the world except the
Indian subcontinent. The persistence of the rural
sector would be even more pronounced statistically
were it not for the phenomenal growth of a few large
cities. Since independence, for example, Kampala,
Dar es Salaam, Nairobi, and Mombasa together accounted for over 60 percent of all urban growth in
East Africa.

The overwhelmingly rural character of East
Africa is given an added distinctiveness when viewed
from a deeper historical and cultural perspective.
There are perhaps no other comparable areas of the
world in which large, indigenous and relatively seden-
tary populations have traditionally shunned so persistently any form of nucleated settlement. Aside from
the ancient trading centers along the Indian Ocean
coast, East Africa was virtually townless until the
last half of the nineteenth century. Occasionally a
chief's compound or the center of one of the larger
states in southern Uganda and northwestern Tanzania
might cluster together a few thousand people, but
this was rare and usually not long-lasting. Furthermore, the predominant settlement pattern in precolonial East Africa was extraordinarily dispersed,
commonly consisting simply of separated, relatively
autonomous homesteads.

Thus not only were there no cities or towns in
the interior of East Africa much over a hundred years
ago, there were precious few settlements which could
be clearly classified as substantial rural villages.
Urbanization has therefore been almost entirely a
twentieth-century phenomenon and quintessentially the
product of European colonialism and economic exploitation. Perhaps nowhere else can we more clearly
glimpse the lasting impact of a colonially-generated
system of cities on the underdevelopment of traditional society.

The location, size, and distribution of urban
centers in contemporary East Africa is almost
entirely the product of British and German decision-
making during the first few decades of colonial rule.
From the 1880s to the first World War was a period of
radical spatial change in East Africa during which
effective administrative control was established and
the basic infrastructure of colonial domination was
implanted. Through the siting of administrative

headquarters, the routing of transport lines, and the identification of areas of strategic and economic importance, a whole new system of locational advantages and productive potential was superimposed over East Africa. By the end of the period, the broad outlines of the present pattern of urbanization had already become solidified.

The new network of settlements was capped by the colonial capitals and key seaports and structured by a hierarchy of administrative centers enforcing colonial control and representing imperial interests. Administrative functions were the primary generative seeds of town growth, particularly when they were locationally associated with the main cash-crop producing areas. Virtually every city over 20,000 in East Africa today was an established administrative post before 1910. The only partial exceptions are Nakuru and Thika, centers of early European settlement in Kenya, the former already by 1910 considered the official "capital of the White Highlands". It is also interesting to note that none of the long string of ancient coastal centers except for Mombasa, Dar es Salaam and Tanga, have a population greater than 20,000 today despite their early origins.

During the past half-century, the system of social and spatial relations implanted earlier was reinforced and elaborated to incorporate most of the population of East Africa into the colonial political economy and thus more directly into the international economic system. This process of underdevelopment or dependent development brought with it many beneficial side effects, such as improved health and nutrition, modern educational facilities, better farming techniques, and easier transport and communications. But the distribution of these benefits served primarily the interests of British and other colonial powers rather than indigenously expressed demands and local development potential. This selective distribution of the more beneficial accompaniments of colonialism is the most crucial aspect of the underdevelopment process. East Africa was never a major source of capital accumulation for Britain and it would be foolish to speak of enormous flows of resources being drained from the three territories during the colonial period to fuel the British economy. But whether the drainage was large or small is not as important as the fact that the social and spatial structures which evolved were designed to distribute scarce resources in such a way as to promote an exploitative emphasis in economic relations, to facilitate control and domination by a nonindigenous colonial elite, and to

38

solidify a condition of dependency within the international market system. Whatever the benefits of
underdevelopment might have been, it has engrained a
framework of social and spatial relations and a
system of unequal exchange between areas and between
different population groups which is inherently anti-
thetical to an autonomously controlled and socially
just process of development.

As E.A. Brett noted in his study of underdevelopment in East Africa,[7] there were four main "layers"
to the colonial political economy: primary producers
almost entirely in agriculture; processors and traders
who handled their products; metropolitan export industries established within the colonial market; and the
colonial administrative and political apparatus responsible for managing the entire system. The ways in
which these layers or subsystems interrelated and
affected the allocation of resources largely determined the patterns of East African urbanization and
economic production and, of course, shaped the East
African modernization surface. This was not a simple
dual economy, with a modern enclave disconnected from
a traditional sector, but a complex and integrated
system which encapsuled virtually everyone in East
Africa in one role or another.

Each of the four layers, for example, was hierarchically structured and geographically focussed
around the colonial primate cities of Nairobi, Dar es
Salaam, and Kampala-Entebbe. These core cities func-
tioned during the colonial period to concentrate the
wealth produced in their increasingly expanding hinterlands — largely through decisions involving infrastructural location and institutional regulations —
and to channel this accumulated wealth for the primary
benefit of the colonial elite, both within and outside
East Africa. By independence, these late nineteenth
century creations, plus the Nairobi outport of Mombasa, contained almost half of the entire urban population of East Africa and proportionately much more
of its industry, employment and urban social services.

Aside from these four cities, plus Tanga and one
or two industrial centers such as Jinja, virtually
all other urban settlements were either administrative centers, serving to maintain political control
and efficient economic management, or trading centers,
functioning essentially as geographical "middlemen"
between agricultural producers and metropolitan
export industries represented in the primate cities.
There was neither need nor reason why any of these
centers should grow to substantial size and not one,
even today, contains much more than 50,000 people.

39

In this context,urbanization and infrastructural development were little more than instruments for the effective management and maintenance of the colonial export economy and the unequal distribution of its derived wealth. Africans were discouraged from settling permanently in urban centers since their labor was needed on the settler estates, the plantations, and where necessary on their own peasant farms. Infrastructural services were notably absent from those agricultural areas which could compete with European plantations and settler farms and thus both divert needed labor and increase wages.

These patterns were most pronounced in Kenya, where the exclusion of an independent African peasantry went furthest due to the necessity of capital accumulation in the settler sector and the resultant net transfer of capital and labor to it from the peasantry. Although Africans produced 70 percent of the exports of Kenya up to the First World War, this percentage dropped to less than 20 percent by 1928 and for many years African productivity declined in absolute value as well. This pattern persisted until the Second World War, when the economy of Kenya began to expand much more rapidly in response to its new strategic importance.

Here was a classical example of underdevelopment which produced an African-subsidized island of European-controlled production amidst a series of densely populated, land-starved, subsistence farming reserves faced with few alternatives other than to supply a dependable source of cheap labor. This was achieved through a mixture of methods: direct expropriation of land and the creation of restrictive Native Reserves; through mass taxation to encourage wage employment — and the diversion of such tax revenues to construct settler-oriented infrastructural services; through the prohibition of certain cash crops in the key Kikuyu and Luo labor reservoirs; through the imposition of special customs and tariff regulations and legal restrictions which, for example, protected European-grown maize from African competition; through the maintenance of low wages regardless of labor supply; and often through coercion.

In Uganda, precapitalist modes of production remained much more important than in Kenya and the colonial political economy came more to resemble West Africa where, in the absence of significant European settlement, the economy revolved around peasant agricultural production dominated by the monopolistic control of colonial import-export houses. This resulted in what Brett called a "less servile" form of underdevelopment than in the labor reserves of Kenya,

40

but one which nonetheless created and accentuated
social and regional inequalities, protected European
firms engaged in marketing and processing from African and to some extent Asian competition, and prevented the accumulation of sufficient capital and entrepreneurial skills on the part of the African population to sustain the structural changes necessary for
autonomous and equitable economic development.

Tanzania mixed both peasant agriculture and a
limited settler economy, but was predominantly affected by the establishment of European agricultural
plantations. Although plantation agriculture did not
require so substantial a net transfer of resources
from the peasant sector as did settler farming, it
did depend upon the availability of cheap labor and
thus upon the inability of certain areas to produce
directly for the world market. As in Kenya, infrastructural services were withheld from the major
labor reservoirs in the southern Highlands, Kigoma
region, and several other areas near the railway
lines, setting in motion a process of selective rural
decay and neglect akin to what occurred along the
coast with the growth of the large colonial port
cities.

Urbanization in East Africa since independence
has been tightly constrained by the colonial legacy
of underdevelopment and the dependent spatial structures it imposed. Despite efforts of the independent
African governments to transform their colonial inheritance, urban development since 1960 has been little
more than an intensification of already existing patterns and relationships and a more open manifestation
of the problems inherent in the political economy of
colonialism. This has been especially evident in
Kenya, the most deeply underdeveloped of the three
territories. The recent ILO Mission on Employment,
Incomes and Inequality, for example, asserted
straightforwardly that:

> Since independence, economic growth has largely
> continued on the lines set by the earlier colo-
> nial structure. Kenyanization has radically
> changed the racial composition of the group of
> people in the centre of power and many of its
> policies, but has had only a limited effect on
> the mechanisms which maintained its dominance —
> the pattern of government expenditure, the free-
> dom of foreign firms to locate their offices and
> plants in Nairobi, and the narrow stratum of ex-
> penditure by a high-income elite superimposed on
> a base of limited mass-consumption.[8]

41

Despite significant ideological, attitudinal, and institutional divergence, all three East African states remain caged within an infrastructure of underdevelopment.

The degree of population primacy of the three colonial core cities, for example, has not only been maintained since independence but has actually increased and, with few exceptions, the same is true of the geographical concentration of industry, employment, urban services and income. Unfortunately, economic expansion has not kept pace with population growth and Nairobi, Dar es Salaam and Kampala-Mengo have become swollen with unemployed laborers and squatter settlements. The mushrooming growth of East Africa's largest cities should surprise no one. The colonial political economy was specifically designed to create a large reservoir of cheap wage laborers primarily for the agricultural export economy and secondarily for the small, dependent industrial sector,which by its nature was almost entirely concentrated in the largest urban centers. Except as needed for industry and related commercial and administrative services, African urbanization was discouraged and controlled. Independence, however, led to many changes. Most restrictions on African settlement were removed and the Asian monopoly of wholesale and retail trade weakened by the departure of many European settlers and land owners. Under these conditions, it is no wonder that the expanding pool of laborers so effectively created by colonial policy flooded the big cities searching for work.

A substantial — if not preponderant — proportion of urban growth in East Africa since 1960 can therefore be attributed to the rapid expansion of a class of African urban poor which was assiduously restricted from urban settlement during the colonial period. In Nairobi in particular, the expansion of this "protoproletariat" was also linked to the increasing role of multinational corporations and foreign capital investment in general. By 1967, fifty-seven percent of all manufacturing industry in Kenya was foreign-owned and accounted for seventy-three percent of all profits — figures which have almost surely increased in recent years. To a significant extent, the growing supply of cheap labor inherent in what has come to be called the "informal sector" — under constant pressure from the similarly growing army of unemployed job seekers — has created since independence the urban counterpart to the rural labor reserves which permitted the underdevelopment of East African agriculture.

42

Through the work of the late Samson Kimani, we also have some interesting descriptive evidence of the spatial impact of underdevelopment at the intra-urban scale in Nairobi.[9] In 1971, for example, individual Asians and Europeans still owned nearly forty-five percent of the city's land, with primarily Asian-owned businesses accounting for another twenty percent. Moreover, most of the Asian-owned land was highly valuable commercial and residential property representing over half of the total assessed value of urban land surveyed. Africans, now making up eighty percent of the total population, owned less than four percent of the city's area rated at 2.7 percent of the assessed value.

Kimani also studied the distribution of land values in Nairobi and demonstrated that they were closely correlated with distance from the city center and secondarily with urban density, thus mirroring the characteristic tentlike structure found in most western cities. At the same time, however, analysis of residuals indicated that land in the European sector was consistently undervalued given its location and density, while land in the African sector was just as consistently overvalued despite its much lower infrastructural and amenity standards. This pattern almost surely evolved early in the colonial period and worked effectively over time to subsidize European and to some extent Asian urban settlement in much the same way that the White Highlands were subsidized through the underdevelopment of the African rural economy. Here is further evidence of the depth to which colonial and postcolonial underdevelopment has tightly structured the spatial organization of East Africa.

What emerges from this brief assessment of the geography of urbanization in East Africa is an immense appreciation for the explanatory power of the radical perspective on development. The subject matter discussed is in many ways similar to most conventional geographic studies of development — the location, size and growth of urban centers, the areal patterns of economic production and infrastructural services; the circulation of people, money and information; the distribution of income and patterns of regional inequality; the internal spatial structure of cities. What differs significantly however, is the degree to which questions regarding the causes and social consequences of these spatial patterns can be effectively and appropriately answered. There is no need to retreat to the comforting logic that all departures from expected geographical models are simply temporary imperfections eventually to be erased in the inexorable

43

march of progress. For these are not departures at all — they are variations of expected patterns of dependent capitalist development. And nearly all the available empirical evidence suggests that they will persist if no radical societal transformation takes place to break the hold of continuing underdevelopment.

It is an inescapable fact that the spatial organization of contemporary East African society has been powerfully shaped by an historical process of capitalist penetration, accumulation, and underdevelopment which still persists in only slightly modified form today. It can also be argued that only within the context of this historical process can the larger-scale patterns of human geography be effectively understood and interpreted. Central place theory, diffusion models, and Western-based locational analysis provide useful tools for macrogeographical description, but to the degree they remain immersed in a simplistic and inappropriate philosophy of development, they have little explanatory potential outside the hypothetical world of isotropic planes and isolated states. Nor is it sufficient to bow occasionally in displaced guilt toward the evils of colonialism if this is no more than an item on a list of possible excuses why Third World countries do not conform to a lognormal city-size distribution.

But I do not wish to conclude on too critical a note with regard to geography and geographical analysis. For one reason, I remain unashamedly a geographer even after the experience I have described and my current position in a school of architecture and urban planning. In any case, geography is certainly not alone in its careful avoidance of Marxism and other forms of radical analysis. But more importantly, geographers appear to me to be in an unusually advantageous position to make major contributions to what might be called social praxis — the creative synthesis of knowledge and action. This will require geographers to become more actively and directly involved in social change than they have in the past. And it will require both a heightened concern for public policy and planning and a significant reevaluation of the political and ideological basis of geographic analysis.

Fortunately, there are indications that such changes are beginning to occur. And from these changes are emerging two key conceptual developments through which I feel geographers are likely to make lasting and significant contributions. The first involves the development of an essentially dialectical

44

analysis of the relationship between social process
and spatial organization in contemporary society,
while the second, growing out of this dialectical
approach, blends both an increasing appreciation for
the relevance of Marxist thought to geographical analysis and an innovative attempt to add a more explicit
spatial dimension to historical materialism.

NOTES

1. Edward W. Soja, The Geography of Modernization in Kenya (Syracuse: Syracuse University Press,
1968).
2. See the review of The Geography of Modernization in Kenya by Philip W. Porter in Geographical
Analysis (1973), vol. 5, pp. 67-73.
3. John Friedmann, "A General Theory of Polarized Development", reprinted in Urbanization, Planning
and National Development (Beverly Hills, Sage Publications, 1973).
4. Edward W. Soja and Richard J. Tobin, "The
Geography of Modernization: Paths, Patterns and Processes of Spatial Change in Developing Countries",
in Ronald Brunner and Gary Brewer (eds.) A Policy
Approach to the Study of Political Development and
Change, (New York: The Free Press, 1974), pp.197-243.
5. See especially Social Justice and the City,
(Baltimore: Johns Hopkins University Press, 1973).
6. Much of the following information and analysis is taken from Edward W. Soja and Clyde E.Weaver,
"Urbanization and Underdevelopment in East Africa",
in Brian J.L. Berry (ed.), Patterns of Urbanization
and Counter-Urbanization (New York: Sage Publications,
1978).
7. E.A. Brett, Colonialism and Underdevelopment
in East Africa: The Politics of Economic Change, 1919-
1939 (New York: Nok Publications, 1973). See also the
excellent volume by Colin Leys, Underdevelopment in
Kenya: The Political Economy of Neo-Colonialism, 1964-
1971. (Berkeley: University of California Press, 1974).
8. International Labour Organization, Employment,
Incomes and Inequality: A Strategy for Increasing
Productive Employment in Kenya (Geneva: ILO, 1972).
9. Samson M. Kimani, "Spatial Structure of Land
Values in Nairobi, Kenya", Tijdschrift voor Economische en Sociale Geografie, (1972), vol.63:2,pp. 105-114;
and _____, "The Structure of Land Ownership in
Nairobi", Journal of Eastern African Research and
Development, (1972), vol.2:2, pp. 101-124.

3. Regional Disparities and the Employment Problem in Kenya

S. H. Ominde

Introduction

The dynamism which has kept Kenya in the forefront of development efforts among the developing
countries of Africa is increasingly facing challenges
in three broad areas. First, there are the physical
constraints which in the absence of technological
breakthrough have continued to place a ceiling on
available land and which underlie the basic framework
of the country's economic regionalization. Second,
there are the emerging regional disparities in population trends and the dynamics of economic change.
Third, as a developing country Kenya faces the stresses and strains associated with transition from a traditional social and economic base to a world monetary
system.

Any attempt to conceptualize the detailed features of emerging regional disparities faces the inherent problem of data. Not only are the tools of
definition of the emergent regions relatively new,
but the effectiveness of available techniques is hampered by scarcity and unreliability of data. The aim
of this chapter is first to consider the conceptual
framework, analyze the main factors underlying economic regionalization, to discuss the macrospatial organization of Kenya and the consequences of emerging
regional disparities.

Conceptual Framework of Regional Disparities

Factors Underlying Economic Regionalization

A central feature of Kenya's regional disparity
is the contrast between the vast area of the country
(582,647 sq. km. including water surface) and the
concentration of its population mainly in the southern

46

half of the country. This disparity is the reflection of the underlying physical constraints on human
activities. That more than half of Kenya is arid and
semiarid land is a well-known fact of the country's
geography. However, within this broad physical framework much of the resource exploitation that supports
the country's population is limited to the humid-to-
dry sub-humid area (53,587 sq. km.) and to restricted
areas of the dry-sub-humid to semi-arid area (53,434
sq. km.). The remaining parts of the country consist
of vast areas of semi-arid,arid and very arid lands
where increased human activities will call for considerable technological and capital investment efforts.
    But apart from the physical geography, regional
disparities are primarily a result of the cumulative
effect of various policies of development. The earliest conceptual framework which tends to be neglected is the changing administrative boundaries. The
present provincial boundaries are the product of suc-
cessive efforts by colonial governments at administrative spatial organization of the country. In the evolving pattern the Nyanza, Rift Valley, Central,Coast
and Northern arid regions reappear. However in most
cases the administrative concept of spatial organization at independence produced cultural provinces which
bore no relation to resource development problems. The
magnitude of the organizational problems of resource
development can best be appreciated by noting the inherent contradictions. Thus while current government
emphasis on physical development planning stresses a
regional approach, the social or administrative framework has aroused conflicting loyalties.
    Among the most fundamental factors playing a key
role in regional disparity is the evolution of land
policy. This began in the early decades of this
century and culminated in the emergence of the "European Highlands" as an area of large-scale commercial
farming. The "White Highlands" emerged as an island
of European settlement surrounded by African land
units on which it depended for labor. Farmers in the
early stages of evolution of this economic heartland
were keen on policies to induce labor to migrate to
the plantation. The establishment of this nucleus
economic region, which had great initial resource
advantages, was strengthened by the emergent urban
structure and provided the core region around which
the Kenya model of evolving regions of economic and
social disparities developed. A center-periphery relationship evolved, based primarily on the exploitation of spatial agricultural resources.

47

Demarcation of the Regional Macrostructure

A closer examination of Kenya's spatial pattern
reveals three basic characteristics (also noted in
the economic regionalization tendencies of other
countries) as follows:

1. a national heartland - hinterland pattern

2. an urban hierarchy pattern

3. an interurban axis linking the main growth
    centers of the heartland with the capital
    city (Nairobi) and Mombasa.

Quantitative definition of these regions of inequality is one of the main tasks facing economists
and geographers. The earliest documented attempt on
Kenya is that of T.J.D. Fair.[1] He proposed five main
development zones based on the controperiphery concept and assumed deteriorating resource and infrastructure facilities as one moved to the outer zone.
In the center is the Nairobi metropolitan zone
formed by the interlinked cities of Nairobi and Mombasa, which form the commercial and industrial hubs
around which the economy of Kenya revolves. Around
this axis is what Fair described as the inner development zone with a high density of traffic movement
both locally and with the capital city. The periphery
of the heartland on the basis of Fair's analysis is
composed of three overlapping regions of increasing
poverty of resources, and inadequate facilities.
Fair's outline of the zones was primarily descriptive. The most detailed quantitative analysis of
Kenya's economic regions is that of R.B. Ogendo,[2] who
outlines in detail the key factors which have given
rise to the spatial differentiation in Kenya's economic life. Using the index of industrial concentration and the location quotient, he suggests a subdi-
vision of Kenya into the following industrial zones:

a. The central zone

    This is the industrial heartland of Kenya.
    Ogendo's analysis based on the 1964 position
    indicated that this region included nearly
    all the existing industrial development. The
    region showed a strongly nucleated pattern
    with the main clusters including the Nairobi
    region complex, Naivasha-Nakuru-Thomsons
    Falls triangle, Ramisi-Mariakani-Mombasa

48

nucleus and a smaller cluster in Kisumu-
Kericho-Nandi area. Nairobi city and district, Thika town and district, Mombasa town
and district, all in this zone, together
accounted for over fifty percent of Kenya's
manufactural employees in 1964. The three
districts had a combined index of industrial
concentration of up to 94.4.

b.   The inner fringe zone

By definition this is primarily the industrially undeveloped part of the high
potential land, a region described by Ogendo
as "depressed industrially". It includes the
main outmigration districts of Nyanza, Western, Central and Eastern Provinces. In 1964
the percentage distribution of manufactural
employment indicated that most districts in
this zone had five percent or less of the
national total.

c.   The outer fringe zone

This includes land agriculturally classified
as having moderate-to-low potential, with
practically no industry. Manufactural employment in the limited resources accounted
for an insignificant share of the nation's
total. In 1964 most centers showed a national share well below one percent of Kenya's
total manufactural employment.

d.   **The** problem zone

This zone agriculturally contains land of
low potential, remote from the central zone
and generally tsetse-infested. It also has
the country's major wildlife reservoirs, of
which Tsavo is the best-known.

e.   The negative zone

This is the semi-desert and desert heart
of northern Kenya.

It should be stressed that the central zone is
the equivalent of the National Heartland concept. For
further studies on the classification of Kenya into
development regions see K. Ivanicka[3] and P.P. Waller
et al.,[4] and R.A. Obudho. Ivanicka's (1968) model as
applied to Czechoslovakia identifies five types of

regions in accordance with the theory of growth as follows:

1. regions - poles of growth

2. regions - axis of development and growth

3. declining regions

4. regions of redevelopment

5. inadequately developed economic regions

Regions 1. and 2. have already been mentioned in the national heartland and interurban axis concepts. Regions 3. and 5. may also be easily identified in Kenya.

In applying the growth concept, Waller, Obudho and others arrive at three broad development regions applicable to Kenya:

a. Core region — characterized by growth at the core, with as growth pole a town or urbanized area with a steadily expanding population and export complex, a region with a positive migration balance compared with other regions.

b. Upward transitional regions — with a positive or stable migration balance, and export activities not concentrated at one growth pole but scattered over the whole region. The region may show a high or low rate of migration.

c. Downward transitional regions or declining regions — where development is below the level necessary for population growth, and where per-capita income can only be improved by outmigration.

With these preliminary conceptual considerations let us now examine the national spatial context in order to facilitate our understanding of the nature of regional disparities and the policies formulated to solve the problems they create.

Major Spatial Patterns and Characteristic Disparities

The national spatial context of Kenya which development planning must take into account consists of a chain of urban growth poles extending from Kisumu

50

through Nairobi to Mombasa, with an agricultural hinterland to which this is linked by a system of communication and other development infrastructure. This urban zone constitutes the core region of a system of urban hierarchy dominated by the growing metropolis of Nairobi. The agricultural hinterland can be subdivided further into five additional development regions:

1. West Kenya

2. The Central Rift and West Rift farming region

3. Nairobi's immediate hinterland: Central Province and adjacent parts of Eastern Province

4. The Coast hinterland of Mombasa

5. The nomadic and pastoral drylands of Kenya

The Urban Core

The level of urbanization in Kenya at the 1969 census was 9.9 percent of the total population. This urbanization process was concentrated in four main centers which accounted for 77.39 percent of the total urban population. In 1969 the four main urban centers, Nairobi, Mombasa, Makuru and Kisumu accounted for 88.6 percent of the total wage employment in the eleven towns with a population of 10,000 or more. Their share of the self-employed and family workers was 87.5 percent. Nairobi alone accounted for 58.4 percent of total wage employment in the main towns and 65.2 percent of self-employed and family workers.

The majority of urban centers show a rapid growth rate attributable to the influx of Africans in search of employment. The main towns mostly draw their population from the national hinterland, whereas the smaller urban centers draw mainly from nearby provincial sources. The national position of Nairobi, Mombasa and Nakuru is well illustrated by comparison with Kisumu. The destination of most provincial migrants is an urban center, usually a major one. In 1969 the city of Nairobi accounted for 55.8 percent of total African migrants including those from outside Kenya. Mombasa accounted for 24.8 percent, Nakuru 5.6 percent, Kisumu 3.32 percent and Thika 2.2 percent.

Of the total African population in the eleven urban areas of Nairobi, Thika, Nyeri, Malindi, Mombasa, Kisumu, Kericho, Nanyuki, Nakuru, Kitale and Eldoret, the 1969 census indicated definite preferences amongst migrants: over seventy percent of Central Province migrants headed for Nairobi. About eighty-nine

51

percent of the Coast migrants were off to Mombasa. The Eastern Province was split between Nairobi (65.12 percent) and Mombasa (28.79 percent). The North Eastern was shared between Nairobi (25.77 percent) and Mombasa (25.4 percent). Nyanza movements were concentrated on Nairobi (52.86 percent), Kisumu (17.43 percent) and Nakuru; Rift Valley destinations show the importance of Nairobi and Nakuru. The remaining migrants were to be found in Kitale, Eldoret, Nanyuki and Kericho. Western Province migrants showed preference for Nairobi and Mombasa. The strength of migration from rural areas may be assessed from the intercensal growth rate figures in Table 3.1 below.

TABLE 3.1
Growth of African Population in the Main Towns
1948 to 1962, and 1962 to 1969

Town	Average Rate of Growth per annum 1948 - 1962	Average Rate of Growth per annum 1962 - 1969
	(a)	(b)
	%	%
Nairobi	6.5	15.2
Mombasa	7.1	7.6
Nakuru	6.3	4.9
Eldoret	7.6	0.4
Kisumu	7.2	8.7
Thika	10.5	5.6
Nanyuki	8.0	3.0
Kitale	3.5	5.5
Nyeri	9.1	5.2
Kericho	7.2	6.2

Source: Column (a) derived from Kenya Population Census 1962, Vol. III, p. 23.
    Column (b) derived from 1962 and 1969 census figures. N.B.: The comparison of 1962/1969 figures may in some cases be subject to boundary changes.

The rapid influx of population into the main urban centers has given rise to an interesting age distribution where thirty-five percent of the total population is aged fourteen years or less. The working age sector in most cases accounts for over sixty percent of the total population. African population figures for Nairobi in these respective age groups were 35.1 percent and 63.0 percent in 1969. For

Mombasa the figures were 40.2 and 58.9 percent, and
Nakuru figures showed proportions within the age
groups of 43.5 and 55.0 percent respectively.

Analysis of personal characteristics of these
immigrants shows a very large proportion with eight
years of schooling (or less), and that they were drawn
mainly from the Kikuyu - Embu, Meru, Luo, Luhya -
Kisii and Kamba ethnic groups.[5] The figures of intercensal growth rates show that the Kikuyu, Luo, Luhya
and Kipsigis increased by over four percent per year
between 1962 and 1969.

The West Kenya Region

This is primarily the rural hinterland of Kisumu
town and includes two of the most populous provinces
in Kenya. In 1962 the region had approximately thirty-
six percent of Kenya's total population. A recent
Swedish Mission indicated that whereas in 1967 the
region's share of reported employment in manufacturing
was eight percent, it had thirty-five percent of the
total population of Kenya. The township which had a
population of 32,000 is expected to have a half a
million by the end of the century, and the region's
total population is expected to increase from about
3.5 million in 1969 to 8.6 million by the year 2,000.

Waller et al. classified the region as downward
transitional, where development is below the level
necessary to support the population. The region for
over thirty years has been characterized by strong
outmigration to urban centers and other growth
regions in Kenya.

Birthplace data from the 1969 census show that
while well over ninety percent of the population were
locally born, a large proportion of migrants to Nairobi came from that region. Nyanza's share of Nairobi's total population was 10.6 percent and that of
the Western Province was 10.8 percent.

During the colonial phase the region now covered
by the Nyanza and Western Provinces formed a major
labor reservoir for the commercial farming of the former "White Highlands". The high potential land in
these areas could not be used for production of some
of the important cash crops of Kenya because of the
discriminatory legislation of a settler-dominated
colonial legislature.

The first settler-grown coffee export from the
Highlands is recorded in 1909. Although the possibility of African-grown coffee was mentioned as early
as 1920, not until 1932 did the Coffee Industry Bill
permit growing of coffee "by natives in the Embu and

Meru Districts on a limited scale and under strict
supervision and control"[6]
    The first planting in the Nyanza area was in
Kisii in the mid-1930s — forty-six acres. It did
not become a part of the government's cash crop
policy until the middle 1950s. Until the mid-1930s
government was mainly preoccupied with European
farming.[7]
    This loss of initial momentum led in the early
and late colonial phase, to large-scale emigration
to the developing lacustrine zone of southern Uganda.
Postindependence changes giving increased preference
to nationals have led to a large influx back into
Kenya. The impact of these returned migrants may
well be noted in the mushrooming periurban developments around the southern, eastern and northern peripheries of Kisumu. Analysis of migration by Census
Survival Ratio for Kakamega district, shows a negative net migration for all cohorts except for males
from fifty-five to eighty years of age.
    The realignment of political forces in indepen-
dent Kenya has merely aggravated the situation through
a slowing-down of the pace of economic growth. Heavy
outmigration has therefore continued into postindependence period as indicated by the following sex ratios
for population age fifteen to fifty-nine, see
Table 3.2:

TABLE 3.2
Western Kenya Sex Ratios, 1969

District	Sex Ratio Total Population	Sex Ratio Urban Areas	Sex Ratio Rural Areas
Kisumu	102.4	155.8	98.1
Siaya	65.5	N/A	65.5
South Nyanza	87.7	180.4	87.1
Kisii	95.7	191.2	94.8
Nyanza	88.2	163.2	86.7
Kakamega	79.1	151.5	78.5
Bungoma	91.4	161.2	90.5
Busia	74.6	N/A	74.6
Western	81.4	155.3	80.8

Source: Based on 1969 population census

The disparity between this region and the rest of the country regarding development of the modern sector of the economy is illustrated in Table 3.3:

TABLE 3.3
Percentage of Total Employed Population in the Modern Sector by Province - 1969
(Total Wage Employment, Self-Employed and Family Workers)

Province	1969 Percentage
Nairobi	33.0
Central Province	5.9
Nyanza	2.2
Western Province	1.4
Coast Province	9.2
Rift Valley Province	8.8
Eastern Province	2.1
North Eastern Province	1.0

Source: Employment Data from Annual Enumeration of Employees 1968-1970 (unpublished)

Among the social differentials is the level of enrolment in primary schools. The proportion of population enrolled ranges from 7.2 percent in South Nyanza to 12.9 percent in Siaya. The Western Province percentage of enrolment ranges from 12.4 for Kakamega to 16.8 in Bungoma. The percentage of trained primary school teachers in Nyanza varies from 46.9 in Kisii to 67.5 in Siaya and Kisumu (combined). In the Western Province the percentage is even higher and varies from 76.4 in Bungoma to 82.9 percent in Kakamega District. Thus to demographic and economic disparities must be added the differences in education opportunities. As a result of historical factors the Nyanza and Western Provinces have a large share of educational facilities, and every year the region contributes a high proportion of job seekers with various education levels.

While the educational system and a poorly developed economy continue to contribute to the growing number of job seekers outside the two provinces, the urban infrastructure remains underdeveloped. At the 1962 census there were only three towns with more

55

than 2,000 people in the whole region. The combined
urban population of these centers was 32,007 out of a
regional population of 3,000,000 — an urbanization
rate of less than one percent. This extremely low rate
of urbanization reflects the subsistence character of
the economy.

The Central and West Rift Farming Region

This is the rich highland farming zone extending
from the Nakuru-Naivasha area to the West Rift Highlands, and includes the bulk of the former "White
Highlands" area with the township of Nakuru as the
largest urban center. In 1962 it had approximately
ten percent of Kenya's total population, which percentage had risen to fourteen in 1969. A recent survey
of employees (1968-1970) indicates that the Rift
Valley accounts for 28.6 percent of total wage employment in the modern sector and 32.1 percent of self-
employed and family workers.

Thus together with the urban Nairobi region, this
is one of the main areas of employment in the modern
sector. Waller et al. clarified it as an upward transitional region. Prior to independence it was the
main focus of rural-to-rural migration of farm workers.
The tendency for the main farming districts to attract
labor migration is well illustrated by the following
data from the 1962 census (Table 3.4):

TABLE 3.4
Labor Migration

District	Percentage of Males & Females Aged 15-59 Born in the District	Percentage of Males & Females Aged 15-59 Born Elsewhere in Kenya
Trans-Nzoia	33.14	60.61
Laikipia	18.70	80.32
Naivasha	32.10	67.53
Nakuru	22.26	77.07
Uasin Gishu	27.36	70.40

Source: S.H. Ominde and R.S. Odingo, "Demographic
Aspects of Regional Inequalities in Kenya". IGU
Commission on Regional Aspects of Economic
Development (Brazil, 1971).

These core districts of the region were in marked
contrast to the surrounding former African Districts
where the proportion of persons between ages fifteen
to fifty-nine born in the district was well over
eighty to ninety percent. This stream of migration
is strongly dominated by males.

The pattern of migration to these farming districts is well illustrated by net migration data calculated by the Census Survival Ratio method which
indicate that in Trans-Nzoia, net migration based on
1969 sex and age data is negative for males and females aged one to four and fifteen to fifty-nine, but
positive for both between ages twenty to twenty-four.
Between twenty-five and thirty-four, both males and
females show negative net migration. From thirty-
five to thirty-nine a positive net migration is recorded throughout. These figures suggest that labor migration favors the twenty-to-twenty-four age group
and laborers in their middle and late maturity. Such
a pattern is in marked contrast to outmigration districts which show a negative net migration up to age
fifty-five to fifty-nine, when retirement begins to
take effect. Nakuru District shows a net migration
pattern closely resembling that of Trans-Nzoia.

The urban infrastructure of this region is more
diverse but is dominated by the small service town.
Towns with a population range of 10,000 to 19,999 in
1969 accounted for 34.68 percent of total urban population. Nakuru alone in 1969 accounted for 31.73 percent of the total urban population of the Rift Valley
Province. Despite the apparent multiplicity of urban
centers, the urbanization level in the whole province
was only 6.7 percent. The former African outlying
district of the Rift Valley Province suffers from extremely poor roads and lack of developmental services.

Life expectancy at birth for females in Trans-
Nzoia in 1969 was 49.2 years, for males 45.6 — in
contrast to the national figure of 51.2 years for
females and 46.9 for males.

Model abridged life tables for Nakuru showed a
life expectancy at birth of 48.7 for females, 46.3
years for males. An interesting feature is the high
mortality under age four. These life expectancy figures compare unfavorably with urban data for the city
of Nairobi where life expectation at birth for males
is 52 years.

The immediate hinterland of the city of Nairobi
includes the whole of Central Province, the Embu,
Meru, Kitui and Machakos districts of Eastern Province and adjacent parts of Kajiado district to the
southwest. Agriculturally it is a diverse region,

57

and includes the heavily populated high-potential
lands of the Aberdares and Mount Kenya slopes and
the populous parts of Machakos. The region also
includes some medium- to low-potential land in the
drier areas east of Nairobi.

In 1962 this region accounted for about thirty-
four percent of the total population of Kenya. The
1969 census indicated it had about thirty-five per- √
cent of the total. Its role is greatly influenced
by the location of the capital city of Nairobi in
the south. The exceptional population concentration
especially in the volcanic highlands and in the highland residuals of Machakos District has already been
noted. The postindependence period has brought about
important boundary adjustments which have had implications for population distribution.

As well as the agricultural potential of the
more productive parts, forestry also plays an important role in the economy. Central Province with an
approximate area of 13,310 square kilometers, includes
substantial forest areas which account for approximately twenty-six percent of that province's total area.

Geographical distribution of population shows a
striking contrast between Nyandarua, the forest areas,
the middle Athi-Tana region, and the lower slopes of
Aberdares where rural densities of 500 to well over
700 people-per-square-kilometer are common. In particular, areas adjacent to the city of Nairobi show
extremely high density.

Within individual districts of Central Province
there are important variations. In Kiambu, two-
thirds of the total population in 1969 were in sublocations with 300 people or more per square kilometer.
For the density range of 500 or more the proportions
were 48.83 percent of the population in fifteen percent of the area. Muranga, the other heavily populated district, indicated that sublocations with more
than 500 people-per-square-kilometer accounted for
twenty-five percent of total land area. At the northern end of the population axis of Central Province,
sixty percent of the total population of the Nyeri
district were crowded in sublocations with densities
of 300 or more per square kilometer.

Inequalities in distribution of population over
the land become more marked away from the Central Province area. In the Mount Kenya area the population
is heavily concentrated on the limited high potential
lands of the mountain slope, leaving vast low-lying
areas to the east sparsely peopled. In Machakos area
population is concentrated largely in the northwestern
highlands. The shortage of land in relation to population needs has always been a crucial factor in the

58

development problems of the Machakos area.

A vital population problem in Nairobi's hinterland area is its rate of growth. Central Province is
still potentially an area of large rural population
increase. The former district of Nyeri showed annual
intercensal rates of increase of two to five percent
per annum between 1962 and 1969. Slightly lower
increases were noted for Murang'a District. It has already been noted that major ethnic groups occupying
Nairobi's hinterland record growth rates well in
excess of the national average.

Migration data from the 1969 census show that
Central and Eastern Provinces accounted for forty-five
percent (46.25 percent) of African migrants into the
city of Nairobi. Central Province contributed 31.10
percent, Eastern Province 15.15 percent. The majority
of Central Province migrants came from Murang'a and
Nyeri. Contributions of the two provinces to total
migrants into Nairobi were: twenty-six percent (Central) and 12.6 percent (Eastern) respectively. In a
study of labor migration, Rempel showed that of the
men who migrated from Central Province, 46.7 percent
went to Nairobi and 21.4 percent to Nyeri.[8] In Eastern Province 39.6 percent migrated to Nairobi, forty-
one percent to Mombasa. In both provinces, over fifty
percent of the men who moved in 1970 to urban centers
were primary school leavers. Primary school enrollment in Central Province is closely approaching uni-
versality.

Rural sex ratios for the fifteen-to-fifty-nine
age group confirm that the impact of outmigration is
felt most in Murang'a (71.5) and Nyeri (76.4). In
Eastern Province low rural sex ratios were recorded
for Embu (81.2), Kitui (74.0), and Machakos (80.7).
These figures compare closely with outmigration
districts of western Kenya such as Siaya (65.5),
South Nyanza (87.1), Kakamega (78.5), and Busia (74.6).

Negative net migration in Kiambu is characteristic
of cohorts up to age fifty-five to fifty-nine when retirement begins to have an effect and a positive net
migration starts for men. For women, positive net migration in Kiambu starts from age forty to forty-four.
In Nyeri positive net migration for males starts from
fifty-five to fifty-nine and for females, from fifty
to fifty-four years of age.

The underdeveloped Kitui district shows a heavy
population outflow leading to a net loss up to the age
of fifty-nine years. Machakos would show a similar
trend.

However, despite heavy outmigration Central Province, part of the hinterland in 1970, recorded fairly

high employment figures in the modern sector compared
with provinces more remote from the capital city such
as Western Province, Eastern and North Eastern Provinces.

Abridged model life tables show a slightly higher
life expectation for Kiambu than for Kitui. Kiambu
female life expectancy for 1969 was 53.4 years, for
males, 50.5 years. Kitui female life expectancy was
43.6 years due largely to heavy infant mortality rising from poorly developed social services and low
rural incomes.

The Coastal Region

This region is isolated from parts of the interior by a broad zone of very low productivity. In 1962
the region accounted for about eight percent of the
total population of Kenya. Mombasa, its urban core
sector, is the second most important industrial town
in Kenya. An expanding growth pole, it caters for
the export services of a wide area including the rest
of Kenya, Uganda, Tanzania, and parts of the Congo. As
with Nairobi, the environmental and income gap between
Mombasa's growth pole and the rest of rural Kenya is
growing, leading to rapidly increasing net migration.
Postindependence changes have also added a thriving
tourist trade for which Mombasa is already catering.

In 1967, Mombasa accounted for sixteen percent
of reported employment in manufacturing. The region's
share of population was eight percent. The city,which
had a total population of 247,000 at the 1969 census,
is expected to grow to 1.4 million by the end of the
century, serving an immediate hinterland whose population should increase from 0.9 million in 1969 to 2.6
million by the end of the century.

Apart from large-scale non-African farming activities begun early in the colonial period, much of
Mombasa's hinterland has stayed relatively undeveloped.
Sugar and coconut plantations of Kwale District in the
south, and coconut and sisal plantations in Kilifi District to the north were among the earliest centers to
attract migrant labor. Her rural districts have a
much lower proportion of high-potential agricultural
land than the Central and Rift Valley Provinces. Percentage of high-potential land varied from 1.1 in
Lamu to 15.3 in Kwale.

Demographically, the hinterland districts of Mombasa form the main source of migration to the city.
Analysis of the distribution of African migrants by
major towns shows that 54.6 percent of the population
were from Coast Province, 15.8 percent from Eastern

Province, 9.28 percent from Nyanza and 6.37 percent
from Western Province. Birthplace data for the total
population showed that of male migrants born in the
Coast Province, 92 percent went to Mombasa. Distribution of male migrants from the other provinces in
respect of major urban centers was more widespread.

1969 data on birthplace shows that of total migrants from Coast Province to the eight main urban
centers of Kenya with population 10,000 or more, just
over 89 percent were in Mombasa. Relatively undeveloped social services in the region are underlined by
the low primary school enrollment except in Mombasa
and Taita.

An important feature of the Coastal region is a
relatively weak urban infrastructure. Most coastal
towns are small administrative centers. Except for
Malindi and Mombasa, the percentage in the working-
age group (fifteen to fifty-nine) is generally less
than fifty percent.

Except for Mombasa, the number of kilometers of
road per 1,000 square kilometers of land is extremely
low; whereas Central, Rift Valley, Nyanza and Western
Provinces average more than 100 kilometers per 1,000
square kilometers, for the Coast Province the figures
are generally below 60 kilometers per 1,000. This
is just one indication of the underdeveloped infrastructure which includes such vital services as
electricity and water supply.

The Arid and Semi-Arid Lands

Physical constraints and the concentration of
development in the high-potential lands have left
vast areas of Kenya undeveloped and largely out of
reach of modern influences. These vast lands of fair-
to-poor resources and limited facilities include the
whole of North Eastern Province, parts of the Rift
Valley and Coast Province.[9] An attempt has already
been made to underline the ways in which this region
differs from other parts of Kenya.

In his suggested "Industrial Development Zones of
Kenya", Ogendo[10] has divided this area into three
main subdivisions: The Outer Fringe Zone, Problem
Zone and Negative Zone, based on distribution of manufacturing industries and the physical disadvantages
the region suffers. The main problem is lack of
a basic service infrastructure and limited agricultural potential.

Colbatch[11] gives an indication of the low level
of development of roads and educational facilities
as follows: (Table 3.5)

61

TABLE 3.5
Levels of Road Construction and Educational Facilities

Province	District	Population per Km.	Percentage of Population in Primary School	Km of Road per 1,000 Km.
Coast	Tana River	1	7.7	14.1
North Eastern	Garissa	1	2.5	11.8
	Wajir	2	1.5	17.9
	Mandera	4	1.5	10.6
Rift Valley	Narok	7	5.0	46.3
	Kajiado	4	9.0	39.0
	Turkana	2	2.0	13.7
	Samuru	3	3.0	20.2

Source: H. Colbatch

     Although more than two-thirds of Kenya's total
area is included in this region the population has
remained small. Comparison of the 1962 and 1969
census figures suggests a growth rate of only 1.1 percent per annum, a slow population increase due to
adverse circumstances. Birthrate data at the 1969
census indicates that despite the harshness of the
environment, people from this region formed a very
small portion of rural-to-urban migrants, their
contribution to the populations of the eleven main
towns remaining below one percent, most of these
to be found in Nairobi and Mombasa.
     Ogendo suggests that the outer fringe zone can
only be developed gradually under strong government
incentives with extensive research based on existing
and introduced agricultural material resources.[12] But
development of the Problem Zone, with its severe conditions, is not seen in terms of agriculture but
through further mineral prospecting, tourism, and
possibly wildlife cropping. Such developments would
require a greatly improved infrastructure including
the provision of water.
     The Negative Zone faces more serious development

constraints. In common with other parts of the region
it suffers from remoteness and extremely poor transport facilities, and it is beset with disasters of
drought and repeated famine.

A Summary of Emerging Policy Issues on
Regional Planning and Development[13]

It is now widely accepted that a part of government involvement in the dynamics of Kenyan development must be the formulation of investment strategies
not only on an overall basis but also to distribute
development across the whole state over the course of
time. A great deal of helpful information now exists
on regional development and planning, especially in
the more developed countries of the world.

However, in most developing countries, where
data is scarce, a major constraint is lack of empirical evidence and comparative studies regarding long-
term relations between overall national development
and its spatial dimensions. The powerful attraction
of the center, and a systematic underevaluation of
investment opportunities on the periphery, continue
to provide a powerful check against any tendency to
narrow disparities. Faster sectoral growth rates at
the center, inability of the periphery to adjust adequately to changing conditions due to lack of local
capital, and effects of selective outmigration all
work against any long-term attempt to spread the
effects of growth beyond the developed areas.

In Kenya, regional planning confronts two sets
of problems, largely administrative in nature: first,
a desire to involve local people in what has been
described as "grassroots planning"; second, the need
to provide local authorities with machinery for their
involvement in the development effort.

The basic weakness of current approaches to
spatial planning is that plans do not deal with the
core, problem of resource allocation. Plans as presently formulated seem to lack specificity. Neither
plans nor organizational structure provide an adequate
basis for choices which must be made by government as
to how national income, investments and welfare services are to be distributed spatially and restructured
to implement the essentials of government policy.

Grounds for Regional Resource Allocation

There are three major aspects in which government policies for regional investment contribute to
spatial dimensions of planning goals, or to planning
constraints:

63

1. First, regional planning must include among
    its policy objectives, the need to alter the
    balance of distribution of industrial produc-
    tion within different areas of the country

2. Further, there is an urgent need to observe
    some restrictions on degree of regional
    income disparities allowable

3. The third objective includes a strategy to
    ease overall constraints by deliberate devel-
    opment of resources of a region. Constraints
    which are the objective of such planning may
    be foreign exchange, capital or administra-
    tive capacity.

    The need for a new attack on problems of regional
development could be translated into a policy objective comprising an admixture of economic, social and
purely political aims.

    In the first case, regional growth policies
would be directed towards a more efficient use of
available resources, such policies to be based on
identification of natural, human and other resources
not now being exploited or mobilized, and which cannot
be easily transferred from one region to another. The
focus of such a policy is based on the assumption
that maximum growth of the economy will not be
reached without planning for locational interdependence of regional resources.
    In the second category are those "welfare poli-
cies" directed towards a more equitable distribution
of the output of the economy between different areas.
Benefits of growth here would be spread on the basis
of some welfare principle.
    Thirdly, programs could be aimed at "regional
integration policies" directed towards achieving some
space preference of the government. Such policies
are based on the recognition of the political influence of given areas in relation to overall state unity.
    However, these three broad policy areas must con-
tribute to a more balanced development of national
spatial units. Balanced development is crucial in
the area of urbanization which will be considered
later. The emerging policy issues can be summarized
as follows:

    a. First, the need to see the long-term effects
        of correcting regional imbalances as a vital
        contribution to the integrity of the state,

and as an instrument for its survival.
This means that among the most important
recommendations of the mission, the instrument for carrying out this broad objective
on a continuing basis must be clearly identified, and must lead to a more efficient
plan formulation, implementation and
evaluation.

b. Second, the widening disparities between
    emerging heartland and hinterland, and the
    tendency of the center to command a dispro-
    portionate share of development effort to
    the detriment of centers on the periphery.
    Policy efforts should be in terms of decen-
    tralization of growth to avoid the implica-
    tions of overurbanization in one or two
    main growth centers.

c. Third, the widening disparities between ur-
    ban and rural areas as a result of differen-
    tial rates of economic and social develop-
    ment, large-scale internal migrations and
    the frustrations that come with lack of
    job opportunities.

d. Finally, the need for physical development
    planning and an urbanization strategy.

However, before making policy suggestions in the
areas indicated it is necessary to comment on the
problem of unemployment as the Select Committee on
Unemployment 1970 saw it.

The Select Committee on Unemployment

The committee's definition of the problem and
its recommendations clearly show that the perception
of the problem was limited by lack of data. Paragraph
(2) of the report underlines lack of adequate statistics which limited the determination of the extent
of underemployment in the country.
The committee was able to comment on the problem
at regional level only in broad terms. It seems the
committee did not have detailed demographic information to guide it in commenting on the spatial aspects
of the problem.
However, it should be noted that despite scarcity of data demographic, economic and social, the
focus on the demographic, economic and social roots
of the problem was essentially in accord with the

65

Mission's emphasis. In the field of education, the problem was seen primarily in terms of curriculum structure. The educational contribution to the unemployment problem is aggravated by the numbers presenting themselves.

The Committee's Recommendations on General Policy Measures

The committee's emphasis was clearly on economic solutions to the problem. Unemployment could be greatly reduced through more development.

Although the committee clearly recognized the problem's demographic roots, serious differences of opinion led to a half-measure suggestion. The committee came to the surprisng conclusion that they could not see programmed family planning as a possible policy measure (para. 20). It saw education as contributing to the long-term solution to excess population growth.

However, the committee's well-directed emphasis on positive rural development aimed at primary school leavers, shows that members were clearly here deliberating on a problem which they were in a much better position to analyze. The committee's criticism of concentration of development funds on urban development, and their emphasis on the need for a more equitable distribution of such funds are some of their most far-reaching recommendations.

The call for a more equitable distribution of funds is in a sense an admission that traditional methods of government planning have failed to overcome widening regional disparities.

More important is the committee's emphasis on the problem of "tribalism". It might be argued that the committee's views represent the backbencher's traditional response to the problem of resource allocation. However, the committee's emphasis clearly underlines the constraints diverse cultural loyalties in Kenya may create in the use of scarce resources. The problem raised at this level of political responsibility suggests that Kenya may well save scarce resources from wastage by considering carefully a structure that would reestablish the essential interrelationship between national and regional development.

Earlier, the cultural context of the administration's machinery within which plan implementation must take place was noted, and the problem of conflicting loyalties was raised. Strong cultural loyalties may intensify problems of unemployment at the provincial, district and urban local authority levels.

66

Conflict arises where cultural loyalties tend to
encourage parochialism, and to obscure the ultimate
national goal of regional development. There must
be a balancing factor to minimize the negative effects
of essentially local loyalties. It is against this
background that the proposed "National Development
Advisory Council" should be assessed.

Physical Development Planning and the Emergent
Problem of Urban Expansion

One of the most serious consequences of regional
inequality is the influx of job seekers into the urban
core region. The relationship between the increasing
volume of urban job seekers and the diminishing share
of good quality land is underlined in the following
paragraph by the Town Planning Department:

> ... Recent regional studies by the Town Planning
> Department of the relationship between the vari-
> able agricultural land and the rate of population
> growth in several provinces of Kenya have shown
> that the pressure of population density in many
> areas will reach serious proportions during the
> next thirty years. Stated simply, there will
> just not be sufficient land for all or even most
> of the grandsons of today's farmers to become
> farmers themselves ... The amount of land with
> surplus population absorption capacity is less
> than might be imagined, due to low rainfall, un-
> suitable soil conditions and other factors, and
> a large proportion of Kenya's future generations
> will need to find nonagricultural employment.[14]

A recent study of the position by the Town Planning Department indicates that if current targets of
economic growth are achieved and population growth is
reduced to three percent per annum, approximately
seven and three-quarters million people will be living
in towns in Kenya, of a total population of twenty-
four to thirty million, by the year 2000. Such a rate
of growth would mean an eight-fold increase in urban
population. Projected figures for major urban centers
indicate that Nairobi will expand to a city of 3.2
million, Mombasa to 1.3 million, and Kisumu to
.5 million.
The consequences on local authorities in the
urban areas can be envisioned: increased pressure on
the already overburdened urban infrastructure and
social services, leading to a further deterioration in
the quality of the urban environment and urban living.
Current trends indicate that continuing regional

disparities will force an even larger proportion of Kenyans into urban living. It is this prospect that underlies the government's sense of urgent need for an urganization growth policy, particularly in physical planning.

Urban Land Needs

Present projections of future urban land needs available to government have been prepared to the year 1980, see table 3.6 below. This projection is based on an assumption that government will achieve some success in diverting economic and social development from the core urban centers of Mombasa and Nairobi to the smaller centers which have stagnated on the peripheries. Stated another way, the tables assume a measure of success in the spatial decentralization of development efforts.

TABLE 3.6   Urban Land Needs 1980

Town	1980 Population Projections	1980 Urban Land Needs (sq.km. @ 50 persons per hectare)	Present Area (sq.km.)
Nairobi	950,000	192	693
Mombasa	410,000	83	214
Nakuru	80,000	16	78
Kisumu	60,000	12	417
Thika	36,000	7	99
Eldoret	34,000	7	25
Nanyuki	20,000	4	22
Kitale	21,000	4	18
Malindi	22,000	4	18
Nyeri	18,000	4	72
Kericho	16,000	3	10
Isiolo	10,000	2	45
Thompson's Falls	14,000	3	16
Lamu	10,000	2	48
Marsabit	10,000	2	26
Naivasha	14,000	3	11
Machakos	15,000	3	19
Kisii	13,000	3	3
Meru	10,000	2	207
Embu	15,000	3	24
Kakamega	16,000	3	49
Voi	12,000	2	8
Athi River	13,000	3	9
Elburgon	6,000	1	2
Towns 2-5,000	100,000	20	1,964
TOTAL	1,925,000	388	4,127

68

TABLE 3.7

Typical Average Land Use in Urban Areas

	Percentage of Total
Residential	33.2%
Industrial	6.2%
Educational	12.5%
Public	12.0%
Commercial	33.1%
Public Utilities	2.4%
Transportation	20.0%
Recreational	10.6%

A proper assessment of actual needs is hampered by lack of adequate data on urban land use. The figures would need to be qualified by a more satisfactory measurement of the migration factor. But inadequate as the figures are, they give a broad indication of the scope of the urbanization process and the problem of resource allocation that is the target of the physical development planning strategy.

Many towns that presently fall within the scope of physical development planning were in existence by the first decade of this century. A growing concentration of economic activity at the center and the increasing volume of rural/urban migration shows that the urban infrastructure has not been expanded adequately to decentralize economic and social activity.

The causes of this failure are complex, and include not only the historical context of the evolution of Kenya's economy, but also the constraints inherent in the center-periphery relationship in the field of local government, and the politicization of policy-making and plan implementation machinery during the postindependence phase.

A Summary of Policy Recommendations

Long-Term Measures

a. Decentralization of the Planning Process

The aim of such a policy is to establish central planning machinery at the local level (local councils and urban authorities), first to continue the process begun with the establishment of planning units within the provincial office and now at the district level. One of the most important objectives here is to transform

existing urban authorities into effective planning units within the framework of physical
development planning. At the central government
level this would include decentralization of
some experienced central staff to the provinces
and districts. This recommendation should be
considered part of the strategy of planning from
below and from above, as recommended in the
macrostrategy section.

b. A Detailed Statement of the Priorities
   of Urban Decentralization

Current government physical development plan
gives priority to a number of growth centers,
but population targets used are based on growth
trends affected by the tempo of economic activity.
It is suggested that for planning purposes, population targets for Kisumu, Nakuru and Eldoret
might be revised upwards for the year 2000 ,
taking into account a new directed industrial location policy which the government is expected
to adopt. A detailed infrastructural development program should be prepared for these
centers along with the industrial location plan.
   The second order of priority should include
intermediate centers (including the remaining
provincial centers). Consideration should be
given to the planning of these towns, choice of
an alternate site and the population level for
which infrastructural investment is to be made
by the national government.
   The third order of priority should include
the smaller towns and district centers. These
centers will draw on the national infrastructural investment resources but will have a lower
population ceiling.

c. Staff Development Policy

The central government should institute a program to train staff in regional planning offices,
the training program to be phased in in accordance with the decentralization policy and aimed
at urban and other local authorities

d. A Satisfactory Plan for Financing Urban
   and Rural Infrastructure

Recommendation b. incorporates a national policy
on infrastructural development. This means that
government should set out specific financial

70

targets to be allocated to growth centers on a
priority basis. It should also include the land
cost incurred in the compensation process. Without a national program of investment in urban infrastructure, the centers will not attract
industries.

Short-Term Measures

a. Development of a Comprehensive Statistical
    Service

The need is for field integration of data collecting and local processing. The present position
of data is confused and further complicated by
unrecorded boundary changes at the local level.
It is recommended that the statistical service
at the district level be reorganized to serve the
functional ministries as well as the district as
a whole, which will require personnel allocation
of a higher caliber.

b. Establishment of a National Industrial
    Location Policy

It is recommended that as part of regional development strategy, the Ministry of Commerce and Industry should set up machinery to direct the location of new industry in accordance with the declared government program of regional development.
The absence of such machinery is a major weakness
in the existing situation and works against a
policy of reducing regional inequalities.

c. A Population Redistribution Policy

The existing government policy of settlement, resettlement and land grants to the landless is part
of the policy of population redistribution. But
in view of the complexity of the land problem, a
thorough survey should be made of the land situation as a basis for such a policy. Among factors
to be considered is the basis for selection.

d. A National Development Council

The national government has a number of avenues
open for stimulating regional development: It
could involve itself in carrying out direct and
indirect investment programs in the downward
transition zones. It could also encourage

71

those willing to invest in these areas by giving
them incentives either directly or indirectly,by
granting concessions such as generous tax relief.
The government could also stimulate development by encouraging local governments and similar
bodies to invest by increasing their share of financial resources. In addition local entrepreneurs
could be encouraged to invest by making funds available from quasigovernment institutions, and
where necessary by acting as their guarantor.
However, it is strongly recommended that in
addition to these measures, government should set
up a National Development Council, advisory to
the Ministry of Finance, such a council to be
composed of the Provincial Commissioners and their
economic consultants, and representatives drawn
from district development agencies. Government
officials from the Ministry of Finance would be
ex-officio members.
The task of such a body would be to advise
the Ministry on regional plan formulation, implementation and evaluation. It would be a meeting
point for a constant review of ongoing and proposed programs and it would consider plans for
distribution of projects among the regions. The
Council should have a professional economist
whose duty would be to advise the Council on
technical matters relating to plan implementation
and evaluation at regional levels.

NOTES

1. T.J.D. Fair, "A Regional Approach to Economic
Development in Kenya". South African Geographic Journal Vol.45 (1963), pp. 57-77.
2. R.B. Ogendo, "The Significance of Industrial
Zoning to Rural Industrial Development in Kenya. A
Study of Facts and Methodology", Cahiers d'Etudes
Africaines, 27: Vol. VII (1967), pp. 444-484.
3. K. Ivanicka, "Problems Connected with Research
of Regions in Czechoslovakia. Function and Forming of
Regions", Acta Geographia, Universatatis Comunenianae;
Economico Geographica No. 8 (Bratislava: 1968).
4. P.P. Waller et al., "Basic Features of Regional Planning in the Region of Kisumu, (Kenya)" (Deut-
sches Institut fur Entwicklungspolitik: Berlin: 1968).
and K.A. Obudho and P.P. Waller, Periodic Markets, Urbanization and Regional Planning — A Case Study from
Kenya (Westport, Connecticut: Greenwood Press, 1976).
5. Henry Rempel, "The Rural-to-Urban Migrant in
Kenya", African Urban Notes VI (Spring 1971), pp.53-72.

6. M.F. Hill, "Planter's Progress. Coffee Board of Kenya" (Nairobi: East African Standard, 1956), p. 94.

7. Hugh Fearn, An African Economy, A Study of the Economic Development of the Nyanza Province of Kenya 1903-1953 (London: Oxford University Press, 1961), p. 224.

8. H. Rempel, op.cit.

9. T. Fair, op.cit.

10. R. Ogendo, op.cit.

11. Colbatch, H., personal communication.

12. R. Ogendo, op.cit.

13. M. Safier, On the Political Economy of Resource Allocation for Planning (Makerere: Makerere Institute of Social Research, 1969).

14. Republic of Kenya, UN Conference on the Human Environment. Case Study: Urbanization and Environment in Kenya (Nairobi: Government Printer, 1971) pp. 1-2.

4. Deriving Planning Regions for Developing Countries: Kenya

David L. Huff and James M. Lutz

Introduction

When the international boundaries in Africa were established in the nineteenth century, they were usually drawn with little or no attention to local circumstances, but rather to meet the needs of European diplomats meeting in Paris or Berlin. These diplomats were primarily interested in other parts of the world and few if any of them had set foot on African soil, let alone become familiar with local conditions on the continent. Similarly, the intranational subdivisions of the African colonies were often established without regard to local circumstances, but rather to facilitate administrative activities, to provide services for European immigrants, to consolidate control, to exploit mineral or agricultural resources, and to achieve similar results. The local boundaries drawn by the colonial administration could thus be less than ideal for an independent nation attempting to organize its political space.

All states, regardless of size and geographical location in the world, face the problem that local units of government may have become outdated as a result of technological, social and economic changes. Edward W. Soja, for example, points out a number of such artifacts in his analysis of the political organization of space in the United States.[1] If the problem exists in a modern country that has had the opportunity to choose its own intranational boundaries, the problem could well be greater in a state where the local governmental boundaries were created by an external colonial power. Local units thus formed may take on a rigid semblance due to political pressures, either from the population at large or from political leaders wishing to preserve an important stronghold for themselves. When a reorganization does take place, it often is influenced by political considerations rather than factors in the best interest of the public.

Some work has been done on urban systems in Kenya, the geographic focus of this study. This work however has generally dealt with problems of urbanization within various cities, without regard to interrelationships that exist between these centers and their hinterlands.[2] Paul G. Clark suggested emphasizing development efforts in "favorably endowed regions" and in "the most promising cities", but he did not delve into the relationships between urban centers and hinterlands.[3] There have been other studies but often as in the case of Clark, the focus was not on the relationships between urban and rural areas. The importance of these relationships has been noted by Soja, who felt that the "identity in the hinterlands of major African urban centers" was an important topic requiring further investigation.[4] Peter R. Gould emphasized that the study of rural problems in African countries must focus "upon those functional relationships that bind urban nodes to their rural hinterlands in general systems of space organizations."[5] Others have noted that in general, or with particular reference to urban African centers, such centers have important effects beyond their legal limits.[6] The delineation of urban spheres of influence, therefore, is one means of more explicitly identifying the areal extent of urban-rural interactions.

Purpose

The present study was undertaken to delineate the spheres of influence of a group of urban places in Kenya, one of the recently independent states in Africa. These urban centers with their associated territorial spheres of influence, would comprise an example of a national set of regions providing a geographical delivery system for serving public interests. A distinctive feature of this study is the use of a model and a computer program, rather than subjective or empirical analysis, in making the delineations. As a result, the same basis will be utilized in delineating the spheres of influence of all urban centers. The procedure is completely replicative. Another important attribute of the method is that delineations can be done comparatively quickly and inexpensively, a quite significant feature if periodic monitoring is desired.

Geometric Properties

The nature of the territory tributary to a given urban center can best be thought of in probabilistic terms. Stated more formally, it is postulated that P_{ij}, the probability of an individual located at point i travelling to an urban place j, is proportional to the ratio $S_j/D_{ij}{}^{\gamma}$, where S_j is the size of an urban place j, D_{ij} is the distance from an individual's travel base i to j, and γ is a constant that reflects the effect of distance on various types of trips, e.g., shopping, recreational, educational, medical, and social. Let n equal the total number of urban places in a given area. Then

$$(1.0) \qquad P_{ij} = A_j D_{ij}{}^{-\gamma} / \sum_{j=1}^{n} A_j D_{ij}{}^{-\gamma}$$

such that $\sum_{j=1}^{n} P_{ij} = 1$

and $0 \leq P_{ij} \geq 1$.

The geographic area comprising the sphere of influence of an urban place consists of a series of attraction gradients, which are isoprobability lines ranging from a probability value of less than one to a value greater than zero except where only one urban place exists, in which case there would be no gradients but rather a plane with a probability value equal to one.[7]

Expected Values

The following equation determines the expected number of individuals traveling to a given urban place:

$$(2.0) \qquad E_{ij} = P_{ij} \cdot I_j$$

where E_{ij} = expected number of individuals at i traveling to j,

P_{ij} = probability of any given individual at i traveling to j, and

I_i = number of individuals at i.

The value T_j, the total expected number of individuals who are likely to travel to $\underline{j}$, is derived by summing the expected values from each of the $\underline{m}$ points of origination. That is,

(3.0)
$$T_j = \sum_{i=1}^{m} E_{ij}$$

Lines of Equilibrium

Given the existence of (a) $\underline{n}$ urban places of unequal size, (b) uniform friction of distance in all directions, (c) a constant value of γ for a particular analysis, and (d) the direction of travel in a straight line, the sphere of influence of any particular urban place can be described as follows:

1. About each urban place are isoprobability lines determined by

$$P_{ij} = A_j D_{ij}^{-\gamma} / \sum_{j=1}^{n} A_j D_{ij}^{-\gamma} = \text{constant}$$

where
$$D_{ij} = \sqrt{(x_i - x_j)^2 + (y_i - y_j)^2}$$

2. The line of equilibrium between any two urban places, $\underline{k}$ and $\underline{h}$, is derived by

(4.0)
$$\frac{S_k / D_{ik}^{\gamma}}{\sum_{j=1}^{n} S_j / D_{ik}^{\gamma}} = \frac{S_h / D_{ih}^{\gamma}}{\sum_{j=1}^{n} S_i / D_{ij}^{\gamma}}$$

or
$$\frac{D_{ik}}{D_{ih}} = \left(\frac{S_k}{S_h}\right)^{1/\gamma}$$

and these lines are circles or parts of circles.[8]
The intersection of like probability contours between each pair of urban places produces a locus of points. Such lines can be interpreted simply as curves upon which any given individual is indifferent between two urban places. Even though the isoprobability contours around an urban place may not be circular, the lines of equilibrium are always circles or parts of circles, and this generalization is true regardless of the number of urban places or the value of γ.

77

Generalizations

On the basis of these geometric properties, the following generalizations can be made about the nature and scope of the sphere of influence of an urban place:

1. A sphere of influence represents a surface consisting of a series of attraction gradients around a particular urban place. An exception would be the rather rare case in which only one urban place existed. In such a case, no gradients but rather a plane would exist.

2. Attraction gradients are probabilistic in character, ranging from a probability value of less than one to a value greater than zero (except in the sole-urban-center situation, in which case the probability value equals one).

3. The total number of individuals within the sphere of influence of an urban place is the sum of the expected number of individuals from each of the originating points.

4. Attraction gradients, i.e., isoprobability contours, of competing urban places overlap and the spatial competitive equilibrium between urban places can be found by drawing a line that connects the locus of points representing the intersection of like probability contours between the pairs of competing urban places.

Application of the Model

In deriving the spheres of influence of Kenyan urban centers by use of the probabilistic model described above, appropriate values were substituted for the size and distance variables as well as the distance parameter.

Size Measure

Different measures have been used to reflect the size of urban places depending upon the type of spatial interaction under study, e.g. population, employment, retail and wholesale sales, commodity output.

Empirical studies have shown that the influence of an urban place is positively related to its functional size. For example, the greater the number of employment opportunities offered by a city, the greater will be the distances associated with the journey to work. The present study sought a measure of

78

functional city size that would encompass different
variables associated with city influence. Population,
public services provided, retail goods and services
offered, and so forth could then be combined to reflect a composite measure of city functional size.

Factor Analysis

In an attempt to derive such a composite measure
of city functional size, fifty-five socioeconomic variables for thirty-two Kenyan urban centers were factor-
analyzed. These thirty-two urban places had populations in excess of 2,000 in both 1962 and 1969 (the
dates of the two most recent national censuses). See
Figure 4.1. Further, demographic, employment and earnings data were reported for these urban places. Fifteen additional urban centers had populations in excess
of 2,000 in 1969, but the necessary economic data were
not reported for them.[9] As a consequence, they had
to be excluded from the analysis. Their probable
impact on the delineated urban spheres of influence
will however be discussed.

Since employment and earnings are likely to be
important determinants of functional size, their inclusion in the list of variables was important. As
W.T.W. Morgan noted in regard to Kenyan urban places,
"the economic 'pull' of the towns is (one) of employment and higher wages."[10] D.R.F. Taylor noted that
some indication of economic activity was necessary to
judge the relevance of a town to the countryside since
administrative functions are often given too much
weight and are reflective of a former colonial system.
Commercial activity serves as a better indicator of
interactions with hinterlands.[11]

While the lower limit of 2,000 population may
appear low, it is important to note that Kenya is
still largely a rural society. Thus, most of the urban centers are comparatively small. Yet despite
their size, they serve as important administrative
centers as well as local markets and distribution
points. Most of the towns were European creations
(except for the old Arab coastal ports), and they
were not always well integrated with the surrounding
countryside.[12] Since independence in 1963, however,
the small centers that served principally as European administrative centers have become increasingly
important as local markets and distribution points
and more integrated with the surrounding countryside.[13]

79

Latent Dimensions

Twelve latent dimensions of variation among Kenyan urban centers resulted from the factor analysis. The twelve dimensions which accounted for eighty-eight percent of the original variance among the fifty-five variables are as follows:

1. Functional size
2. Age - education makeup
3. Age - sex makeup
4. Internal migration
5. Transportation - mining sectors
6. Non-African ethnicity
7. Service sector
8. Commerce sector
9. Agricultural sector
10. External migration
11. Density
12. Social service sector

Functional size proved to be the most important of the twelve latent dimensions in the structure of Kenyan urban centers. Table 4.1 lists the variables that had the highest loadings on this dimension, as well as their respective loadings:

TABLE 4.1   Kenya: Variables with High Loadings on Functional Size Dimension

Variable	Loading
Area, 1969	.9947
Earnings in Manufacturing, 1971	.9942
Total Earnings, 1971	.9938
Employment in Commerce, 1971	.9925
Earnings in Utilities, 1971	.9911
Earnings in Commerce, 1971	.9909
Total Employment, 1971	.9909
Employment in Services, 1971	.9890
Employment in Utilities, 1971	.9858
Employment in Mining, 1971	.9845
Earnings in Services, 1971	.9835
Employment in Construction, 1971	.9816
No. of Firms Employing 100 or more, 1970	.9783
Population, 1969	.9769
Earnings in Mining, 1971	.9751
Employment in Manufacturing, 1971	.9749
Earnings in Construction, 1971	.9721
Earnings in Agriculture, 1971	.9607
No. of Firms Employing 500 or more, 1970	.9596
Employment in Agriculture, 1971	.9493
Earnings in Transport, 1971	.9147
Employment in Transport, 1971	.8446

The functional size dimension reflects the aggregate economic power or more generally the status of each urban center within the Kenyan urban hierarchy. Factor scores were derived for each of the thirty-two places in the hierarchy. These centers, their populations and their functional-size factor scores are shown in Table 4.2, with the urban centers ranked on the basis of their population in 1969. Although Nairobi, and to a lesser extent Mombasa, are clearly dominant in terms of both population and factor scores, the relationship between population size and factor scores as a measure of functional size is less evident for the remaining centers. For all centers, the correlation between the two measures is quite high (R^2 = .98), but if Nairobi and Mombasa are excluded the correlation between the two measures for the remaining urban places is much lower (R^2 = .43). As a result, population alone could not be used in this instance as a reliable measure for the status of various centers in Kenya's urban system. Morgan noted that in Kenya population does not necessarily parallel rank in a hierarchy since the number of functions performed in a given place determines the rank in an urban hierarchy.[14] M.A.A. Smout made the same observation for the hierarchy he derived in a study of urban centers in Natal.[15]

Previous Factor-Analytic Studies

There have been several factor-analytic studies of the urban systems of different countries. Early noncomputer studies of American cities were followed by the Jeffery K. Hadden and Edgar F. Borgatta study of 644 American cities. This study used factor-analytic methods to determine the characteristics of American cities and to classify them into general types.[16] Brian J.L. Berry also developed a major functional classification of American cities, updating the Hadden and Borgatta work.[17] Berry's study included 1,762 urban centers in the United States and 92 variables designed to measure aspects of urban life and structure. C.A. Moser and Wolf Scott analyzed the structural characteristics of 157 English and Welsh urban communities and utilized factor analysis to create a classification scheme for these communities.[18] Similar studies were done by Leslie J. King for 106 Canadian cities, by Berry for the Chilean urban system, and by Qazi Ahmad for 102 Indian cities.[19] Robert H.T. Smith developed a functional classification of Australian urban places using a clustering routine that is related to factor analysis. With twelve

TABLE 4·2
Populations and Factor Scores of Functional Size
Dimension for Thirty-Two Kenyan Urban Centers

Urban Center	Population 1969	Factor Score*
Nairobi	509.286	5.8389
Mombasa	247,073	1.7799
Nakuru	47,151	.4706
Kisumu	32,431	.4697
Thika	18,387	.3950
Eldoret	18,196	.2779
Nanyuki	11,624	.1430
Kitale	11,573	.2097
Malindi	10,757	.0892
Kericho	10,144	.2276
Nyeri	10,004	.2779
Isiolo	8,201	.4071
Thomson's Falls	7,602	.3438
Lamu	7,403	.5942
Naivasha	6,920	.2482
Marsabit	6,635	.2693
Machakos	6,312	.2338
Kakamega	6,244	.1799
Kisii	6,080	.2130
Athi River	5,343	.2434
Elburgon	5,343	.3702
Voi	5,313	.2851
Fort Hall	4,750	.2608
Meru	4,475	.2384
Molo	4,240	.3803
Gilgil	4,178	.1359
Embu	3,928	.1455
Kitui	3,071	.2129
Londiani	2,994	.3592
Kiambu	2,776	.1344
Eldama Ravine	2,692	.3899
Kilifi	2,662	.1199

*
Factor scores have been linearly transformed so
that all of them are positive.

industrial-occupation-category data sets for 1954, he
clustered urban centers across the variables and derived seventeen types and subtypes of urban places.[20]
Studies that have used factor analysis to classify urban centers of African countries are of obvious
importance for the present analysis. Akin Mabogunje

factor-analyzed the age and sex characteristics of 329 urban centers in Nigeria.[21] While the availability of only demographic variables limited the scope of his work, Mabogunje was able to identify probable expanding and declining centers within the country on the basis of age and sex structures. For example, he found that in western Nigeria many small centers had declined, most likely as a result of being poorly linked with the larger urban centers or having limited access to the major transportation routes.[22] Herbert C. Weinand similarly used factor analysis to ascertain the presence of spread or backwash effects in the economic development of Nigeria. His analysis, however, revolved around characteristics associated with the thirty-six preindependence provinces, rather than those of Nigerian urban centers.[23] Michael L. McNulty carried out a factor analysis of forty-three urban centers in Ghana based on data from the 1960 census.[24] Perhaps his most surprising conclusion was that very few cities in Ghana could be clearly classified as to explicit functional types. This conclusion may have been due to the limited amount of data available to him precluding the inclusion of characteristics that would have been more important in differentiating the urban areas.

A study by R.A. Obudho is yet another in which factor analysis was employed to differentiate city types, this time forty-seven urban centers in Kenya.[25] Although his study, like McNulty's and Mabogunje's, was limited in some respects by data availability, he utilized variables reflecting ethnic backgrounds (both African and non-African), household and demographic characteristics, and physical development that had occurred or was occurring in urban areas. His variables did not include data related to urban economic functions but did however permit the inclusion of the other urban places over 2,000 in 1969 (but not in 1962), that the present study cannot include for lack of data. Soja also used factor analysis in his study of modernization in Kenya, but his data were collected for districts, not for urban centers.[26] He did find four distinct groups into which individual districts fell. Thus, his work constituted a functional classification of local political units in Kenya.

The Kenyan Urban Hierarchy

The next step involved in determining urban spheres of influence for Kenyan urban places was the separation of the centers into different ranks. A number of methods have been used to create urban

83

hierarchies in both developed and underdeveloped
countries: Gerald Hodge for Saskatchewan, Smout for
Natal, Josephine Oleduron Abiodun for Nigeria, and
Obudho for Kenya used variations of the point system.[27]
Berry in his study of American cities, used a cutoff
in the factor scores for urban centers to separate
first- and second-order cities.[28] Morgan developed a
hierarchy of places in Kenya based on population, administrative function, and his estimation of commercial significance.[29] Ann E. Larimore relied on population size and position in the governmental administrative setup (i.e., provincial capital, district capital).[30] For the present study, the hierarchy of urban
centers in Kenya was derived through a clustering routine that divided the thirty-two places into groups on
the basis of their factor scores on the functional
size dimension.[31]

Distance Measure

    It would be virtually impossible to compute ac-
tual road distances from the multitude of originating
points to each of the thirty-two urban places in the
study. As a consequence, the Cartesian coordinates
of each originating point i and each center j were
determined and the straight-line distance between
each pair was calculated.

Distance Parameter

    In addition to the variables just described, spa-
tial interaction is also affected by a distance parameter. This parameter, as reflected in the model,
takes the form of an exponent of distance. The rationale underlying the use of such an exponent is that
some specific kinds of spatial interaction are more
sensitive to distance than others. For example, the
distance exponent in most cases would be larger for
shopping trips than for recreation trips, and as a
consequence, distances people travel for shopping
will be shorter than for recreation trips. The distances traveled for major purchases might be larger
than those for everyday items. The larger the value
of the distance exponent, therefore, the more sensitive is a given type of spatial interaction to distance. In the present study the distance parameter
was varied depending upon the levels of hierarchy involved in the delineation of urban spheres. For first-
and second-order centers in the Kenyan hierarchy, a
value of 2.00 was assigned to γ. For third- and
fourth-order places, a value of 3.00 was used, on the
assumption that the impact of distance would be greater

84

for those functions provided by smaller places. Support for this assumption is in the study by Illeris, who found the friction of distance to be greater when smaller urban centers were included in a delineation of urban spheres of influence of urban places in Denmark.[32]

Computational Procedure

After the appropriate values for the variables were specified, a computer program was utilized to calculate the lines of equilibrium between all pairs of cities.[33] The output stemming from the program includes the coordinates of the points representing these lines of equilibrium. The values were then used as input for the plotter in drawing lines of equilibrium on a map. The area encompassed within the line of equilibrium encircling a given urban place constitutes that urban center's sphere of influence. Although the sphere of influence of an urban place actually extends beyond the line of equilibrium, it is within this area that this urban center, in contrast to others, has its greatest influence or attraction.

Results

First-Order Urban Centers

Nairobi, the only first-order urban center in Kenya, serves as the political, higher-education, and major commercial center of the country. Thus, the urban sphere of influence for Nairobi encompasses the entire country.

Second-Order Urban Centers

Mombasa, the only second-order urban center in Kenya, does not compare with Nairobi in terms of functional size , but is substantially larger than any of the remaining urban centers. The existence of only one first-order and one second-order urban center is somewhat unusual, but the level of functional complexity involved has created such a situation. Smout found a similar situation for one level in the hierarchy he derived for Natal, which contained only two centers.[34]

The factor scores were modified in delineating the urban spheres of influence for Nairobi and Mombasa for second-order functions. The factor score for Nairobi reflects the influence of that city as a first-order as well as a second-order center. As a result,

a comparison of Nairobi and Mombasa as competing
second-order places should not include the first-
order effects of functional size for Nairobi. Instead
of using the absolute value for Nairobi, the difference between the averages for first-order places
(5.8389, the factor score for Nairobi, the only first-
order place) and the second-order places (1.7799, the
factor score for Mombasa, the only second-order place)
was computed (4.0590). The halfway point between these
two averages (3.8094) was assumed to be the dividing
line between the first-order and second-order centers.
Since Nairobi was in the first rank, it was assumed to
have the maximum of the second-order functions present
in the hierarchy and was assigned the value representing the halfway point.
     The urban spheres of influence for Mombasa and
Nairobi as second-order places are shown in Figure 4.2.
Mombasa's sphere includes the coastal area of Kenya,
and does not extend a great distance inland. Nairobi's
hinterland encompasses by far the largest portion of
the country. The respective spheres appear to support
Soja's observation that Mombasa has become a relatively
modernized enclave of the highlands area, rather than
a center that affected the surrounding area.[35]
     The district is the basic geographical unit for
which economic and social data in Kenya are consistently reported; therefore the urban spheres of influence shown in Figure 4.2 were altered to conform to
district boundaries. The following criteria were established in deriving these district delineations:

     1. A district was assigned to the urban center
     whose sphere of influence encompassed the largest
     proportion of the district's total area.

     2. If the sphere of influence of an urban place
     encompassed less than the major portion of a
     district, it was eliminated.

     The district boundaries in Kenya are shown in
Figure 4.3. Based on the above criteria, multidistrict
delineations were derived for Nairobi and Mombasa. The
resulting districts encompassed by each city's sphere
are shown in Figure 4.4. Mombasa's hinterland includes
the districts in Coast Province, of which it is the capital. The other districts in the other provinces fall
within Nairobi's sphere of influence.

     Third-Order Urban Centers

     Spatial spheres of influence were derived for
the ten third-order urban centers as well as for

86

FIGURE 4.1

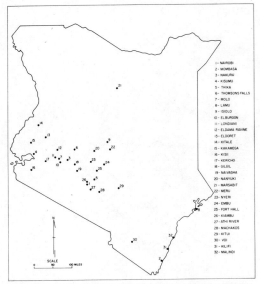

1 - NAIROBI
2 - MOMBASA
3 - NAKURU
4 - KISUMU
5 - THIKA
6 - THOMSONS FALLS
7 - MOLO
8 - LAMU
9 - ISIOLO
10 - ELBURGON
11 - LONDIANI
12 - ELDAMA RAVINE
13 - ELDORET
14 - KITALE
15 - KAKAMEGA
16 - KISII
17 - KERICHO
18 - GILGIL
19 - NAIVASHA
20 - NANYUKI
21 - MARSABIT
22 - MERU
23 - NYERI
24 - EMBU
25 - FORT HALL
26 - KIAMBU
27 - ATHI RIVER
28 - MACHAKOS
29 - KITUI
30 - VOI
31 - KILIFI
32 - MALINDI

DISTRIBUTION OF CITIES IN KENYA WITH POPULATIONS IN EXCESS OF 2,000 PERSONS IN
1962 AND 1969

FIGURE 4.2

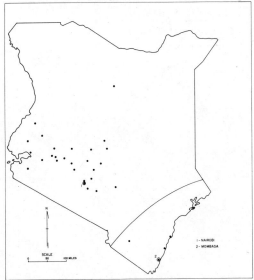

1 - NAIROBI
2 - MOMBASA

SECOND-ORDER URBAN SPHERES OF INFLUENCE IN KENYA

87

FIGURE 4.3

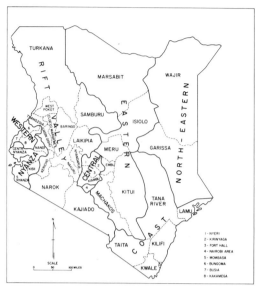

PROVINCES AND DISTRICTS IN KENYA IN 1968

FIGURE 4.4

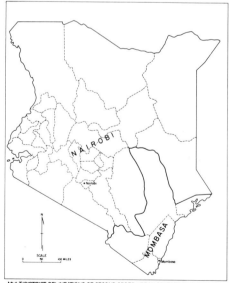

MULTIDISTRICT DELINEATIONS OF SECOND-ORDER URBAN SPHERES OF INFLUENCE

Nairobi and Mombasa. The factor scores for Mombasa and Nairobi were modified to reflect their areas of influence in terms of third-order functions. The scores used for these two centers were derived by finding the midpoint between the factor score for Mombasa, the only second-order place, and the average of the scores for the ten third-order centers. This midpoint was assumed to be the upper limit of a functional measure of third-order centers, and as such, was assigned to both Mombasa and Nairobi. As was mentioned above, the distance parameter was increased for the delineation of the spheres for third-order places.

Spheres of influence for the third-order centers are shown in Figure 4.5. Mombasa no longer dominates the coast, but shares that area with Lamu. Lamu's relatively large area of influence is somewhat misleading, as this area is sparsely populated. The population concentration along the coast and the near interior is centered on Mombasa. Nairobi is dominant in south-central Kenya, and Thika has an "island" sphere of influence in this densely populated area. Six of the third-order centers are closely grouped west of Nairobi, resulting in relatively small spheres of influence for some such as Molo and Londiani. The situation in this area contrasts with that to the east, where Nairobi and Thika are the only third-order centers.[36] However, the presence of Nairobi may have inhibited the growth of other potential centers.

Kisumu and Isiolo have two of the largest geographical spheres of influence. Isiolo's sphere encompasses the sparsely populated northern and northeastern areas which lack sufficient rainfall and are populated largely by nomadic peoples. Isiolo itself is basically an outlier of the densely populated Central Highlands, rather than an urban center of the north. Some urban centers which had fewer than 2,000 persons in 1962 but passed that threshold by 1969, are in this northern region. Kisumu in the west also has a large areal sphere of influence. The northern portion is sparsely populated, but the other parts include the relatively densely populated areas of Western and Nyanza Provinces. Thus Kisumu's sphere of influence encompasses not only a large geographic area but also a large portion of Kenya's population.

A multidistrict delineation of the urban spheres of influence for third-order centers was developed as had been done for the second-order centers of Mombasa and Nairobi. Two third-order centers, Molo and Elburgon, were not included in the multidistrict delineation. Both were in Nakuru District and they had lower factor scores than Nakuru, the third-largest city in

89

Kenya. Their spheres also did not include the majority of the area of any of the districts. The multidistrict delineations are shown in Figure 4.6. Of
the four other centers in the area of Molo and Elburgon, Nakuru and Londiani have only single-district
hinterlands, while Thomsons Falls and Eldama Ravine
have multidistrict spheres since they encompass parts
of the north which have no third-order centers among
the urban places included in this study. The districts of Coast Province are all in the spheres of
Lamu and Mombasa. Nairobi's sphere is restricted to
its own district, Nyeri, which is isolated to the
north by Thika's sphere of influence and to the south
and east by relatively thinly populated districts.
Thika is the only other center in this area, and
other than Nyeri District, the whole of Central Province is in its sphere of influence. Isiolo's sphere
includes most districts in the north, while Kisumu
in the west includes all the districts in Western and
Nyanza Provinces as well as Trans-Nzoia and Turkana
districts in Rift Valley Province.

Fourth-Order Urban Centers

    Spheres of influence for fourth-order urban cen-
ters were delineated for all thirty-two urban places
used in the study. The first-, second- and third-
order centers had modified factor scores for the delineation. The midpoint between average scores for
third- and fourth-order centers was assumed to be the
maximum measure of the functions of fourth-order centers and was assigned to all higher-order centers. The
distance parameter of 3.00 was also used in delineating the spheres of influence for fourth-order centers.
    Fourth-order spheres of influence are shown in
Figure 4.7. Centers associated with population concentrations in western Kenya, the Central Highlands,
and the southern portion of the coastal area have
relatively small spheres of influence. The larger
spheres serve the more sparsely populated areas of
the country. Marsabit in the north and Kitale in the
west have the largest areal expanses encompassed in
their spheres. In the fourth-order delineation, the
spheres for Nairobi and Mombasa are relatively small,
indicating that the remaining centers are competitive
for a limited range of functions.
    The multidistrict delineations were also deter-
mined for fourth-order urban centers (see Figure 4.8).
Nine of the centers — Kilifi, Kiambu, Gilgil, Londiani, Molo, Naivasha, Nanyuki, Athi River, and Elburgon) are not included since they do not encompass the

FIGURE 4.5

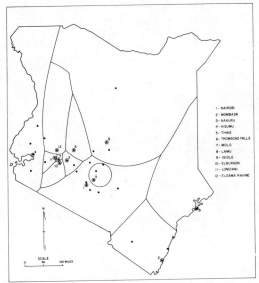

THIRD-ORDER URBAN SPHERES OF INFLUENCE IN KENYA

FIGURE 4.6

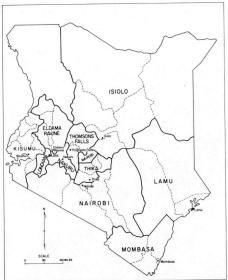

MULTIDISTRICT DELINEATIONS OF THIRD-ORDER URBAN SPHERES OF INFLUENCE

91

FIGURE 4.7

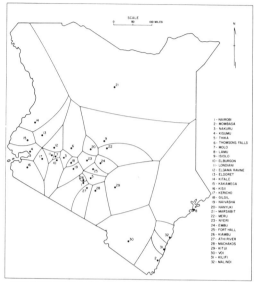

1 - NAIROBI
2 - MOMBASA
3 - NAKURU
4 - KISUMU
5 - THIKA
6 - THOMSONS FALLS
7 - MOLO
8 - LAMU
9 - ISIOLO
10 - ELBURGON
11 - LONDIANI
12 - ELDAMA RAVINE
13 - ELDORET
14 - KITALE
15 - KAKAMEGA
16 - KISII
17 - KERICHO
18 - GILGIL
19 - NAIVASHA
20 - NANYUKI
21 - MARSABIT
22 - MERU
23 - NYERI
24 - EMBU
25 - FORT HALL
26 - KIAMBU
27 - ATHI RIVER
28 - MACHAKOS
29 - KITUI
30 - VOI
31 - KILIFI
32 - MALINDI

FOURTH-ORDER URBAN SPHERES OF INFLUENCE IN KENYA

FIGURE 4.8

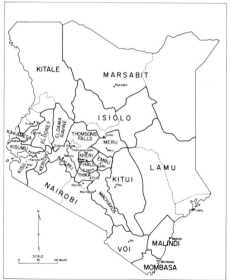

MULTIDISTRICT DELINEATIONS OF FOURTH-ORDER URBAN SPHERES OF INFLUENCE

largest portion of any district within their spheres
of influence. Londiani, even though it was present
in the third-order delineation, disappears in the
fourth-order multidistrict delineation because Kericho
includes the largest portion of Kericho district in
its sphere.

Of the twenty-three urban centers included in
the fourth-order delineation, over half (twelve) include only one district in their spheres; another
seven include two districts, and four centers — Lamu,
Kitale, Nairobi and Eldoret — include more than two
districts. Lamu dominates the sparsely settled northern coast and nearby interior, while Kitale dominates
the northwest. Nairobi's sphere includes the Nairobi
area and the two Masai districts of Kajiado and Narok.
Eldoret includes three Rift Valley Province districts
in its sphere. In terms of population, Eldoret is the
largest of the fourth-order places. It was the sixth-
largest place in Kenya in 1969 even though its population declined between 1962 and 1969. The fact that
its factor score on functional size placed it in the
fourth order reflects its declining importance in the
Kenyan urban system relative to other urban places.

The Effect of the Excluded Urban Places

Urban spheres of influence that have been delineated for thirty-two urban places in Kenya will undoubtedly be affected by those urban centers excluded
from the analysis for lack of data. Since these urban places would at least have been included in the
fourth order, the discussion of them will be based on
their relationship to those urban spheres of the thirty-two urban centers for which data were available.

Fifteen of the excluded urban places had populations over 2,000 in 1969 (see Table 4.4). Three of
these centers are proximate to existing centers and
share parts of their present urban spheres. Kinango
in Kwale district is close to Mombasa, and would have
only a small sphere since it would be in competition
with this major city. Wundanyi is near Voi in Taita
district and would draw upon the southern part of that
center's present sphere as delineated. The proximity
of Njoro to Nakuru and the other third-order centers
in the western highlands area would likely limit its
area of influence.

The other excluded places are located either in
the peripheral areas of the country or in the interstices of the present spheres. They possibly have grown
up in these areas because they are less well served by
the present urban centers. Homa Bay, Migori, Narok,
Bungoma and Lokitaung are all near the borders of the

93

country with no intervening centers. Their locations enable them to serve area populations better than the existing centers, at least in terms of accessibility. Wundanyi and Kinango also share this characteristic to a certain extent. Wamba, Marala and Baragoi are all in Samburu District and are located near the line of equilibrium between Marsabit to the north and Isiolo to the south. Large geographic spheres occur in this area of Kenya, and these new centers may serve as dispersal centers for government programs in northern areas. The other excluded urban places are similarly located: Galole is near the line of equilibrium between Lamu and Kitui; Karatina, between Nyeri and Embu; Lubwa, between Londiani and Kericho; and Kapsabet between Kisumu, Eldoret and Kakamega. Due to their locations, these urban places need to be considered in any effort which uses the derived urban spheres as a basis for planning, as their growth possibly reflects the lack of centers in certain areas such as the north and southwest.

Conclusion

The above derived spheres of influence provide a potentially important planning input in Kenya. "The integration of economic, social, and spatial policy permits an optimum comprehensive solution to difficult and complex problems produced by modern development of the national economy, its regions and metropolitan areas."[37] The urban spheres derived provide a useful input for spatial policy at a number of different levels. Since the spheres have been delineated for four orders of centers, it is possible to determine the optimum location and potential effects of different types of planning activities. Thus, major projects might be initiated in either Nairobi or Mombasa,[38] while projects requiring decentralized applications might be diffused to third- or fourth-order centers. The multidistrict delineations pinpoint the optimal centers if the existing political-administrative structure is deemed useful in a planning project, either because of the need for data collected only at these levels for political reasons, or to avoid creating overlapping administrations between the existing districts and special project districts. Some present urban centers as a result would appear illsuited as centers for certain projects.

The urban spheres of influence as delineated might be useful in other respects. New districts might be drawn to reflect the urban spheres (taking into account local geographic factors) or the present seven provinces

94

(and the Nairobi area) might be reorganized to reflect third-order spheres of influence. Ten provinces would thus exist, although such a reorganization might have to take into account the existence of both the sparsely settled areas and the small geographic spheres of influence of some centers.

Two examples illustrate the utility of these spheres of influence in an administrative reorganization. Meru seems poorly situated to serve as the capital of Eastern Province. It is not even a third-order center, while the province itself is split between Nairobi, Thika and Isiolo among the third-order centers. If present boundaries are preserved, Isiolo might be a more functional provincial capital. In the western part of the country, urban spheres indicate that Western and Nyanza Provinces might be profitably consolidated, with Kisumu serving as provincial capital.

Some caution must be expressed in regard to the above observations. First as was mentioned in the introduction, present boundaries are political artifacts, and therefore may be resistant to changes. Second, some relatively new urban centers were not included in this study, and any changes would have to take them into account. Finally, the location of planning projects, industries and administrative services will have an effect on the extent of various urban spheres of influence. In a sense the spheres reflect the presence of these activities, and their locations may weaken or strengthen the dominance of some centers. The delineated spheres can still be useful in this sense, as they indicate those areas, such as northern Kenya, which are presently underserved by existing urban centers.

In summary, the areas of urban spheres of influence as delineated provide one objective measure for matching particular functions with appropriate scales of organization. Obviously however, the distribution of population within these spatial units must also be considered. Further, it would be constructive to derive comprehensive socioeconomic profiles for each of the delineated regions. It would also be advantageous to examine the stability of boundaries outlining the urban spheres of influence. This last consideration is extremely important in assessing the expected duration of a given regionalization before it becomes outdated.

95

NOTES

1. Edward W. Soja, The Political Organization
of Space, Resource Paper No. 8 (Washington, D.C.:
Association of American Geographers, 1971), pp.45-46.
2. See for example Nikos Georgulas, "An Approach
to Urban Analysis for East African Towns with Particu-
lar Reference to the African Population", Maxwell Gra-
duate School of Citizenship and Public Affairs Occas-
ional Paper No. 4 (Syracuse, New York: Program of
East African Studies, Syracuse University, 1963);
Harm J. deBlij, Mombasa: An African City (Chicago:
Northwestern University Press, 1968); B.S. Hoyle, The
Seaport of East Africa: A Geographical Study (Nairobi:
East African Publishing House, 1967); and W.T.W.Morgan,
"The 'White Highlands' of Kenya", Geographical Journal,
Vol. 129, 2 (June, 1963), pp.140-155.
3. Paul G. Clark, "Towards More Comprehensive
Planning in East Africa", East African Economics Re-
view, Vol. 10, 2 (December, 1963), p. 73.
4. Edward W. Soja, "Rural-Urban Interaction",
Canadian Journal of African Studies, Vol. 3, 1 (Winter
1969), p. 286.
5. Peter R. Gould, "Research Strategies for
Rural Spatial Planning", Canadian Journal of African
Studies, Vol. 3, 1 (Winter 1969), p. 281.
6. See for example Kasimierz Secomski, "Modern
Factors in Development Policy of Metropolitan Areas",
in Alan A. Brown, Joseph A. Licari, and Egon Neuberger,
(eds.), Urban and Social Economics in Market and Planned Economies: Policy, Planning and Development, Vol.
1 (New York: Praeger Publishers, 1974), pp.249-257;
Raymond Bunker, Town and Country or City and Region?
(Melbourne: Melbourne: Melbourne University, 1971),
particularly pp. 22-29; and John W. Sommer, "Spatial
Aspects of Urbanization and Political Integration in
the Sudan", in Salah El-Shakhs and Robert Obudho (eds.),
Urbanization, National Development, and Regional Planning in Africa, (New York: Praeger Publishers, 1974),
pp.27-46.
7. David L. Huff and George F. Jenks, "A Graphic
Interpretation of the Friction of Distance in Gravity
Models", Annals of the American Association of Geographers, Vol. 58, 4 (December 1968), pp. 814-824.
8. Raymond Gambini, David L. Huff and George F.
Jenks, "Geometric Properties of Market Areas," Papers
of the Regional Science Association, Vol. 20 (1968),
pp. 85-92.
9. Complete information was also available for
two other centers, Kajiado and Magadi, but these two
centers had less than 2,000 population in 1969 so
demographic data could not be gathered for them.

10. W.T.W. Morgan, "Urbanization in Kenya: Origins and Trends", Transactions, Institute of British Geographers, No. 46 (March 1969), p.176.

11. D.R.F. Taylor, "The Role of the Smaller Urban Place in Development: The Case Study of Kenya", in El-Shakhs and Obudho, Urbanization, National Development and Regional Planning in Africa, pp.157-158.

12. Ibid. pp.143-160 and R.A. Obudho, "Urbanization and Regional Planning in Western Kenya", in El-Shakh and Obudho, Urbanization, National Development, and Regional Planning, (New York: Praeger Publishers, 1974), pp. 161-176.

13. Obudho, "Urbanization and Regional Planning," p.170.

14. Morgan, "Urbanization in Kenya", p. 175.

15. M.A.H. Smout, "The Hierarchy of Central Places in Natal", Tijdschrift voor Economische en Social Geografie, Vol. 61, 1 (1970), pp. 25-31.

16. Jeffery K. Hadden and Edgar F. Borgatta, American Cities: Their Social Characteristics,(Chicago: Rand McNally, 1965).

17. Brian J.L. Berry, "Latent Structure of the American Urban System, with International Comparisons", in Brian J.L. Berry (ed.), City Classification Handbook: Methods and Applications (New York: Wiley-Interscience, 1972), pp. 11-60.

18. C.A. Moser and Wolf Scott, British Towns: A Statistical Study of their Social and Economic Differences (Edinburgh: Oliver and Boyd, 1961).

19. Leslie J. King, "Cross-Sectional Analysis of Canadian Urban Dimensions: 1951 and 1961", Canadian Geographer, Vol. 10, 4 (1966); Brian J.L. Berry, "Relationships between Regional and Economic Development and the Urban System: The Case of Chile", Tijdschrift voor Economische en Sociale Geografie, Vol. 60, 5 (1969), pp. 283-307; and Qazi Ahmad, Indian Cities: Characteristics and Correlates, Department of Geography Research Paper No. 102 (Chicago: University of Chicago, 1965).

20. Robert H.T. Smith, "The Functions of Australian Towns", Tijdschrift voor Economische en Sociale Geografie, Vol. 56, 3 (1965), pp. 81-92.

21. Akin Mabogunje, "Urbanization in Nigeria: A Constraint on Economic Development", Economic Development and Cultural Change, Vol. 13, 4, Part I (July 1965), pp. 413-438.

22. Ibid., p. 430.

23. Herbert C. Weinand, "Some Spatial Aspects of Economic Development in Nigeria", Journal of Developing Areas, Vol. 7, 2 (January 1973), pp. 247-264.

24. Michael L. McNulty, "Urban Structure and Development: the Urban System of Ghana", Journal of Developing Areas, Vol. 3, 2 (January 1969), pp. 159-176.

25. R.A. Obudho, Development of Urbanization in Kenya: A Spatial Analysis and Implication for Regional Development Strategy (New Brunswick, New Jersey: Ph.D. Dissertation, Rutgers University, 1974).

26. Edward W. Soja, The Geography of Modernization in Kenya: A Spatial Analysis of Social, Economic, and Political Change, Syracuse Geographical Series No.2 (Syracuse: Syracuse University Press, 1968).

27. Gerald Hodge, "Developing Regional Statistics for Policy Purposes: The Prediction of Trade Centre Viability in Saskatchewan", in Sylvia Ostry and T.K. Rymes (eds.), Papers on Regional Statistical Studies, Canadian Political Science Association Conference on Statistics, 1964 (Toronto: University of Toronto, 1966), pp. 53-74; Smout, "The Hierarchy of Central Places in Natal"; Josephine Olu Abiodun, "Urban Hierarchy in a Developing Country", Economic Geography, Vol. 43, 4 (October 1967), pp. 145-154; and Obudho, Development of Urbanization in Kenya.

28. Brian J.L. Berry, "Latent Structure", and David L. Huff, "The Delineation of a National System of Planning Regions on the Basis of Urban Spheres of Influence", Regional Studies, Vol. 7 (1973), pp.323-329.

29. Morgan, "Urbanization in Kenya," pp.173-175.

30. Ann E. Larimore, "The Africanization of Colonial Cities in East Africa", East Lakes Geographer, Vol. 5 (December 1969), pp. 50-68.

31. This program is an iterative clustering program developed by D.J. McRae on file at the University of Texas Computation Center. The program is briefly described in D.J. McRae, "MIKCA: A FORTRAN IV Iterative K-Means Cluster Analysis Program", Behavioral Science, Vol. 10, 4 (1971), pp. 423-424.

32. Sven Illeris, "Hierarchies of Functional Regions: Theoretical Models and Empirical Evidence for Denmark", reprinted in Brian J.L. Berry and Frank E. Horton (eds.), Geographic Perspectives on Urban Systems with Integrated Readings (Englewood Cliffs, New Jersey: Prentice-Hall, 1970), pp. 200-207.

33. Raymond Gambini, A Computer Program for Calculating Lines of Equilibrium between Multiple Centers of Attraction (Lawrence, Kansas: Center for Regional Studies, University of Kansas, 1966).

34. Smout, "The Hierarchy of Central Places in Natal", p. 30.

35. Soja, The Geography of Modernization, p.85.

36.   Morgan, "Urbanization in Kenya", p. 175,
noted the lack of intermediate centers in his hierarchy for this area.   In his analysis; Thika did not
have the importance indicated by the factor score
in this study.
37.   Secomski, "Modern Factors in Development
Policy", p. 257.
38.   Obudho, Development of Urbanization in
Kenya, p. 228, noted that the Kenya government had
decided to concentrate major projects in these two
cities, partially because they were the best developed urban areas in the country.

5. Urban Primacy in Kenya

R. A. Obudho

Introduction

Before the colonization of present-day Kenya,
there were no towns to mention except for small
agglomerations in the form of trading centers, found
in the coastal parts of Kenya. Most of these coastal
central places were founded by Arab traders over 700
years ago. Inland traditional periodic or daily
markets, however, were important nucleation points
and they formed a spatial system in the hierarchy of
central places. These central places were paramount
to intra- and interethnic trade during the precolonial
era. Thus during this era there were several spatial
systems which were ethnic-based without any form of
natural primacy.

This spatial pattern was altered drastically
with the onset of colonialism at the turn of the century. This transformation was particularly altered
with construction of the Mombasa-Kisumu rail line
between 1896 and 1902. Important towns such as Mombasa, Nairobi, Nakuru and Kisumu were established at
this time. Nairobi as the national capital, and Mombasa as the chief entrepôt for eastern Africa, grew
in importance with the political and administrative
consolidation of the country. The colonial government introduced an administration based on provinces,
districts, and subdistricts, each centered on a settlement. In establishing the colonial central places,
popularly known as bomas, existing traditional nucleation points were not only ignored but often

---

The views and opinions expressed in this chapter
are those of the author, and do not necessarily
reflect those of JOHNSON & JOHNSON and family of
Companies.

deliberately avoided.

An urban center in Kenya is defined as any nucleated settlement with a population of 2,000 and over.[2]
Based on this definition there were seventeen towns
in 1948, with a total population of 285,445. At the
time of the 1963 census the urban population had increased to 670,445 and the number of towns to thirty-
four. The latest census in 1969 gave the total urban
population as 1,079,908, and the number of towns had
risen to forty-seven. See the following population
growth table (Table 5.1):

TABLE 5.1
Kenya: Growth of Urban Population 1948 to 1969

Size of Urban Center	Number of Towns					
	1948	% Total	1962	% Total	1969	%
100,000 +	1	5.9	2	5.9	2	4.2
20,000 - 99,999	1	5.9	2	5.9	2	4.2
10,000 - 19,000	2	11.8	3	8.8	7	14.9
5,000 - 9,999	3	17.6	11	32.4	11	23.4
2,000 - 4,999	10	58.8	16	47.0	25	58.3
Total	17	100.0	34	100.0	47	100.0
Annual Growth Rate, No. of Towns	5.1		4.7			
Total Urban Population	285,445		670,945		1,079,908	
Percentage of Population Growth Rate	5.3		7.8		9.9	

Source: Kenya Population Census 1948, 1962, and 1969.

Urban Primacy

Primacy, according to Jefferson,[3] is present when
the largest city in a country or region has several
times the population of the second-or third-ranking
city. Primacy also exists when a stratum of small
central places is dominated by one, two, or three
very large cities and there are fewer cities of intermediate size than would be expected from Zipf's rank
size rule theory. Most spatial development strategies
have been an attempt to investigate the relationship

101

between primacy and development ?— without conclusive
results. El-Shakhs has contributed a major study to
support the imbalance argument, contending that primacy as related to development will follow the path
of an inverted U.[4] Although there is still controver-
sy on the theory of primacy and development, no countries exhibit this theory more than urbanizing third-
world countries. This primacy of central places can
be observed at supranational, national, regional and
local levels. Primacy is one of the most important
characteristics of colonial and postcolonial urbanization. It is especially notable in a country such as
Kenya, where the level of urbanization was nonexistent
prior to colonial urbanization.
        Analysis of Kenya's urban population between 1948
and 1962 shows that Nairobi dominated all the urban
centers.[5] (See Table 3.1 on page 52). During the
three censuses, about seventy percent of the total
urban population were in Nairobi and Mombasa; Nairobi
has therefore maintained its primacy role. For example, in 1962 the total population of Nairobi accounted
for 3.1 percent of the national population, and this
increased to 4.8 percent by the 1969 census. The
increase in Nairobi's share of the urban population
by 1969 meant that her share of the total population
of the ten centers increased from 46.5 percent in
1962, to 55.6 percent in 1969. Nairobi at this time
had 47.16 percent of Kenya's total urban population.
        The 1969 census, the most comprehensive census in
Kenya's history to date, provides certain information
which may serve as an indicator of the primacy of urban centers in the different regions of the country.
Based on this census, the Central Highlands Region
(including Nairobi Extra-Provincial District, Central
Province, the District of Nakuru, Laikipia, Trans-
Nzoia, Uasin Gishu, Baringo, and Elgeyo Marakwet of
Rift Valley and the Districts of Meru and Embu of Eastern Province) has 63.33 percent of the urban centers
and 42.55 percent of the urban population (see Tables
5.2 and 5.3). The Coastal Region (the present Coast
Province) is second in population, and the Western
Region second in number of centers. The Masai -
Northern Frontier Region (including Northeastern Province districts of Narok, Kajiando, West Pokot, Samburu, Machakos, Northern Laikipia, Isiolo,and Marsabit) is the least-urbanized region in Kenya. Least-
urbanized regions historically have very few non-
African settlements. Non-Africans who settled in
the Central Highlands and Coastal Region developed a
diversified urban economic base which helped sustain
a larger number of urban centers than other regions.

TABLE 5.2
Kenya's Urban Centers: Analysis of Urban Centers by Size, Group and Number

Size	Region				Total Population	Percent of Total
	Western	Central Highlands	Coastal	Masai – Northern Frontier		
Towns with population						
over 500,000	–	1	–	–	509,286	47.16
100,000 – 500,000	–	–	1	–	247,073	22.88
40,000 – 100,000	–	1	–	–	47,151	4.37
20,000 – 40,000	1	–	1	–	32,431	3.00
10,000 – 20,000	1	5	1	–	90,685	8.40
5,000 – 10,000	1	4	2	3	71,396	6.61
2,000 – 5,000	6	9	4	6	81,886	7.58
Grand Total	9	20	8	9	1,079,908	100.00
Percentage of Total	21.27	42.55	17.02	19.16		

Source: R.A. Obudho, Development of Urbanization in Kenya: A Spatial Analysis and Implications for Regional Development Strategy (New Brunswick, New Jersey: Rutgers University), unpublished Ph.D. Thesis, 1974, p. 76.

103

TABLE 5.3
Kenyan Urban Centers: Analysis of Urban Centers by Size and Population

Size	Region			
	Western	Central Highlands	Coastal	Masai – Northern Frontier
Regional urban population	4,138,546	4,036,571	–	1,823,506
Towns with population over 500,000:	–	509,286	–	–
100,000 – 500,000	–	–	247,073	–
40,000 – 100,000	–	47,151	–	–
20,000 – 40,000	32,431	–	–	–
10,000 – 20,000	10,144	–	–	–
5,000 – 10,000	12,324	25,208	10,757	21,148
2,000 – 5,000	17,588	32,512	13,106	18,680
Grand Total	72,487	683,941	283,652	39,828
Percentage of Total Urban Population	6.72	63.33	26.27	3.68

Source: Obudho, Development of Urbanization in Kenya, p. 77.

104

The overwhelming dominance of Nairobi with a population of 509,286 is only rivaled by Mombasa, the second-largest urban center, with a population of 247,073. In 1967 Nairobi accounted for 56.34 percent of employment in industrial manufacturing. Mombasa's population accounts for 22.88 percent of the urban population, but it should be remembered that Mombasa is a seaport for Kenya as well as for other east African countries, which explains why its population is half that of Nairobi. The largest urban population in Kenya was and still is concentrated in Nairobi and Mombasa, and this proportion is increasing.[6] These two cities accounted for 446,369 or sixty-six percent of total urban residents (670,945) in 1962. By 1969 this proportion had increased to 756,359 out of 1,057,494, or seventy-two percent. But the low population of the third urban center Nakuru, with 4.37 percent of the total, and the fourth urban center Kisumu, with only 1.70 percent, proves the primacy of Nairobi over the years, as shown in Table 5.4. Thus Nairobi dominates the country in terms of population and in the provision of urban social amenities. Nairobi according to Soja is the national nucleus or core area. In his words, "It is clearly the most modernized part of Kenya and the hub of the nation — an easily identifiable hub core area . . . (it has) dominance in the network of communication and transportation — as well as in the overall social, economic and political organization of Kenya."[7]

Regional, provincial and district urban primacy is even more discernable than national urban primacy (see Table 5.4). In the Western Region (including Nyanza Province, Western Province and the districts of Kericho and Nandi), Kisumu with a population of 32,431 dominates the region. The next-largest urban center, Kericho, had a population of 10,144 at the 1969 census. Kisii town enjoys such primacy in Abagusii district, Homa Bay in South Nyanza district, Kericho in Kericho district and Kapsaset in Nandi district.

Although Kakamega and Bungoma have populations of 6,244 and 4,401 respectively, the former is more important in Western Province for the following reasons: First, Western Province was until 1962 a part of Nyanza Province, and as such was only a district, with economic functions relegated to district level. Also, Kakamega's economic, cultural and social importance has been heavily dominated by Kisumu town because of the close proximity of the two towns. According to Waller, " . . . the southern Kakamega district belongs to the catchment area of Kisumu. Kisumu

TABLE 5.4
Primate Urban Centers of Kenya in Relation to Second, Third, and Fourth Rank
Urban Centers of their Province and Urban Geographic Regions, 1969

Province or Urban Region	Percentage of Primacy of First, Second, Third and Fourth Urban Centers	Urban Centers			
		First	Second	Third	Fourth
1. Central Province	100-54-41-26	Thika 18,387	Nyeri 10,004	Nyahururu 7,602	Fort Hall 4,750
2. Coast Province	100-8-3-2	Mombasa 247,073	Malindi 19,757	Lamu 7,403	Voi 5,313
3. Eastern Province	100-81-77-65	Isiolo 8,201	Marsabit 6,635	Machakos 6,312	Athi River 5,343
4. Nyanza Province	100-19-10-6	Kisumu 32,431	Kisii 6,080	Homa Bay 3,252	Migori 2,066
5. Rift Valley Province	100-39-25-25	Nakuru 47,151	Eldoret 18,196	Nanyuki 11,624	Kitale 11,573
6. Western Province	100-70-17-12	Kakamega 6,244	Bungoma 4,401	Busia 1,057	Kimilili 723
7. Central Highlands Region	100-9-4-4	Nairobi 509,286	Nakuru 47,151	Thika 18,387	Eldoret 18,196

(continued on next page)

106

TABLE 5.4 (continued)

Province or Urban Region	Percentage of Primacy of First, Second, Third and Fourth Urban Centers	Urban Centers			
		First	Second	Third	Fourth
8. Western Region	100-31-19-19	Kisumu 32,431	Kericho 10,144	Kakamega 6,244	Kisii 6,080
9. Masai-Northern	100-81-77-65	Isiolo 8,301	Marsabit 6,635	Machakos 6,312	Athi River 5,343
10. Coast Province	100-8-3-2	Mombasa 247,073	Malindi 10,759	Lamu 7,403	Voi 5,313
11. Kenya 1969	100-49-9-6	Nairobi 409,286	Mombasa 247,073	Nakuru 47,151	Kisumu 32,431
12. Kenya 1962	100-79-16-10	Nairobi 226,794	Mombasa 179,595	Nakuru 38,181	Kisumu 23,526
13. Kenya 1948	100-71-14-9	Nairobi 118,976	Mombasa 84,746	Nakuru 17,625	Kisumu 10,899

Source: Based on data from Republic of Kenya, Kenya Population Census 1969, Vol. II, Data on Urban Population (Nairobi: Statistics Division, Ministry of Finance and Economic Planning, 1971).

NOTE: The percentages after the provinces or urban regions, for example 100-8-3-2, give values of populations of the four largest urban centers of each province or urban region as percentages of the value of the ranking urban center, and are arranged in order of the relative importance of that urban center.

107

carries out not only the higher-order functions for the entire region but also the medium-order functions for its Kakamega hinterland."[8] The primacy ratio percentage of Western Province is 100:70:17:12 compared to Nyanza Province, 100:19:10:6.

In considering intraregional and intraprovincial primacy, no region shows this factor more clearly than Coast Province and the coastal region. Mombasa, with a population of 247,073, dominates the whole region, only rivaled by Malindi and Lamu. The primacy percentage ratio for the province as well as the region is 100:8:2:3. Despite the fact that there are a number of towns and trading centers in Coast Province, there is a lack of centrality because "the demand for many kinds of services, especially of an economic nature, which create growth of such places is not very large."[9] The Central Highlands, the most urbanized area of Kenya, shows the highest level of primacy, with Nairobi (509,286) and Nakuru (47,151), Thika (18,387) and Eldoret (18,196) resulting in a primacy ratio of 100:9:4:4. According to the 1962 census, the population of Nairobi city accounted for 39.79 percent of the urban population and 3.7 percent of the total population. This compares with 47.16 percent of urban population and 4.65 percent of total population for 1969. The primacy tendency as shown on Table 5.4 is not common in Eastern Province or the Masai – northern frontier region because this is the least-urbanized part of Kenya. Urban primacy is and will continue to be a common aspect of urbanization in a developing country such as Kenya. This urban primacy can only be bridged by adopting viable spatial planning schemes to narrow the gap between urban and traditional subsystems. Primacy, however viewed, will be a crucial part of Kenya's spatial system in the foreseeable future.

NOTES

1. R.A. Obudho, "Urbanization and Development in Kenya: An Historical Appreciation", African Urban Notes Vol. 1, 3, (Fall 1975), pp. 1-56; R.A. Obudho (ed.), Urbanization and Development Planning in Kenya (Nairobi: East African Literature Bureau, 1978); and R.A. Obudho and P.P. Waller, Periodic Markets, Urbanization and Regional Planning, A Case Study from Western Kenya (Westport, Conn., Greenwood Press, 1976).

2. J.C. Blacker, "Demography", in W.T.W. Morgan (ed.) East Africa, Its Peoples and Resources (Nairobi: Oxford University Press, 1972) p. 47.

3. Mark Jefferson, "The Law of Primate City, Geographical Review Vol. XXIX (1939), pp. 226-232.

4. Salah El-Shaks, "Development, Primacy and Systems of Cities," Journal of Developing Areas (1972) Vol. XII, pp. 11-36.

5. S.H. Ominde, The Population of Kenya, Tanzania and Uganda, (Nairobi: Heinemann Educational Books, 1975), pp. 93-96.

6. R.A. Obudho, The Nature of Kenya Urban Hierarchy: Implication for Regional Planning Strategy, (Nairobi: East African Publishing House, 1978); R.A. Obudho, "Spatial Dimension and Demographic Dynamics of Kenya's Urban Subsystems", Pan African Journal, Vol. IX, 2 (1976), pp. 103-134; and G. Gaile, The Spatial Reorganization of Development Around Growth Centers, (Los Angeles: University of California at Los Angeles: unpublished Thesis, 1976).

7. Edward W. Soja, The Geography of Modernization in Kenya: a Spatial Analysis of Social, Economic and Political Change (Syracuse, New York: Syracuse University Press, 1968), p. 197.

8. Peter P. Waller et al., Basic Features of Regional Planning in the Region of Kisumu (Kenya), (Berlin: Deutches Institut fur Entwicklungspolitik, 1960), p. 60; see also Obudho and Waller, Periodic Markets.

9. D.R.F. Taylor, Development of Central Places in the Coast Province of Kenya, (Ottawa: Department of Geography, Carleton University, 1974).

6. A Comparative Analysis of the Functional Structures of Central Business Districts in East Africa

R. C. Tiwari

Introduction

This chapter will concentrate on an analysis of the central business districts (CBD's) of Nairobi and Dar es Salaam. Nairobi, the capital of Kenya, came into existence in 1899 as a changing station of the Uganda railway, with the "capital" function being added in 1905. At present it is the largest city of East Africa with a population of nearly 500,000. The regional headquarters of the United Nations is located in Nairobi, which has enhanced the city's prestige beyond the continent of Africa.

Dar es Salaam was founded by Seyyid Majid, the Sultan of Zanzibar, in 1862. It became the capital of German East Africa in 1891, and is the main port of Tanzania with railway links to Zambia. The city has an estimated population of over 200,000. Figures 6.1 and 6.2 show the location of central commercial areas along with the generalized land-use pattern of these two cities.[1, 2]

This study is divided into three parts: first, methodological arguments are considered; secondly a comparison between the functional structure of the two CBD's is attempted; and finally, the cultural duality observed in central commercial areas of cities in developing countries is explored.

Methodological Considerations

There have been numerous studies of the central business district as a region for geographical analysis. The most intensive studies have been made in the United States, and the well-accepted models of city growth, (i.e., the concentric zone model, the sector theory, and multiple nuclei theory) label the central areas as CBD's.[3] The central business district

FIGURE 6.1

CITY OF NAIROBI

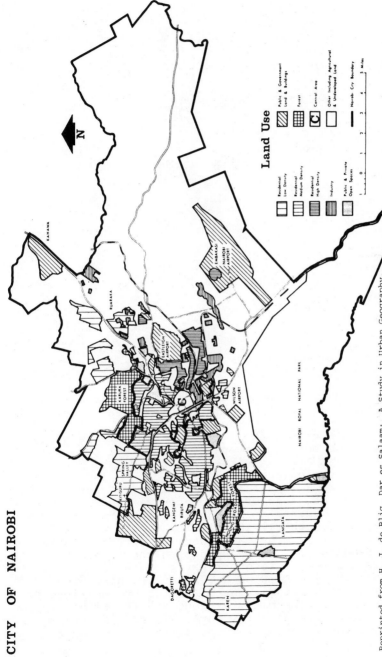

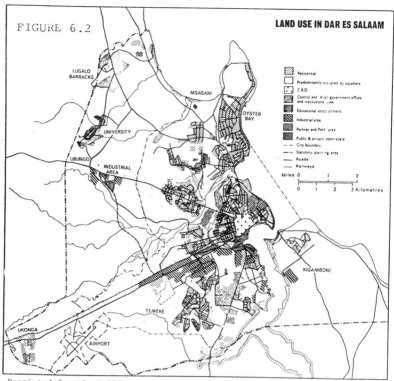

FIGURE 6.2

LAND USE IN DAR ES SALAAM

LUGALO BARRACKS

MSASANI

OYSTER BAY

UNIVERSITY

UBUNGO

INDUSTRIAL AREA

KIGAMBONI

TEMEKE

UKONGA

AIRPORT

Residential
Predominantly occupied by squatters
C.B.D.
Central and local government offices and institutional uses
Educational establishment
Industrial area
Railway and Port area
Public & private open space
City boundary
Statutory planning area
Roads
Railways

Miles 0   1   2

0   1   2   3 Kilometres

Reprinted from D. Halliman and W. T. W. Morgan, "The City of Nairobi," in
<u>Nairobi: City and Region</u>, edited by W. T. W. Morgan, by permission of Ox-
ford University Press, Nairobi, copyright © 1967 by Oxford University Press,
Nairobi.

of American cities has gradually lost or is losing its
importance, and has become a problem area. Many functions have migrated to regional shopping centers. In
developing countries however, the central areas still
dominate the business scene. The central business
areas of East African cities are typical of most
cities in developing countries.

The term "central business district" incorporates
three distinct geographical concepts: location, function, and a defined spatial unit. In terms of location a CBD is central in relation to the whole city
(or urban area). The main function of this spatial
unit is business, which depends on the accessibility
of this areal unit to other parts of the city. This
creates linkages between a CBD and its hinterland.
With continuous migrations of different functions to
other parts of the city, present-day functions of this
areal unit represent "the survival of the fittest".
In other words, the more central the functions the

more centrally they are located, and this is the case with central business districts in both developed and developing countries.

Although Proudfoot[4] classified the commercial areas within a city, and Hartman[5] studied the shapes of CBD's, Murphy and Vance[6] were the first geographers to devise a standard method for delimiting the CBD's of medium-sized American cities. Application of this method of delimiting CBD's of various cities has made comparative studies possible. It was Murphy and Vance who classified land use of central areas into central business district uses and non-central business district uses. The following were considered non-central uses:

a. permanent residences, including apartment houses and rooming houses

b. government and public (parks and public schools as well as establishments carrying out city, county, state and federal government functions)

c. organizational institutions (e.g., churches, colleges, fraternal orders)

d. industrial establishments (except newspapers)

e. wholesaling

f. vacant buildings or stores

g. vacant lots

h. commercial storage

i. railroad tracks and switching yards

Weiss[7] has shown that this grouping of land uses was quite arbitrary, and " . . . while there would be agreement on the uses classified as central business, city planners however, might not agree with certain of the land uses which were considered to be noncentral business in character . . ."

After the detailed mapping of functions (by blocks) in the central area, two indices were derived: "height index, i.e., floor space used by central business activities in relation to the space on the ground floor, and intensity index, i.e. floor space in central business activities as the percentage of total floor space."[8] Consequently the two indices, central business height index (CBHI) and central business intensity index (CBII) were obtained for each block. The method of delimitation as outlined by Murphy and Vance is as follows:

113

1. To be considered part of the CBD, a block
must have a CBHI of 1 or more and a CBII of 50
percent or more, and it must be one of a contiguous group of blocks surrounding the PLVI (peak
land value intersection) that meet these index
requirements. Even though a block touches another only at one corner they are considered to
be contiguous.
2. A block that does not reach the required
index values but is surrounded by blocks that do
is considered part of the CBD.
3. A block completely occupied by the buildings
and grounds of a city hall or other municipal
office building, a municipal auditorium, city
police or fire department headquarters, or a central post office is included within the CBD if it
is adjacent to (or contiguous with) blocks meeting the standard requirements. In some cities
it will be necessary to add to this list the buildings and grounds of certain other government establishments: the courthouse in a county seat,
the capitol buildings of a state capital, and
occasionally certain Federal buildings in addition to the post office, e.g., a Federal court
building or other Federal office building the
activities of which are closely integrated with
those of the city and its region. In no instance
should such government buildings as those described in this paragraph result in the extension
of the CBD for more than one block beyond normal
CBD blocks. And a group of such government buildings cannot be split. Thus where there is a cluster of state buildings occupying several blocks
that border the CBD, as in some state capitals,
the whole group is considered to lie outside
the CBD.
4. If the structures mentioned in Rule 3 occupy
only part of a block which is contiguous with normal CBD blocks and if the inclusion of these establishments as central business would bring the
two indexes of the block to the required totals,
then the block is considered part of the CBD.
5. Blocks located beyond railroad tracks or beyond a freeway are not considered contiguous to
the main body of CBD blocks unless the tracks
and freeway are so completely underground (or
overhead) as to allow free access to the main
mass of CBD blocks.

A number of valid objections have been raised
about the areal unit so defined. Murphy himself
" . . . emphasized that the boundary which results

114

from application of the method in any city is not the
boundary of the CBD of that city . . . Moreover, the
edge of the CBD is unquestionably a zone and our boundary is a line."[9] Lord Curzon[10] may have wished to
define the international boundaries like a "razor's
edge", but one must acknowledge the limitations of
defining a boundary of a central business district.
Therefore the aim of delimitation of a central business district should be not only the definition of an
areal unit but also the use of this unit for purposes
of further analysis.

This method, with slight adjustments to the CBHI
and CBII indices, has been used in Australia for delimitation of the CBD,[11] as well as South Africa,[12]
Great Britain,[13] and West Germany.[14] It is interesting to note that the cities where the Murphy and
Vance method has been successful are the product of
"western culture". Many cities of developing countries
are the product of different cultures, and several were
established prior to contact with the west. The Murphy
and Vance indices do not accommodate the diverse functions observed in blocks of cities of developing countries.

Consider, for example, a block of single storied
buildings performing central functions and another adjacent block made up of three storied
buildings in which the central functions are limited to the ground floor. On the basis of Murphy and Vance indices, the latter block will not
qualify as a part of the CBD. Since such blocks
are fairly common in the commercial areas of developing countries and form an integral part of
the CBD of those cities, de Blij attempted to
overcome this problem by devising a system to
accommodate these differences. de Blij[15] used
the retail frontage as a percentage of the total
frontage of the block. In this method, only
ground floor functions are taken into account,
and the delimited CBD would include buildings
performing Commercial and Residential functions
in addition to those that are wholly commercial
in function. The resultant CBD, in consequence,
is much larger than delimited by the Murphy and
Vance method.[16]

The basic advantage of using the de Blij method is
that it defines "a broader central area as the region
for geographical analysis". de Blij derived this
method for analysis of the central business district
of Lourenco Marques and subsequently used it to study

the CBD's of Dar es Salaam and Mombasa.[17]   Khan and
Salehuddin[18] defined the central business district of
Chittagong using the de Blij method (while other re-
searchers, e.g., Majid[19] in Dacca, had adjusted the
Murphy and Vance indices).   In the case of Nairobi,
Murphy and Vance indices only delimit that part of
the central commercial area which is occidental in
character, and do not include the oriental or bazaar-
type area.[20]   In this study initially, de Blij's
method [21] for delimitation of CBD's has been used,
and Figures 6.3 and 6.4 show the CBD's of Nairobi
and Dar es Salaam respectively.

    As the basic aim of this chapter is to compare
the functional structure of the central business districts of two East African cities, the question of
method or methods to be utilized for this purpose
arises.   Garner[22] suggested the application of such
procedures as factorial ecology, so that underlying
dimensions of variations could be identified.   Factorial ecology is the application of factor analysis to
the problem of areal differentiation,[23] and "factorial
analysis is concerned with discussing the underlying
structure exhibited by a group of variables."[24]

FIGURE 6.3

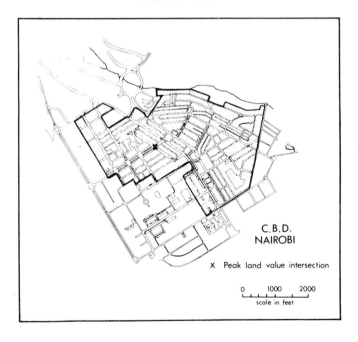

C.B.D.
NAIROBI

X Peak land value intersection

0   1000   2000
scale in feet

116

FIGURE 6.4

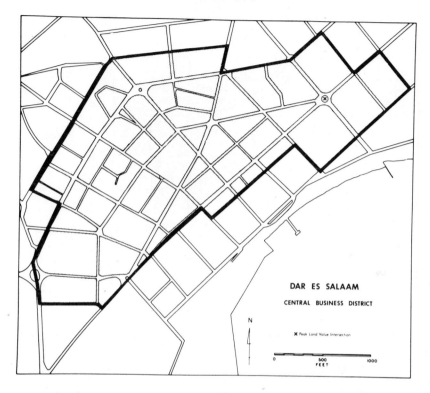

DAR ES SALAAM

CENTRAL BUSINESS DISTRICT

N

X Peak Land Value Intersection

0   500   1000
           FEET

A flow diagram (Figure 6.5) explains the procedures involved in this analysis.

Functional Structures of CBD's

Data

In North American cities a block is fairly well defined, and consequently easily recognized. In West European cities this is not so. In cities in developing countries, defining a block in itself can be quite problematical. In the case of Nairobi, a block was defined as that area lying between two marked roads. In certain cases however, exception had to be made and a narrow lane was used as a demarcation line. For Dar es Salaam, blocks as depicted by de Blij[25] were used. A block thus became the enumeration unit and the retail functions were treated as variables. The data were then registered in an X matrix. The data for Dar es Salaam were obtained from the work of

FIGURE 6.5

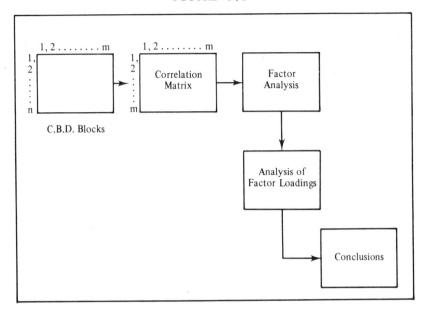

de Blij. For Nairobi the data were collected in 1969.

Analysis

The data were analyzed by using a principal component analysis and the components (factors) with
eigenvalue of over one were retained.

	Nairobi	Dar es Salaam
Number of blocks	101	50
Number of variables (functions)	40	23
Number of factors (Eigenvalue over 1)	14	8
Percentage of Variation explained	72.4	70.3
Number of factors retained after Screen Test	6	6

Tables 6.1 and 6.2 show details of functions
along with their factor loadings. The tables also
show that the functions have been categorized into
three broad groups: professional, semiprofessional
or specialized, and retail. Figure 6.6 attempts to
illustrate the interrelationship between the factor
loadings and the three groups. It is suggested that
the professional functions are, or are becoming, the
primary functions for a CBD. However, the definition

118

FIGURE 6.6

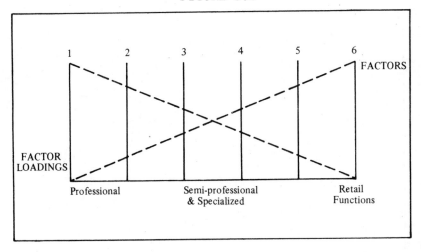

of "primary" functions in a CBD depends on the culture and age of the city. In other words, the central functions for a city in different parts of the world would require different definitions. Similarly central functions also have a temporal dimension, i.e., what was a central function in 1940 may not necessarily be a central function today.[27] Retail functions usually have more functional units but do not occupy the same position on the "importance" scale, and consequently are first to migrate from this area.

Factor I

An examination of this factor in Nairobi confirms the domination of professional functions, e.g., lawyers, solicitors, and accountants. In the second group of semiprofessional or specialized functions, chemists and curio shops appear. The inclusion of crockery shops in this group needs explanation. These shops are usually patronized by a selected few, and in this city they are "specialized" shops. The loadings on this factor show that these service-oriented functions are fairly similar to what one would expect from a CBD in a developed country.

In the case of Dar es Salaam the function "office" includes doctors, dentists and lawyers. This may be why this function does not appear as a dominant one and only appears in Factor III. The dominant proffessional group to emerge in this city is tailors.

119

TABLE 6.1   Nairobi: CBD (Central Business District)

Functions	Rotated Factor Loadings	Professional Functions	Semi-Professional or Specialized Functions	Retail Functions
Factor I				
Lawyers & Solicitors	.8037	Lawyers & Solicitors		
Accountants	.7926	Accountants		
Insurance	.7238	Insurance		
Chemists (Drugstore)	.7018		Chemists (Drugstore)	
Doctors & Dentists	.3408	Doctors & Dentists		
Crockery Shops	.3099		Crockery Shops	
Curio Shops	.3096		Curio Shops	
Factor II				
Shoeshop	.7807			Shoeshop
Radio & Electricity	.7772		Radio & Electricity	
Photographers	.6833		Photographers	
Hairdressers	.6789		Hairdressers	
Builders & Contractors	.5249	Builders & Contractors		
Factor III				
Plumbers	.8595		Plumbers	
Furnishers	.7420		Furnishers	
Decorators	.7271		Decorators	
Tire Retreaders	.6437		Tire Retreaders	
General Merchants	.6312			Gen.Merchants
Wholesalers	.4007			Wholesalers
Factor IV				
Metal & Metal Engineers	.8961		Metal & Metal Engineers	
Cars & Accessories	.8738		Cars & Accessories	
Stationers	.5940		Stationers	
Factor V				
Opticians	.8830	Opticians		
Agents & Auctioneers	.7935		Agents & Auctioneers	
Travel & Safari Agents	.7510		Travel & Safari Agents	
Photographers	.3324		Photographers	
Architects	.3202	Architects		
Educational	.3073	Educational		
Factor VI				
Groceries	.8657			Groceries
Butchers	.8397			Butchers
Wholesalers & Bars	.7198			Wholesalers
Restaurants & Bars	.5184			Restaurants,Bars
Clothing	.3835			Clothing

TABLE 6.2   Dar es Salaam: CBD (Central Business District)

	Functions	Rotated Factor Loadings	Professional Functions	Semi-Professional or Specialized Functions	Retail Functions
Factor I	General Merchants	.878			
	Furnishers	.862		Furnishers & Drapers	
	Hotels	.417		Hotels	
	Cars & Accessories	.334		Cars & Accessories	
	Tailors	.318	Tailors		
	Hardware				Household Hardwares
Factor II	Clothing	.908			Clothing
	Shoeshops	.871			Shoeshops
	Tailors	.442	Tailors		
	Radio ...	.311		Electrical	
Factor III	Hairdressers	.777		Hairdressers	
	Furniture	.743		Furniture	
	Restaurant	.618			Restaurants, Bars
	Offices*	.524	Offices		
Factor IV	Photographer	.852		Photographer	
	Theaters	.825		Theater	
	Chemists	.511		Chemists	
	Stationers	.383		Stationers & Office Material	
Factor V	Travel Agents	.862		Travel Agents	
	Radio & Electricity	.772		Radio & Electricity	
	Hardware	.532			Household Hardwares
Factor VI	Jeweller	.758	Jewellers& Opticians		
	Groceries	.666			Groceries & Liquor
	Tailors	.529	Tailor		
	Hardware	.404			Household Hdw.

*See bottom page 119.

121

This function is closely associated with clothing stores, and in many developing countries a tailor operates as an integral part of a clothing store. The semiprofessional or specialized group in Factor I includes furnishers and drapers, car and accessories, and hotels. As de Blij[28] has pointed out, though the hotels in the CBD are uniformly distributed, the sizes and mode of operation differ considerably. The same comment could be applied to the other two functions.

In the retail function, the appearance of general merchants and household hardwares is not surprising. General merchants are jacks-of-all-trades and sell practically everything. In a way these are glorified versions of the small "duka" through which commerce was carried to the interior of East Africa.

Factor II

The professional and semi-professional function continues to dominate the loadings in Nairobi. The only retail function to appear is shoe shops. In the case of Dar es Salaam, tailors reappear as a professional function and electrical shops fall into the specialized category. These shops sell not only electrical goods but also records. In the retail function clothing and shoe shops are fairly closely related and tend to locate adjacent to one another.

Factors III to VI

An analysis of loadings on these factors only confirms the pattern depicted in Figure 6.6. In Nairobi, professional and semiprofessional functions continue to dominate, and only in Factor VI is this dominance taken over by retail functions.

A similar trend can be recognized in Dar es Salaam. However, these loadings must be carefully interpreted because (a), the data was collected in 1962; (b) a number of functions have been grouped together, e.g., jewellers, opticians, and offices; and (c) only twenty-three variables were used in the analysis, which is rather a small number for a CBD analysis.

The main limitation of this type of study is lack of complete data. However, on the basis of analysis of selected functions it can be inferred that the CBD of Nairobi is more "westernized" than the CBD of Dar es Salaam. Evidence of this is readily seen in the loadings of the first few factors. These functions (e.g., lawyers and solicitors, accountants, and insurance), reflect the similarity between Nairobi's CBD and the CBD's of cities of the developed world.

The real explanation possibly lies in the differences
observed in the colonial past of these two countries,
for example Kenya has always had larger immigrant
(European and Asian) communities compared to Tanzania.

Cultural Duality and the CBD's

The Murphy and Vance method for defining CBD's
was discussed earlier, and attention was drawn to the
fact that this method only accommodates the commercial areas of Western cities. Therefore it is inferred that such central business indices are only capable of delimiting those central business areas which
display Western characteristics. In Nairobi, the application of this method results in defining[29] that
part of a commercial area which is more-or-less occidental in character (Figure 6.7). Therefore this area
has been named the occidental central business district. Figure 6.3 shows the larger CBD as defined by
de Blij's method. The additional area incorporated
by de Blij's method has been labelled the oriental
central business district.[30] It is recognized that a
zone separates these two business districts but a
line is being drawn to facilitate a comparative analysis.

FIGURE 6.7

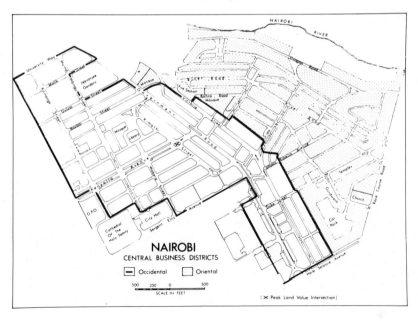

123

For Dar es Salaam de Blij calculated the retail
nodes of individual functions, and then these were
shown in terms of increasing distance from the peak
land value intersection. In subsequent discussion the
CBD is shown to have a European and a non-white region.[31]
For the purpose of comparative analysis these zones
have been demarcated and are shown in Figure 6.8.

The basic aim of this section is to study the
cultural duality as expressed in the distribution of
functions in these business districts. Do the differences or similarities observed justify the division
of these spatial units into occidental and oriental
business districts? These differences must be viewed
carefully because a partial duplication of functions
is expected. But this duplication does not reflect
the dissimilarities observed in operational characteristics of these business outlets.

The data were again analyzed using the principal
component analysis as described earlier, except that
two spatial units in each of the business districts
were used. The partial findings are as follows:

	Nairobi		Dar es Salaam	
	Occidental CBD	Oriental CBD	Occidental CBD	Oriental CBD
Number of Blocks	56	46	20	30
Number of Variables	40	40	23	23
Number of Factors above the eigen-value of 1	14	13	9	9
Percentage of Variance explained by the factors	79.02	83.36	84.5	80.3
Number of Factors obtained after Scree test	5	3	6	4

From the detailed analysis for Nairobi, the following
generalizations can be made: (a) the professional
and semiprofessional functions dominate the occidental CBD; (b) the professional functions load nega-
tively in the case of the oriental CBD, thus indicating the differences between the two CBD's; and
(c) in partially duplicating the retail functions,
the "mode of operation" is not accommodated in this
type of analysis, therefore this duplication does
not fully explain the differences observed.

For Dar es Salaam, the duplication of functions
emerges more strongly. This may be due to the fact
that a number of professional functions have been

124

FIGURE 6.8

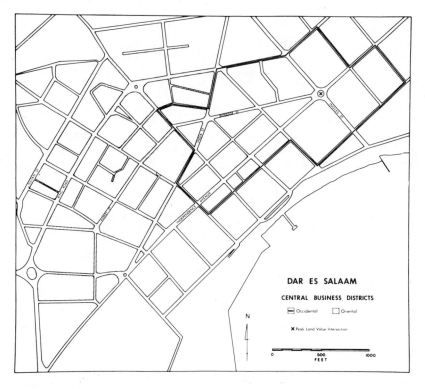

DAR ES SALAAM

CENTRAL BUSINESS DISTRICTS

⊟ Occidental   ☐ Oriental

X Peak Land Value Intersection

N

0   500   1000
       FEET

grouped together; therefore when the function "office"
loads on factor I, it may be indicative of the proffessional group. Also the absence of functions like
travel agents, stationers and office materials from
the oriental CBD indicates the minor differences
which separate the two CBD's. However, the mode of
operation of these functional outlets differs considerably, so that the division into two CBD's can be
readily justified. For example, in Nairobi photographic establishments in the oriental CBD in contrast
to those in the occidental one, usually depend on
local clientele and rarely deal with tourists. de
Blij made similar observations in Dar es Salaam.[32]
Similarly, chemists (drugstores) in the oriental CBD
rely exclusively upon local customers and do not
carry additional items such as photographic supplies
and souvenirs. Therefore this duplication of functions proves the point made earlier, that in performing the same functions, operational characteristics
have been altered to accommodate the cultural differences of the clientele.

125

Study of these commercial areas shows that it may be more realistic to treat these divisions in central commercial areas as distinct central business districts. After all, locationally these two areas in the city are central; their main function is business; and by serving two different groups of people, business agglomerates in different locations thus form distinct spatial units. R.J. Davies and D.S. Rajah[33] in Durban, South Africa have recognized such a duality. Unlike Durban,in Nairobi and Dar es Salaam this duality is the consequence of voluntary segregation. Although only Davies and Rajah have explicitly recognized this phenomenon, other studies have indicated the presence of dual CBD's. Hamadan[34] in his study of Khartoum has written that:

> The business center has both a European and an Arab market, a duality reflecting the heterogeneity of a cosmopolitan population. The two markets are physically ... separate. Khartoum, like Cairo, shows a definite binucleation in the market.

Similarly, Khan and Salhendin[35] in Chittagong and Majid[36] in Dacca, noted that either the hard core was divided into two physically distinct sections or there were two distinct commercial nodes. Both these cities were in existence prior to the coming of the British and therefore the two nodes or parts of the hard core may in fact be two culturally distinct CBD's which have not been distinguished as such — as it has been customary to look for one unified CBD.

Conclusions

This study explored the usage of the principal component method for analyzing the functional structures of central business districts. Because of the use of selected data, the technique's full potential may not be apparent. However, if the loadings on these factors can be equated to the importance of functions then this data reduction process could be extremely useful in revealing the underlying dimensions either in terms of temporal crosssections of one CBD or for a comparative study of many CBD's at the same time.

It has already been mentioned that the CBD of Nairobi is more Westernized than that of Dar es Salaam. This conclusion was drawn on the basis of the factor loadings shown in Tables 6.1 and 6.2.

With respect to the duality observed in these

CBD's, the two CBD concepts should be taken into consideration, especially as they are in developing
countries.   Future research into the commercial
structure of these two cities should treat these
divisions as separate units.   Further too, the city
planners should not ignore this duality, because
oriental central business districts may not attract
many tourists but they still fulfill a very important
function, and as a region, should not be allowed to
deteriorate.

NOTES

1.   D. Halliman and W.T.W. Morgan, "The City of
Nairobi", in Nairobi: City and Region, ed. W.T.W.
Morgan (Nairobi: Oxford University Press 1967), p.113.
2.   A. Mascarenhas, "Land Use in Dar es Salaam",
in Tanzania in Maps, ed. L. Berry (New York: Africana
Publishing Corporation 1972), pp. 136-137.
3.   E.W. Burgess, "The Growth of the City", Proceedings of the American Sociological Society, Vol.18,
1923, pp. 85-89.
C.D. Harris and E.L. Ullman, "The Nature of Cities",
Annals of the American Academy of Political and Social
Science, Vol. 142, 1945, pp. 7-17.
4.   M.J. Proudfoot, "City Retail Structure",
Economic Geography, Vol. 13, 1937, pp. 425-428.
5.   G.W. Hartman, "The Central Business District:
A Study in Urban Geography", Economic Geography, Vol.
26, 1950, pp. 237-244.
6.   R.E. Murphy and J.E. Vance, Jr., "Delimiting
the C.B.D.", Economic Geography, Vol. 30, 1954, pp.
189-222.
7.   S.F. Weiss, "The Central Business District
in Transition", Research Paper No. 1, City and Regional Planning Studies, University of North Carolina,
Chapel Hill, N.C., 1957, p. 18.
8.   A.E. Smailes, "The Central Business District
of Cities", Geographical Review, Vol. 45, 1955,
pp.574-577.
9.   R.E. Murphy, The Central Business District,
(Chicago: Aldine Press 1972), p. 37.
10.   Lord Curzon of Keddleston, Frontiers,(Oxford:
Clarendon Press 1907), p.7.
11.   P. Scott, "The Australian C.B.D.", Economic
Geography, Vol. 30 (1955), pp. 290-314.
12.   D.H. Davies, Land Use in Central Capetown:
A Study in Urban Geography (Capetown: Longmans, 1965.)
13.   D.R. Diamond, "The Central Business District
of Glasgow", in Proceedings of the I.G.U. Symposium
in Urban Geography.

Lund, 1960,"Lund Studies in Human Geography Series B",
Human Geography No. 24,(1962), pp. 525-534.

14. W. Harttenstein and G. Staack, "Land Use in
the Urban Core", in Urban Core and Inner City, W.F.
Heinemeijer et al.,(Leiden: E.J. Brill, 1967), pp.35-
52.

15. H.J. de Blij, "Functional Structure and
Central Business District of Lourenco Marques, Mocam-
bique", Economic Geography,Vol. 38 (1962) pp. 56-77.

16. R.C. Tiwari, C.B.D. Delimitation in Devel-
oping Countries: A Case Study of Nairobi, Kenya,
Paper read at the 4th Annual Conference, The Canadian
Association of African Studies, Halifax, 1974.

17. H.J. de Blij, Dar es Salaam: A Study in
Urban Geography (Evanston: Northwestern University
Press, 1963); Mombasa: An African City (Evanston:
Northwestern University Press, 1968).

18. F.K. Khan and A. Salehuddin, "The City Centre of Chittagong", Oriental Geographer, Vol. 11, 1967,
pp. 1-37.

19. R.Majid, "The C.B.D. of Dacca, Delimitation
and Internal Structure", Oriental Geographer, Vol.14,
1970, pp. 44-63.

20. R.C. Tiwari, "C.B.D. Delimitation in Developing Countries,"op.cit.

21. de Blij had used a cut-off point of twenty-
seven percent for Lourenco Marques and twenty-nine
percent for Dar es Salaam. In Nairobi no such break
was obtained. Some of the blocks with very low values
were completely surrounded by blocks with values of
over eighty percent, consequently the blocks with low
values had to be included in the CBD delimited by de
Blij's method.

22. B.J. Garner, "Review of Murphy's 'The
Central Business District'", The Canadian Geographer,
Vol. 17 (1973), p. 95.

23. P.H. Rees, "Factorial Ecology: An Extended
Definition Survey and Critique of the Field", Economic Geography, Vol. 47, No. 2 Supplement, 1971,p.220.

24. M. Yeates, An Introduction to Quantitative
Analysis in Human Geography (Toronto: McGraw Hill 1974)
p. 208.

25. H.J. de Blij, "Dar es Salaam", op.cit.,p.51.

26. The analysis for Nairobi used a package
program FACTAN of the University of Waterloo. The
factors were rotated according to the varimax method.
The data for Dar es Salaam were analysed by using
Biomed-BMDP4M and the factors in this case were also
rotated by varimax method. This method has generated
a methodological debate in Human Geography. However,
in this study the principal component analysis is solely used for a comparative purpose. For details of

this method, see R.J. Rummell, Applied Factor Analysis, (Evanston: Northwestern University Press 1970); Also: D. Clark, W.K.D. Davies and R.J. Johnson, "The Application of Factor Analysis in Human Geography", The Statistician, Vol. 23 (1974), pp. 259-281.

27. J.E.Bohnert and P.E. Mattingly, "The Delimitation of C.B.D. through Time", Economic Geography, Vol. 40, 1964, pp. 334-337.
M.J. Bowden, "Downtown through Time", Economic Geography, Vol. 47, 1971, pp. 121-135.
28. H.J. de Blij, "Dar es Salaam", op.cit.,p.67.
29. In addition to the central business uses defined by Murphy and Vance, wholesaling, printing and storage were also included as central business uses. In many cases storage was the integral part of a shop.
30. R.C. Tiwari, "C.B.D. Delimitation in Developing Countries", op.cit.
31. H.J. de Blij, "Dar es Salaam", op.cit., pp. 64-65.
32. H.J. de Blij, "Dar es Salaam", op.cit.,p.73.
33. R.J. Davies and D.S. Rajah, "The Durban C.B.D.: Boundary Delimitation and Racial Dualism", The South African Geographical Journal, Vol. 47, December 1965, pp. 45-58.
34. G. Hamadan, "The Growth and Functional Structure of Khartoum", Geographical Review, Vol. 50 (1960), pp. 21-40.
35. F.K. Khan and A. Salehuddin, "The City Center of Chittagong", op.cit.
36. R. Majid, "The C.B.D. of Dacca", op.cit.

7. Location and Functional Structure of Shopping Centers in Nairobi

S. M. Kimani

Introduction

Commercial activities form a large part of the economic activity in urban areas. They provide not only goods and services, but also employment opportunities for large numbers of rural and urban residents.

Interest in the study of the internal commercial structure of urban areas makes it quite clear that a thorough understanding of the distributive retail system of goods and services is a prerequisite to sound formulation and implementation of urbanization and development policies, especially in order to determine current and future land use needs and development within our cities. With this realization in mind the Urban Study Group of the Nairobi City Council in preparing a master plan, included among other tasks, preparation of a report on the existing retail structure of Nairobi.[1] While many studies of this sort have been carried out in the western world, relatively few appear in the existing literature on nonwestern urban systems. It would appear therefore that the time is ripe to extend both theory and empirical research to more cities in developing countries, to see whether the generality of these studies extends to cases other than those for which they were devised.[2] The primary purpose of this chapter is to examine the location and functional structure of shopping centers in Nairobi in the light of western-based theories.

This chapter is divided into two major parts: the first outlines an overall view of the retail distributive system, the second attempts an analysis of the retail structure of shopping centers outside the central business district (CBD).[3]

The author wishes to gratefully acknowledge the assistance of Nairobi City Council and the University of Nairobi in the preparation of this article.

Distributive System of Retail Trade

It may be useful first to examine the overall distributive system of retail trade in order to gain a proper perspective of the place of shopping centers within the urban spatial system.

According to Murphy,[4] retail structure in American cities can be viewed as having two basic forms: nucleation, and the string - street or ribbon development. Nucleation is a cluster of retail outlets which grade from the CBD on the one extreme, down to isolated store clusters on the other. Ribbon development amounts to retail use of property along a traffic artery with only minor extensions on intersecting streets. The principal business thoroughfare and the neighbourhood business street are two examples of ribbon development catering for transients and residential areas, respectively. Many attempts have been made to provide detailed classification and characterization of these basic forms in America and elsewhere. One of the earliest was evolved by Proudfoot[5] who saw the hierarchy in American cities as comprising the following:

a. the CBD

b. the outlying business center

c. the principal business thoroughfare

d. the neighborhood business street

e. the isolated store cluster

Later studies by Ratcliff, Murphy and Vance, Kelly and Hoyt confirmed the presence of these types in many other cities with only minor variations in classification and additional characterization.[6] In his study of Chicago in 1963 Berry's[7] classification differed from the others in matters of theoretical grounding and a more detailed business structure. He identified three major types: centers, ribbons and specialized areas, each further subdivided into several components. Studies with similar classifications have also been carried out in Britain by Thorpe and Carruthers, and in Australia by Logan.[8] But most relevant to our study is that of Berry which has been modified to reflect nearly all types of retail outlets in Nairobi.

At the conceptual level, five major forms of retail outlets were specified. They are: centers, ribbons, specialized spots, markets and "others". (See Figure 7.1).

131

FIGURE 7.1

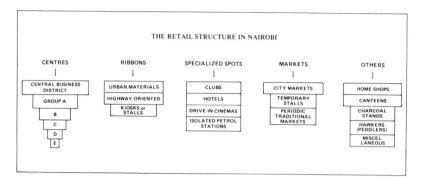

Centers

The centers consist of nucleations or business clusters, spatially separated from other uses by alternate types of land use such as residential, manufacturing, or even undeveloped tracts.[9] Six orders were identified. At the top of the list is the CBD whose characteristics in Nairobi are similar to those of other cities. It is the pinnacle of a complex and varied commercial activity which includes public offices and law courts serving areas far beyond the city's limits. Groups A through E represent the lower levels in the hierarchy of shopping centers, and will be discussed later in this chapter.

Ribbons

There are several types in this category properly termed ribbon or strip development. The first consists of those commercial functions which seek out accessible urban arterial locations in cities. They tend to locate in such a manner as to have reasonable access to the urban market; but because of space requirements and the way consumers use them, they function most efficiently outside the nucleated business centers.[10] Examples are found along Mombasa Road where establishments for vehicle repairs, sales of road and agricultural machinery, and lumber yards are located near the industrial area.

The second group comprises functions serving demands originating on highways, and in general the greater the traffic volume, the greater the demand for and density of highway-oriented uses.[11] Functions such as petrol stations, groceries and restaurants

are to be found along Ngara/Fort Hall, Park, Jogoo
and Pumwani Roads. An interesting combination of
small-scale functions such as clothing, hardware, groceries, restaurants, etc., is found on Jogoo and Pumwani Roads. Nearly all these functions are in temporary building structures called kiosks (or stalls)
where pedestrian traffic is very heavy. Apart from
the demand side, the existence of these small-scale
businesses can readily be understood from the point of
view of the small capital outlay required, compared to
that involved in areas officially earmarked for
business development.

Specialized Spots

Specialized areas, unlike those in cities of comparable size in the west, are relatively undeveloped.
The three functional areas mentioned are to be found
singly with a combination of other ancillary integrated services such as bars, restaurants, etc. Most
clubs, although designed to serve private membership,
are open to the public and located mainly in the formerly exclusively European and Asian areas of the city.
Likewise hotels which are, in terms of bed capacity,
smaller than those in the CBD and its immediate sur-
roundings, are found in similar locations. There are
only two drive-in cinemas outside the hub of the city,
on Thika and Mombasa Roads. Considering the distance
that moviegoers have to travel to reach them, a third
one on the western side of the city (now more and more
heavily populated) should become a viable business proposition in the near future.

Markets

Even in traditional societies, markets have always been the major focus of the distributive retailing system. Within the city boundaries three types
of markets are to be found: first, city daily markets,
mainly in large buildings owned by the city council,
offering groceries, fruits, vegetables, flowers, meats,
and carvings. One is in the CBD, two are at the edge
on Landies and Racecourse Roads, and one in the Westlands shopping center.
A second type of daily market consists of stalls
in closely built temporary structures conducting fairly small-scale individual business operation. In addition to some of the functions usual in city markets,
this group offers a wide range of goods: new and used
clothing, utensils, and so forth — mainly of lower
quality and therefore cheaper. The two biggest such

markets are Bama on Jogoo Road and Gikomba on Pumwani Road, both on principal mass-transportation routes.

The third type are periodic open-air markets, mainly in trading centers outside the main effective urban area. (See Figure 7.2). The major markets of this type are in Dagoretti Corner West, Kawangware, Riruta and Uthiru, and purvey goods similar to those of the second group. The majority of customers in the last two groups are Africans in the low-income bracket. It is reported that nine semicovered markets are to be constructed in outlying areas at Kariobangi North and South, Kibera, Embakasi, Kenyatta National Hospital, Ngara, Eastleigh, Kahawa, and Jerico. Four more markets at Dagoretti, Kawangware, Riruta and Kangemi will be considered. In these markets traders will be provided with reasonably big stalls to match the nature of their existing businesses or expected prospects.

Others

The rest of the retail outlets were classified as "others". But this category comprises what the International Labour Office (ILO) calls the "informal sector".[12]

In many mud-walled and tin- or corrugated-iron-roofed houses in Kariobangi, Mathare Valley, Pumwani/Majengo and Kibera areas (to mention only a few), dwelling rooms facing a street or public thorough-fare have been converted into small shops selling groceries and a few other items through the windows. They are small shops during the daytime, reverting to their basic purpose of sleeping at night when items for sale are set aside to give way to night accommo-dation. These home shops are mainly found in high-density, relatively low-income areas. The preponder-ance of these shops has to some extent inhibited the growth of the few shopping centers within their trade areas. As their large numbers suggest, very small resources are required to open such shops and they provide an important source of employment to large numbers of residents who would otherwise be jobless.

Other retail outlets of local significance are the kioski or stalls scattered in nearly all areas of the city except the core of the CBD: Small wooden or sometimes cardboard structures whose sale items may vary from tea and cooked food only to groceries such as vegetables, bananas, milk, soft drinks, cigarettes, etc., depending on local demand. They tend to locate at strategic places — sometimes near existing shop-ping centers, in heavily travelled streets of residen-tial areas and in sites not officially designated

FIGURE 7.2

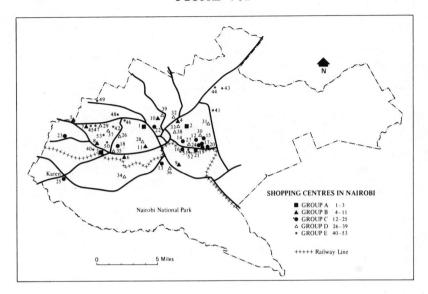

SHOPPING CENTRES IN NAIROBI

■ GROUP A   1-3
▲ GROUP B   4-11
●̇ GROUP C   12-25
△ GROUP D   26-39
★ GROUP E   40-53

+++++ Railway Line

Nairobi National Park

0   5 Miles

MAP KEY

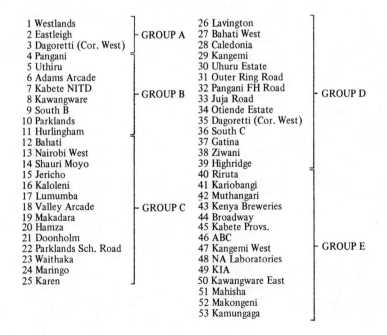

1 Westlands		
2 Eastleigh	GROUP A	
3 Dagoretti (Cor. West)		
4 Pangani		
5 Uthiru		
6 Adams Arcade		
7 Kabete NITD	GROUP B	
8 Kawangware		
9 South B		
10 Parklands		
11 Hurlingham		
12 Bahati		
13 Nairobi West		
14 Shauri Moyo		
15 Jericho		
16 Kaloleni		
17 Lumumba		
18 Valley Arcade	GROUP C	
19 Makadara		
20 Hamza		
21 Doonholm		
22 Parklands Sch. Road		
23 Waithaka		
24 Maringo		
25 Karen		

26 Lavington
27 Bahati West
28 Caledonia
29 Kangemi
30 Uhuru Estate
31 Outer Ring Road
32 Pangani FH Road   GROUP D
33 Juja Road
34 Otiende Estate
35 Dagoretti (Cor. West)
36 South C
37 Gatina
38 Ziwani
39 Highridge
40 Riruta
41 Kariobangi
42 Muthangari
43 Kenya Breweries
44 Broadway
45 Kabete Provs.
46 ABC
47 Kangemi West   GROUP E
48 NA Laboratories
49 KIA
50 Kawangware East
51 Mahisha
52 Makongeni
53 Kamungaga

135

commercial areas. Perhaps they are similar to the
"counters" found in Lagos, Nigeria — except that
most proprietors in Nairobi are men, whereas in Lagos
they are owned by women.13 Like the home shops, they
provide reasonable incomes to a large number of people
who would otherwise remain unemployed.

Canteens are another type — small shops within
the precincts of a government post such as a police
station, or perhaps on a company's working premises,
designed to serve the population residing or working
there. Low-threshold goods such as groceries, other
catering services, and beverages, are the common
items for sale.

The sale of charcoal is another — charcoal is a
fuel commodity in great demand in Nairobi. Charcoal
stands are located in many parts of Nairobi outside
the CBD, in three types of location: Inside some
shopping centres; or just a few yards from most shopping centers (this latter designed to capture customers from shopping centers, but because of the high
capital investment required within the center's designated area, they locate next to them in an open plot);
or third, in a residentially-oriented location where
a strategic point (particularly in undeveloped property) has been chosen for selling to nearby residents.
Here hardly any capital or overhead input is necessary
except a small fee for licence, because they are in
open-air plots.

Fruit and vegetable hawkers form another group.
Itinerant traders, they constitute a prominent feature
of small retail enterprise in Nairobi's Eastlands and
in many other areas. Commodities are carried in bas-
kets and push-carts for sale to passers-by, to passengers at bus stations or to some homes. Although a lot
of energy is required in most businesses, this is one
of the most demanding of all and these people toil
tirelessly to make a hard living.

Mention should also be made of other street newspaper vendors, sweepstakes ticket sellers, of combination newspaper,magazine and shoeshine boys, generally
located in the CBD's busy streets under the canopy of
an already existing shop. Maize roasters, and a few
auto parts sellers are also found in the city.

Thus it can be seen that distribution of retail
goods and services is a highly complex system even
in such a modest-sized city as Nairobi with a population of 600,000 in 1971.14 For this reason we will
focus on one element of the system, the shopping
centers outside the CBD.

Shopping Centers

The Underlying Theory

Perhaps some of the most important theoretical contributions to spatial analysis of commercial activities within urban areas are those of Berry. His interest stemmed from his early concern with the central-place theory originally evolved by Christaller in the early 1930s, focussing mainly on locational and hierarchical systems of urban places.[16] Berry applied similar ideas to the internal structure of urban areas, particularly in Chicago.

According to him shopping centers display spatial patterns that conform to geographic distribution of consumers, being centrally located with respect to the maximum number of consumers they can serve. Shops which cluster in such locations thus require similar trade areas for their support, and experience mutual benefits from agglomerating at a central place where consumers round about can converse easily.

From the point of view of supply, different functions have different conditions of entry or thresholds, and thus demand minimum trade areas of different sizes for their support. On the demand side, consumers spend differing proportions of their income on different goods and services, and frequency of purchase varies. Hence those functions with low-threshold requirements, those most frequently needed, will be found in lower-level nucleations; and those functions requiring a high threshold to become economically viable, will be found in higher-level centers serving larger trade areas. Thus the distribution of functions should be closely related to distribution of consumers. For these reasons there emerges a regular pattern in the location of retail and service outlets, known as the hierarchy of functions, and of centers.

Berry argued further that competition between centers at any one level in this hierarchy reduces their trade areas nearly to threshold, and spreads the centers throughout the city, each central to its own trade area. Besides higher-order goods, higher-level centers should also handle lower-order functions and should have somewhat larger trade areas than centers exclusively on the lower level, as the existence of better shopping opportunities induces consumers to travel further to purchase convenience goods. "Low-order centres in terms of the provision of higher order goods and services to the consumers who visit the lower order centres for their offerings, and at the extreme all outlying centres, 'nest' within the sphere of influence of the CBD for its most specialized functions."[16]

Though they are basic to understanding the pattern, supply and demand functions are not the only factors which explain the character of the urban hierarchy of centers. In common with the rest of the landscape of which they are a part, retail patterns result from a complex interplay of economic, political, social and historic factors. This is clearly demonstrated by many subsequent efforts made in the reformulation of the central-place theory to allow for deviations from the classical pattern[17] and to incorporate some concepts which have evolved from studies of consumer and entrepreneurial behavior as in works of Pred, Curry, Horton, and many others.[18] Moreover the importance of scale economies and agglomeration, business organization, attitudes and values in a given society must also be stressed.

It is within this theoretical framework that the retail structure of Nairobi's shopping centers is examined.

Some Basic Definitions

A Shopping Center

There is a big problem in defining a shopping center. Apart from function, a researcher is faced with the problem of physical form and delimitation and ultimately, the classification of shopping centers. These problems have been well reviewed by Scott.[19] It suffices to regard a shopping center as a concentration of economic and other related activity. The system of shopping centers embraces all retail areas whether nucleated or linear and includes all centers whether planned or unplanned.[20]

Establishment, Function and Functional Unit

In attempting to assess the importance of a shopping center, several data measurements have been proposed: e.g., business turnover, employment payroll, floor-space, frontage, land valuation, and functions of retail establishments.[21] In this study data were not readily available, hence a field survey had to be carried out. Then the question was which could be collected with ease and in the shortest time possible, and a number of establishments, functions and functional units were arbitrarily selected. It was necessary to define these clearly before going to the field.

The definitions were basically those commonly used in central-place studies and in particular by Thomas:

138

An _establishment_ is essentially the physical
manifestation of an activity and is generally
the unit in which an activity is performed;
e.g., the building in which the office for a
filling station is located or the office of a
physician are examples of establishments. In
contrast, the term 'function' refers to the activities which are performed in the establishments. According to these definitions, it is
possible for more than one function to be associated with a particular establishment. Each
occurrence of a function constitutes one functional unit . . . Each of these indices illu-
minates a somewhat different aspect of the overall distribution of activities . . . Differences between these may be illustrated as follows.
Let us assume that there is a place with three
establishments, A, B, C. Three functions are
performed in establishment A: it is a gasoline
filling station, bulk oil distribution station,
and used car lot. Two functions are associated
with establishment B: it is a combination of
food store and filling station. Two functions
are associated with establishment C: it is a
combination of food store and livestock feed
store. There are, in this case, three establishments, five functions, and seven functional units.[22]

In adopting these definitions, it was necessary
to include those functions neither performed in nor
associated with an establishment. For example, charcoal stands and building materials which are in the
open air without any kind of structure, temporary or
permanent, associated with them were included if
located within the centers.
The gravest defect in these indices however lies
in that they mask significant and substantial variations in size and trading characteristics. For example a grocery function in a department store in Westlands was treated the same as a small grocery shop
in, say, Kariobangi. Yet the amount and variety of
stock as well as business turnover and returns are
vastly different. In the former the returns are col-
lossal — while in the latter the business barely
manages to survive. What effect does this have on
land or retail space available?

Data Collection

It was also our intention to seek additional information about customers' perception of the centers
as well as their travel and shopping behavior. A

139

questionnaire to this effect was prepared.

Initial and trial stages of the field work were carried out by University of Nairobi students during field-day excursions. Procedures and modifications of the prepared list of functions were established in the early part of 1972. Thereafter two people were employed full-time for six months and the desired information was collected at each of the centers. These data are analyzed in the following sections:

Main Features of Retail Structure

A. Functions and Functional Units

A total of forty-three functions were identified and arranged in order of their frequency of occurrence among the fifty-four centers of business. Groceries were to be found in every shopping center since they have the lowest threshold requirement. The frequency of occurrence decreased from the most frequent, such as butchers and meats, hardware, bars and clothing stores, through to petrol stations, restaurants, barbers and chemists, with the cinema at the other extreme end found only in one shopping center (Adams Arcade). Further examination of the data reveals that the number of functional units tends to decrease from the lowest-order goods (groceries, meats, etc.,) towards the higher-order goods (laundromat, insurance, and cinema). A comparison of this ordering of functions with what has been found elsewhere does show striking similarities. For example, in many countries such as Britain, the United States, Australia and Nigeria, groceries, bars and restaurants are in the category of low-order goods, and hence occur most frequently, while sporting goods and cinemas, to mention only a few, are generally higher-order goods and thus locate in higher-level places.

There are also notable differences. For instance bank and postal services, laundromats, and insurance agencies which appear as higher-order goods, are low-order goods occurring frequently in Western urban centers. This is perhaps a reflection of the difference in economic, social and technological conditions prevailing in different countries.

B. Aggregate Retail Structure

Table 7.1 shows the number of aggregate functions at each center. The number of establishments and the estimated population served by each center are also given.

Examination of table 7.1 shows too that centers formerly serving predominantly European communities have a wider range of functions offered to relatively fewer people. This is because both Europeans and

140

TABLE 7.1 AGGREGATE RETAIL STRUCTURE&POPULATION SERVED

		No.of Establishments	No.of Functions	No. of Functional Units	Population Served
GROUP A	Westlands*	81	35	150	83,110
	Eastleigh	104	19	133	18,617
	Dagoretti Corner W.	47	19	70	2,857
GROUP B	Pangani*	43	16	486	21,146
	Uthiru	38	19	46	–
	Adams Arcade*	23	28	47	4,428
	Kabete NITD	32	19	46	–
	Kawangware**	30	16	61	8,763
	South B. **	31	9	72	10,007
	Parklands *	20	22	51	2,260
	Hurlingham *	20	22	48	3,210
GROUP C	Bahati W.	26	10	54	19,040
	Nairobi W.	23	10	54	13,663
	Sharui Moyo	30	10	35	24,364
	Jericho	22	9	44	9,083
	Kaloleni	17	14	39	8,829
	Lumumba	20	10	33	13,133
	Valley Arcade*	14	15	28	3,496
	Makad	18	9	37	11,086
	Hamza	17	9	37	5,204
	Donholm	18	10	31	8,223
	Parklands Sclaters Rd*	6	18	22	4,239
	Waithaka	18	8	25	6,768
	Maringo	15	9	28	8,731
	Karen*	11	13	21	1,334
GROUP D	Lavington*	13	11	14	6,035
	Bahati E.	11	8	24	19,040
	Caledonia*	7	12	15	1,599
	Kandemi	8	10	18	2,222
	Uhuru Est.	9	8	22	7,029
	Outer Ring	7	9	23	1,442
	Pangani FH Road *	10	9	16	12,381
	Juja Road *	10	8	17	31,190
	Otiende Est.	9	8	19	995
	Dagoretti*C.E.*	8	8	12	1,224
	South C.	12	4	17	19,751
	Gatjra	8	7	13	412
	Ziwani	9	6	11	37,858
	Highridge *	7	7	10	795
GROUP E	Riruta	8	4	9	1,381
	Kariobangi	8	4	9	1,021
	Muthangari	7	5	7	1,955
	K. Breweries	7	5	7	1,159
	Broadway*	2	7	7	1,264
	Kabete Province	2	7	7	478
	ABC*	2	6	7	1,223
	Kangemi W.	3	5	7	234
	NA Lab	2	6	6	808
	KIA*	3	4	55	639
	Kawangware E.	3	4	4	1,224
	Mahisha	2	3	4	3,922
	Makongeni	2	3	4	4,479
	Kanungaga	2	3	3	807
	Karen Market	2	2	2	632

Asians have had relatively greater purchasing power
to support a wider range of functions than poorer
Africans residing around their respective centers.
Centers such as Dagoretti Corner West, Kawangware,
Jerico and Shauri Moyo with relatively greater numbers of establishments, contain fewer functions
with a larger number of duplicated functional units
of mainly low-order or convenience goods, sometimes
of poor quality, which theoretically require a small
support threshold. This could be construed as an indication of the lower purchasing power of the predominantly African consumer and the perhaps unsophisticated level of their business organization. Interes-
tingly, in his study of Leeds, Davies[23] found a similar situation in lower income areas of that city, and
it is likely that it may be found in many other cities.

C. Some Empirical Relationships

It seems appropriate to examine here some of
the relationships that may be expected within the
framework of the theory of intraurban retail location
discussed previously.
If regularities of occurrence of functions exist
as postulated in the theory, then some direct relationships obtain between population served by a center and the number of establishments, functions and
functional units. Thus the greater the number of establishments, functions and functional units, the larger the population served by the centers. Some of
these relationships have been empirically verified in
many central-place studies even in urban areas.
In order to test the hypothesis, scatter diagrams
were drawn as shown in Figure 7.3. At first sight
the reader is tempted to think that such relationships are not revealed in the diagrams. However a
closer examination of the scatter of plots (which
appear almost identical) does reveal some interesting
observations, especially in B. There are two distinct
groups of centers represented by the dots below and
above the dashed line. The scatter of those below
the dashed line definitely suggests a fairly reasonable relationship between population and number of
functions. The dots represent those serving European
or Asian communities in the outskirts of the city.
The scatter of dots above the line does not suggest
the existence of such a relationship. In other words,
an increase in population does not necessarily lead to
an increase in number of functions. It is interesting to note that dots above this line represent centers inside the "effective" urban area serving predominantly African masses (with the exception of

142

FIGURE 7.3

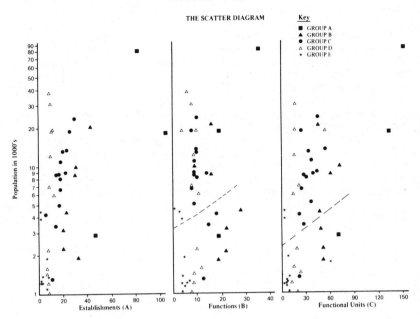

THE SCATTER DIAGRAM

Key
■ GROUP A
▲ GROUP B
● GROUP C
△ GROUP D
* GROUP E

Westlands — Europeans or Asians). Their functional paucity can be attributed to several factors:

First, although it is well-known that the areas served by these centers have experienced the most rapid population growth, a time lag exists between population growth and the introduction of additional functions. Secondly, freedom of entry by prospective entrepreneurs is restricted by lack of space for expansion of facilities. Apart from space limitations, the preponderance of home shops, kiosks, itinerant sellers or hawkers (which were not included in this study) could conceivably retard new development of services, since they share the patronage with these centers. Third, since there exists a remarkable heterogeneity in the purchasing power of customers, the use of population as an indicator of market conditions (which should induce establishment of additional functions as it grows) may come under question just as it has in central-place studies in the light of the theory of consumer spatial behavior.

D. Classification of Centers

According to Scott, spatial systems of shopping centers may be regarded as comprising complex hierarchies, each made up of discrete groups of centers

143

with each group distinctive in its retail functions.
The problem of hierarchical classification is far from
being resolved. "Almost all hierarchical classification, despite the claims of a few classifiers, are to
a greater or lesser degree arbitrary." Scott continues to assert that in the light of what is known concerning entrepreneurial and consumer behavior this
would seem to be true of almost all studies to date.[24]
In this study, sophisticated techniques normally called
for were not at our disposal, therefore recourse was
to an unsophisticated method.

It is observed from the literature that a combination of number of establishments, functions and
functional units may serve a useful purpose in illum-
inating the importance of a center. A combination of
number of establishments and functions has been used
by Garner,[25] and one of functions and functional units
by Logan,[26] both of whom employed different classification techniques. In this study however it seemed
reasonable to use a combination of all three and em-
ploy a weighting system. Thus for every establishment,
function and functional unit a center has, it received
3, 2 and 1 points respectively, and total scores for
each center were obtained. Centers were then ranked
in descending order according to these scores. In
order to identify groups, a major break between any
two consecutive scores was deemed to isolate one group
from the other except in the first three treated as
one group which, according to this rule, would otherwise have formed three separate levels. Hence a five-
level hierarchy was obtained with a range of scores
as follows:

Group A	221-463
Group B	154-180
Group C	82-136
Group D	45-73
Group E	12-37

Obviously the method is not very rigorous, but it is
not completely arbitrary.

Of the fifty-four centers, three are in group A,
eight in B, fourteen in C, fourteen in D and sixteen
in group E. This is quite in keeping with other empirical findings where shopping centers tend to exhibit
a hierarchical spatial arrangement with an increasing
number of centers in successively lower orders.

We now turn our attention to the spatial arrangement and trade areas of these centers:

144

E. Spatial Distribution and Trade Areas

The spatial arrangement of the hierarchy of
centers and population distribution is shown in Figures
7.2 and 7.4 respectively. It is apparent that the
centers of low density are in the west, north and south
of the city. This situation could have resulted from
market conditions, but more likely as creations of land
developers and city planners deliberately designating
these sites for commercial purposes. Each site was
associated with one or more residential estates.

In order to delineate the trade areas of the
centers, shoppers were asked whether they normally
buy their goods in that particular center, and if so,
where they lived.[27] An attempt was made in the field
to locate their homes as accurately as possible with
a dot on the map and directed lines drawn to the center. The outermost dots were considered to mark the
edge of a trade area for a given center, and the boundary was drawn around them. To supplement this procedure however, a variation of the gravity model was
used. This is the well-known "breaking point" between
two centers which marks the theoretical extent of influence of each of the competing centers. In its revised form the formula is written as:

$$Bx = \frac{Dyx}{1 + \frac{Py}{Px}}$$

where:

Bx is the distance of the breaking point from
center x

Dyx is the distance between centers x and y

Px, Py are measures of the importance of centers
x and y.

In this investigation D was represented by straight-
line distances between paired centers, and P by the
number of functions at each center. Lines were then
drawn joining the breaking points around each center.
These lines in conjunction with those enclosing customers' home locations[28] were used as guides in drawing the trade area boundaries.

Having delineated service areas for the centers,
population numbers enclosed by the boundaries were
then determined by enumeration of areas and also by

145

interpolation whenever necessary, and are given in
Table 7.3.[29] The proportion of population circumscribed
by these boundaries is about seventy-six percent of
the total for the city. It is therefore likely that
the larger part of any center's patronage is drawn from
its bounded area.

The patterns revealed by the trade areas are interesting. Most obvious among these are the barrier
effects of nonresidential areas which do not produce
customers for the centers. For example, the effect of
the industrial area to the southeast is to separate the
eastlands from that sector to the south; Ngong Road
forest isolates the Karen areas from areas to the
northeast; while Otiende Estate and Broadway are separated from the rest either by vacant or other non-resi-
dential land. It should be noted however that many of
the gaps in Figure 7.4 do not necessarily indicate complete absence of shopping facilities. The preponder-
ance of numbers of scattered stalls in temporary structures and home shops in many areas of the city does
fulfil many shopping needs, especially for convenience-
type goods.

Another interesting feature is the size , shape
and "nesting" of trade areas. Deduction from the underlying theory postulates that larger centers will have
larger trade areas. Likewise, smaller centers will
have smaller service or trade areas; and the ideal
arrangement would be a system of interlocking hexago-
nal-shaped trade areas. It should be remembered however that the size, shape and nesting of trade areas
will also depend upon spatial distribution and density,
wealth and purchasing power of the population served,
and the transportation. Several Nairobi examples
can be cited.

A comparison of group A centers comprising Westlands, Eastleigh and Dagoretti Corner West reveals
some interesting contrasts. Westlands serves a larger
area with a more dispersed, wealthier population, most
of whom travel in their own cars to centers. The shape
of its trade area approximates a hexagon. The area served by Eastleigh is much smaller, densely populated —
largely by poor people most of whom walk to the center
and buy their goods and services, and its trade area
is almost oval in shape. Characteristics similar to
those of Eastleigh also obtain for Dagoretti Corner
West, but the more elongated shape of its trade area
is influenced by the two major roads forking around it
from which some of the motoring customers originate.

Further examples could be cited, but it suffices
to state that in general, trade areas are more compact
and smaller in areas of high population density, and
larger in low density areas for any given level of

FIGURE 7.4

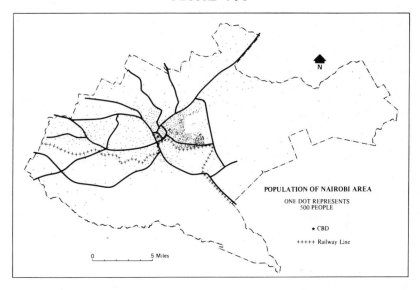

POPULATION OF NAIROBI AREA

ONE DOT REPRESENTS
500 PEOPLE

★ CBD

+++++ Railway Line

0   5 Miles

the hierarchy (compare those in the eastern and western parts of the city). They are more elongated for
centers whose patronage mostly originates from the
major roads (e.g., Hurlingham, Pangani Highway and
Broadway); and the centers themselves are far from
being centrally located: they are at the edge of their
respective trade areas. Those serving surrounding populations seem closer to the geometric centers of their
trade areas. Although they do not measure up to the
standard postulated in the central-place theory, there
is ample evidence of nesting and interlocking of market
areas, for various levels of centers.[30]

Conclusion

Several important points have emerged from this
investigation. First, although not all centers could
be analyzed, it has been shown that the distributive
retail trade in Nairobi is a rather complex one. Evidence shows that on the one hand Nairobi shares with
many Western cities the main features of urban retail
activities. On the other hand, the city has its own
idiosyncrasies, particularly at the lowest level of
retail outlets when compared with cities of the west,
and many of these "peculiarities", (for example the
existence of counters, home shops, etc.) can also be
found in other African cities.

Secondly, the functional structure and spatial arrangement of shopping centers and their trade areas were examined in the light of existing Western-based theories. Even though rigorous techniques were not employed in our analyses, it has been demonstrated that some theoretical notions can be usefully applied to empirical research in areas other than those for which they were devised.

Third, it has been shown that it is not uncommon to expect certain departures from well-known hypothesized relationships — departures which reflect local influences (as for example the apparently weak correlation between population served and establishments, functions,and functional units).

Finally, this study has provided a useful base for a dynamic approach to examination of changes that must be expected to take place in the near future.

Some Planning Implications

And now a word for the city planners, which perhaps renders testimony to the value of this study. The process of population redistribution within the city is taking place continuously and is rapidly calling forth a bold and imaginative policy of expansion and improvement of public services. In the matter of shopping center systems, policy should include two lines of action:

First, an improvement of existing services and the establishment of new services within the same centers. It was considered a useful exercise during this field survey to solicit information from adult customers about services and improvements they would like to see established. Responses in two categories are summarized in Table 7.2. We find services suggested by a majority of customers, and others mentioned by from twenty-five to fifty percent of those interviewed. Information in the Table is self-explanatory and will provide a useful guide in improvement efforts. It is interesting to note that telephone and postal services (especially at predominantly African-serving centers) were mentioned by an overwhelming majority, and the need to establish new service facilities long denied is quite apparent. Serious note should also be taken that information in Table 7.2 suggests a need to reserve some land adjacent to these centers to accommodate reasonable current and future expansion.

Second, the high rate of population growth in the city, coupled with property acquisition and development, would indicate a need to establish new shopping centers or at least designate and set aside land for

148

commercial purposes in various areas. From the viewpoint of existing locations and likely population redistribution, new sites have been proposed,and it is
also proposed that the policy of providing service
sites in any new development of residential estates
be encouraged — as is happening in many newer housing estates east and south of Nairobi.

TABLE 7.2   SERVICES NEEDED

Center	Suggested by Majority	Suggested by More Than Twenty-five Percent
Westlands	Traffic control	Recreation facility/tarmac/resurfacing/fish & chips
Eastleigh		Security/social hall
Dagoretti C.W.	Telephone	Post office/mailbox/tarmac/resurfacing
Pangari		Chemist/clothing/shoe shop
Uthiru	Telephone/tarmac Resurfacing	Clinic/dispensary/social hall/security
Adams Arcade		Bank/restaurant
Kabete NITD	Tarmac/resurfacing	
Kawangware		Variety shop
South B		Post office/mailbox
Hurlingham	Chemist	Post office/mailbox
Bahati		Post office/mailbox/telephone/restaurant
Nairobi West		Chemist
Shauri Moyo	Post office/Mailbox	Clinic/dispensary/chemist/clothing
Jericho	Post office/Mailbox/telephone	Restaurant
Kaloleni		Chemist/clothing/night club/shoe shop
Lumumba	Telephone	Post office/mailbox
Valley Arcade	Chemist	Post office/mailbox/dry cleaner/veg.-fruit shop
Makadana	Telephone	Post office/mailbox
Hamza	Post office/mailbox/telephone	Clothing/restaurant
Donholm		Telephone/clothing/nightclub
Parklands Sc.Rd.		Clothing/shoeshop/variety Shop
Waithaka	Telephone	Drycleaner
Maringo	Telephone	Social hall/chemist/cinema/restaurants
Karen		Butcher/variety shop
Lavington	Chemist	Clinic/dispensary
Bahati West	Telephone	Post office/mailbox/restaurant
Caledonian Market		Post office/mailbox/dry cleaner/variety shop
Kangemi	Telephone	Butcher/chemist/dry cleaner/restaurant
Uhuru Estate	Post office/mailbox	Dry cleaner/restaurant
Outer Ring	Clothing	Post office/mailbox/restaurant
Pangani FH Road		Chemist/clothing/shoeshop
Juja Road	Butcher	Post office/mailbox/clothing

Table 7.2 (cont'd.)

Dagoretti	Butcher	Post office/mailbox/bank/vegetable/fruit shop
South C		Post office/mailbox/petrol station/restaurant
Gatina		Tarmac/resurfacing/street lighting
Ziwani	Telephone	Post office/mailbox/security/shoeshop
Parklands Av. 5		Variety shop
Riruta		Variety shop
Kariobangi		Clinic/dispensary/clothing/petrol station
Kenya Breweries		Variety shop
Broadway		Variety shop
Kabete Prov.		Butcher/variety shop
ABC		Butcher/hardware/vegetable/fruit shop
NA Lab.		Variety shop
Mahisha	Restaurants	Telephone/drycleaner/night club/
Kanungaga		Tarmac/resurfacing/street lighting

NOTES

1. Colin Buchanan and Partners in association with East African Engineering Consultants, Programmes of Urban Studies (Nairobi: Final Draft Monograph 1970), pages 2, 18.

2. William Alonso, "The Form of Cities in Developing Countries", Papers and Proceedings of the Regional Science Association, XIII (1964), p.165, and for application of Western theories to urban and regional planning see El-Shakhs and Obudho, Urbanization, National Development and Regional Planning in Africa.

3. Since another task force was to study the Central Business District, the author undertook to examine the shopping centers outside the Central Business District.

4. Raymond Murphy, The American City: An Urban Geography (McGraw-Hill, New York 1966) p. 263.

5. M.J. Proudfoot, "City Retail Structure", Economic Geography, 13 (1937), pp. 425-428.

6. R.V. Ratcliff, "Internal Arrangement of Land Uses", Urban Land Economics (New York: 1949), pp.386-397; R.E. Murphy and J.E. Vance, "Delimiting the CBD", Economic Geography, 30 (1954), pp.189-222; E.J. Kelly, "Retail Structure of Urban Economy", Traffic Quarterly, 9 (1955) pp. 411-430; Homer Hoyt, "Classification and Significant Characteristics of Shopping Centres", Readings in Urban Geography, H.M. Mayer and C.F. Kohn (eds.) (Chicago: Chicago University Press 1959), pp.454-461.

7. Brian J.L. Berry, Commercial Structure and Commercial Blight (Chicago: University of Chicago Department of Geography Research Paper No.85, 1963), p.20.

8. D. Thorpe and G.A. Nader, "Customer Movement and Shopping Centre Study: A Study of a Central Place System in Northern Durham", Regional Studies, 1, (1967) pp. 173-191; W.I. Carruthers, "Service Centres in Greater London"; Town Planning Review (1962) pp. 5-31; and A. Logan, "The Pattern of Service Centres in Warringah Shire", Sydney University, Sydney Planning Research Centre (1968).

9. W.L. Garrison et al., Studies of Highway Development and Geographic Change (Washington: 1959) p.69.

10. Berry, Commercial Structure and Commercial Blight, p. 23.

11. Ibid.

12. International Labour Office (ILO), Employment, Incomes and Equality: A Strategy for Improving Productive Employment in Kenya (Geneva: ILO, 1972), pp.5-6.

13. Akin L. Mabogunje, "The Evolution and Analysis of the Retail Structure of Lagos, Nigeria," Economic Geography, 55 (1964), p. 321.

14. A. Vukovich, "Population and Employment", Unpublished draft paper Technical Appendix No. 1 (Nairobi: 1971), p. 2.

15. W. Christaller, Central Places in Southern Germany (Englewood Cliffs, N.J.: Prentice-Hall, 1966) (translated by C.W. Baskin).

16. Berry, Commercial Structure and Commercial Blight, pp.19-23.

17. cf. M.F. Dacey, "A Probability Model for Central Place Locations", Annals of the Association of American Geographers, 56, pp.550-568 .

18. Allan Pred, "Behaviour and Location: Foundations for a Geographic and Dynamic Location Theory", Land Studies in Geography (1967) Series B, No.27; L. Curry, "Central Places in the Random Spatial Economy", Journal of Regional Science (1967) 7, pp.217-238; F.E. Horton, "Location Factors as Determinants Consumer Attraction to Retail Firms", Annals of the Association of American Geographers (1968), 58, pp.787-801.

19. Peter Scott, Geography and Retailing (London: Hutchingson, 1970).

20. Scott, Geography and Retailing, pp.92-93.

21. Scott, Geography and Retailing, pp.95-97.

22. E.N. Thomas, "Some Comments on the Functional Bases of Small Iowa Towns", Iowa Business Digest (1960), p. 11.

23. R.L. Davies, "Effects of Consumer Income Differences on the Business Provisions of Small Shopping Centres," Urban Studies, 5, (1968), pp.144-164.

24.   Scott, Geography and Retailing, p. 106.

25.   B.J. Garner, "The Internal Structure of Retail Nucleations", Northwestern University Studies in
Geography (1966), No. 12.

26.   Logan, "The Patterns of Service Centers in
Warringah Shire".

27.   About 2,000 customers were interviewed and
the number at each center depended upon size of center
in terms of establishments.

28.   It is interesting to note that in some instances there were overlaps of the two types of lines on
the map.

29.   The 1969 Population Census provided figures
by enumeration areas, the boundaries of which did not
necessarily coincide with those of trade areas,espec-
ially at the edges of the latter. In such cases where
an enumeration area is shared by two or more trade
areas, the population in a segment falling in a given
trade area was interpolated using the average density
figure for the enumeration area as a whole. The
resulting figures were then raised by a compounded
seven percent (which is the city's average annual
growth rate) to reflect a population increase for
the years 1970/71 so as to bring the numbers closer
to 1972.

30.   It should be noted that no attempt was
made to assess the significance of the deviations
of centers and their trade areas from the expected
theoretical spatial arrangement.

8. An Analysis of the Variation in Modern Sector Earnings Among the Districts and Major Urban Centers in Kenya

William J. House and Henry Rempel

Introduction

Much discussion has been generated by the International Labor Organization report, Employment, Incomes and Equality, on the extent of income inequalities in Kenya.[1] The determinants of wages in the various industrial, occupational and regional labor markets will identify to a certain extent the major causes of earnings inequality. This paper analyzes these various labor markets using a large body of unpublished data centered mainly on 1968, the first year for which such data were generated in Kenya.

The extent of interoccupational wage differences in competitive markets will be a function of the relative supplies and demands for different skills of labor. In a developing economy we would expect to find large-scale premiums being paid to skilled labor and in the long run, as the output of qualified persons from the educational institutions increases, that these occupational wage differences would decline.[2] Interindustry earnings differences will be a function of the skill requirements of the various industries and the degree of interoccupational differences. The extent of regional income differentials will in turn be a function of the interregional distribution of occupations and industries as well as of the extent to which market forces fail to contract wage differences for similarly skilled workers in different industries.[3]

The significance of wage differentials (i.e. the relationship of wages in any particular structure) is derived from the role that wages play in the economy. A wage represents the price of a

---

An earlier version of this paper appeared as Working Paper No. 243, Institute for Development Studies, University of Nairobi.

153

specific kind of labour services and shares the function of other prices. Specifically, the wage structure influences the allocation of labour resources among the various kinds and places of employment. For example differences in earnings of engineers and school teachers may influence the career choice of students entering a university. Wage differences among regions of a country will influence the direction and magnitude of internal migration as well as the location of certain kinds of productive activity. Differences in wages paid among firms or industries will influence the ease of recruitment and the quality of the recruits. Differences in the relative prices of different classes of labor may influence the choice of production techniques of managements seeking to minimize costs of production.[4]

Factor mobility would tend to narrow interregional wage differentials if wages are responsive to the varying degree of unemployed labor. Indeed,

. . . competition and mobility in labour markets may be sufficient to ensure that earnings for the same work are the same throughout the country, so that all regional differences in earnings of otherwise similar workers are due to differences in their marginal value product arising from differences in skill.[5]

It may be argued that wages of similarly skilled workers in different industries or regions might reflect differences in industry or regional productivity because of variation in the utilization of nonhuman factors of production. Yet,

. . . theoretically there is no a priori reason to expect a flow of productivity gains to wages. They could equally well be passed on to consumers in the form of lower prices or to owners in the form of higher profits. One would expect higher wages to result from increased productivity if, at the same time, labour was in short supply relative to the demand at current wage levels.[6]

In Kenya the rate of growth of the labor force has exceeded the rate of growth of modern sector job creation, especially in recent years. The purpose of this paper is to analyze the various wage structures, both for districts and the larger towns, under conditions where supply of labor available exceeded the

154

observed growth in demand for labor. Specifically it
is our intent to sort out the relative contribution of
interdistrict and intertown differences in the occupational and industrial mixes of the employed labor force
and the pure area effect where different wages are paid
for the same type of labor.

Given a mobile labor force, and assuming competitive market conditions, we hypothesize that (1) variations in occupational and industrial mixes of employed
labor will be the dominant determinant of observed
differences in interregional wage levels; (2) area
effects that do exist will be declining over time because of growth in modern sector employment; and
(3) the reduction in interarea effects over time will
be greater than the reduction in interoccupational
wage differences because the lead time required to ac-
quire appropriate skills exceeds the time needed to
make an interdistrict move.

The Data

The data source is the unpublished results of the
Annual Enumeration of Employees of the Central Bureau
of Statistics which provides employment levels and average monthly earnings for June of each year. At the
district level it provides a breakdown of earnings and
employment for the private sector only, of thirteen occupational categories (excluding casual workers). Another set of data at the district level presents earnings and employment, combining both the private and
public sector, for forty-six two-digit (I.S.I.C.) industries including casual employees. A third set of data
commencing in 1972, presents information on occupational and industrial structures, public and private sectors combined for the largest towns of Kenya. (see
Table 8.1).

1968 was chosen for analysis at the district level
because it is the first year for which such detailed
information is available while the analysis of the urban centers concentrates on 1972, the initial year of
detailed town data. According to our data base the
modern sector is defined as: "the entire urban sector,
public sector activity outside the urban sector as
well as large scale enterprises such as large farms
and sawmills in the rural areas."[7]

At the district level the coverage of total employment is rather limited, although the large majority of
regular wage employees are covered by the modern sector.
Most economic activity in the towns is included except
for the "informal sector", consisting of small-scale
(less than five employees), labor-intensive industries
and services.

155

TABLE 8.1
The Two-Digit Industries Showing National Average
Earnings per Month in Shillings and Relatives for 1968

I.S.I.C.		Shillings	Relative
01	Agriculture	119	30
02	Forestry & logging	130	33
03	Hunting & trapping	138	35
04	Fishing	467	119
12	Metal mining	740	188
13	Crude petroleum	740	188
14	Stone quarrying	246	62
19	Nonmetallic mining	871	221
20	Food manufacturing	559	142
21	Beverage industries	1,021	259
22	Tobacco manufacture	852	216
23	Textiles	318	81
24	Footwear and clothing	450	114
25	Wood and cork	215	55
26	Furniture & fixtures	475	121
27	Paper and paper products	586	149
28	Printing & publishing	934	237
29	Leather & fur products	475	121
30	Rubber manufactures	699	177
31	Chemicals	806	205
32	Petroleum products	1,753	445
33	Non-metallic mineral products	669	170
34	Basic metal industries	557	141
35	Metal products	557	141
36	Non-electric machinery	637	162
37	Electrical machinery	889	226
38	Transport equipment	713	181
39	Miscellaneous manufacturing	647	184
40	Special trade contractors	721	183
41	General trade contractors	437	111
51	Electric light & power	820	208
52	Water supply	676	172
60	Joint wholesale & retail	1,010	256
61	Wholesale trade	973	247
62	Banks & financial institutions	1,237	314
63	Insurance	1,263	321
64	Real estate	704	179
66	Retail trade	496	126
71	Transport	704	179
72	Storage & warehousing	826	210

(Continued on next page)

TABLE 8.1, continued

73	Communication	826	210
81	Government services	519	132
82	Education & welfare services		
		444	113
83	Other social & related services	1,106	281
84	Recreational services	471	120
85	Personal services	218	55
	Kenya Average	394	100

Source: Unpublished data from Kenya, Statistics Division, Ministry of Finance and Planning, Annual Enumeration of Employees.

Occupational and Industrial Wage Structures

At the national level both occupational and industrial wage structures exhibit a high degree of earnings inequality. Elsewhere a large part of inter-industry average earnings differences is explained by the occupational makeup of the industries.[8] The national occupation wage structure is presented in Table 8.2 while the industrial wage structure is included in Table 8.1.

In general relative differences amongst occupational wages in the public sector are smaller than those in the private sector. For the category "unskilled laborers", where the majority of workers is found, the public sector pays much more than the private sector.

As can be seen in Table 8.1, interindustry differences in average earnings are very large. The greatest differences occur between industries in the agricultural sector and those in manufacuring and commerce.

The Variation in Interdistrict Wage Levels

Table 8.3 presents the level of monthly wages relative to the Kenya average for 1968. One set of data refers to private sector activities only and is taken from the occupational breakdown of activities. The second combines public and private activities, includes casual workers, and is taken from the industrial breakdown of activities.[9]

The table demonstrates the wide variation in

TABLE 8.2
Average Monthly Income by Occupations for Private and
Public Sectors, 1968   (Shillings)

Occupation	Private Sector		Public Sector	
	Absolute	Relative	Absolute	Relative
Directors and top administrators	2,040	560	3,020	620
Professional	1,900	522	2,109	433
Executive and managerial	2,462	676	2,167	445
Technicians & works managers	1,306	359	1,204	247
Teachers	337	93	558	115
Secretaries & typists	1,074	295	977	201
Clerks	705	194	512	105
Bookkeepers & cashiers	934	257	1,145	235
Office machine operators	786	216	560	115
Technical sales representatives	1,240	341	813	167
Shop assistants	381	105	406	83
Other skilled and semiskilled	369	101	288	59
Unskilled laborers	142	39	253	52
TOTAL	364	100	487	100

Source: Unpublished data from Kenya, Statistics Division, Ministry of Finance and Planning, Annual Enumeration of Employees.

earnings amongst the districts of Kenya. Nairobi and Mombasa are the dominant industrial centers in the country and are leaders in both level of earnings and size of modern sector employment. Districts of little consequence in terms of numbers employed in modern sector economic activity — such as Tana River, Siaya, Baringo and Elgeyo Marakwet — have very low average earnings. The coefficients of variation are very high and are indicative of the high degree of regional inequality in Kenya.[10]
The greatest inequalities in relative earnings are found in private-sector employment. When the public sector is included together with casual workers, there

158

TABLE 8.3
Relative Monthly Earnings per Worker and Percent of
Kenya Modern Sector Employment in Each District, 1968

District	Private Sector Based on Occupations**		Public and Private Sectors Based on Industries***	
	Relative Wage	Percent of Total Employment	Relative Wage	Percent of Total Employment
Nairobi	177	31	178	31
Kiambu	64	9	66	8
Kirinyaga	64	*	88	1
Muranga	44	2	72	2
Nyandarua	40	1	58	1
Nyeri	68	2	90	3
Kilifi	53	1	70	1
Kwale	40	2	69	1
Lamu	56	*	99	*
Mombasa	163	8	158	9
Taita	36	1	57	2
Tana River	23	*	90	*
Embu	74	*	102	1
Kitui	64	*	84	1
Machakos	54	2	74	2
Meru	46	1	69	2
Kisii	65	1	78	1
Kisumu	89	3	96	4
Siaya	22	*	104	*
S. Nyanza	77	1	82	1
Kajiado	159	*	105	*
Kericho	42	10	51	6
Laikipia	51	2	52	2
Nakuru	58	10	75	9
Narok	45	*	84	*
T. Nzoia	40	4	49	3
U. Gishu	54	5	67	4
Baringo	31	*	68	*
E. Marakwet	28	*	71	*
Nandi	37	3	43	2
W. Pokot	12	*	50	*
Bungoma	50	*	79	1
Busia	55	*	95	*
Kakamega	49	1	95	2
Kenya Total	100	100	100	100

Coefficient of Variation:6
- Weighted   59.8%   53.4%
- Unweighted   55.5%   33.6%

* District employment is less than 0.5% of total
** Casual workers excluded
*** Casual workers included
Source: (Same as Table 8.2)

is a dramatic rise in relative earnings in low-wage districts and a sharp fall in the unweighted coefficient of variation. However, the overall degree of regional inequality in average earnings remains very large.

The Determinants of the Variation in Interdistrict Wage Levels

The next step was to establish the extent to which district average earnings reflect differences in earnings of persons of a given age, sex, skill and education level working in a stated occupation and in a particular industry, and the extent to which district earnings reflect differences in the population mix with respect to characteristics specified. But as stated by Denison, if nearly all the interdistrict differences in average earnings can be explained in terms of differences in the composition of the labor force, the reason for the small remaining differences would not be crucial.[11]

However, the only readily accessible information on the composition of employees in Kenya's various districts was the breakdown by occupational categories, and a separate breakdown by industries. An attempt was made to attribute the difference between average earnings for each district and the national average earnings per worker to the occupational and industrial makeup of the district, and the extent to which similarly classified occupations and industries receive varying amounts of remuneration in different districts.[13]

Economic theory suggests that in static equilibrium, if workers within each occupational classification in industry were truly similar, with perfect competition in the various labor markets, the "area effects" should be negligible. Therefore the extent to which competitive forces are working in labor markets in Kenya can be gauged tentatively, assuming a reasonable degree of homogeneity within occupational and industrial classifications, by the relative importance of the "area effect".[14]

In attempting to establish the relative importance of the "mix effect" and the "area effect" for the thirty-four Kenya districts, the standardization technique was used.[15] The amount by which each district's average earnings would differ from the national average, can be calculated as the difference between D, actual district earnings per worker, and O, the occupation-constant district earnings per worker — or as the difference between D and I, the industry constant district earnings per worker.

If national occupational or industrial employment weights are used the calculation becomes the difference between R, the rate-constant district earnings per worker, and K, the actual Kenya average earnings per worker.

Following Denison, however, there is no reason to prefer one set of weights over the other, so an average of the two differences was used. The result provides the amount by which a district's earnings per worker would differ from Kenya averages if only their occupational or industrial composition varied: that is, the "mix effect".

Similarly the "area effect" can be measured in two ways: If each district has the same occupational or industrial composition so that the geographic variation is limited to differences in earnings per worker within an occupation or industry, the measure would be D - R, if district weights are used, or O - K or I - K if Kenya weights are used. Again an average of the two approximates the amount by which each district's average earnings would differ from the Kenyan average if their occupational or industrial compositions were the same: that is, the "area effect".[16]

A. Analysis of the Information on Occupations

Results of the standardization exercises for 1968 were as reported in Table 8.4. Of the shs.6,438 total difference between the average for each district and the Kenyan average earnings, it was estimated that thirty-one percent was attributable to the "mix effect" and sixty-nine percent to the "area effect". Almost identical allocations were made to these separate effects using the 1971 data. In most cases the two separate effects reinforce each other and work in the same direction.

When account is taken of the wide variation in number of employees in each district by weighting the difference between district's average earnings and the Kenyan average by the number employed in each district, then the average difference between the "representative" employee and national average earnings would be shs.209. Of this amount, fifty-three percent was attributable to the "mix effect" and forty-seven to the "area effect". For 1971 each factor's contribution was approximately equal.[17]

In addition, in 1968 the difference in earnings between the district average and the Kenyan average attributable to the "area effect" exceeds that which can be attributed to the "mix effect" in sixteen of the thirty-four districts. In the seven districts

161

TABLE 8.4

Analysis of Sources of Variation in Average Monthly
Earnings by District in 1968 (in shillings) from Information on Occupations for Private Sector Only

District	Average Earnings				Measures of Determinants of Variation in Earnings		
	K	D	R	O	Total	"Mix Effect"	"Area Effect"
Nairobi	364	644	523	480	+281	+162	+119
Kiambu	364	233	286	295	-131	-70	-61
Kirinyaga	364	324	285	312	-130	-79	-51
Muranga	364	161	238	239	-230	-102	-101
Nyandarua	364	147	227	217	-217	-104	-113
Nyeri	364	247	328	268	-117	-29	-88
Kilifi	364	194	279	271	-170	-81	-89
Kwale	364	145	208	239	-219	-125	-94
Lamu	364	204	379	670	-160	-226	+66
Mombasa	364	593	508	480	+229	+129	+100
Taita	364	131	406	155	-233	+9	-242
Tana River	364	83	337	83	-281	-14	-267
Embu	364	268	472	259	-96	+68	-164
Kitui	364	234	317	273	-130	-43	-87
Machakos	364	198	243	317	-166	-120	-46
Meru	364	166	348	191	-198	-20	-178
Kisii	364	235	406	229	-129	+24	-153
Kisumu	364	323	389	309	-41	+19	-60
Siaya	364	80	396	168	-284	-28	-256
S. Nyanza	364	279	392	277	-85	+15	-100
Kajiado	364	580	288	1,031	+216	-263	+479
Kericho	364	153	209	291	-211	-147	-64
Laikipia	364	186	237	291	-178	-116	-62
Nakuru	364	212	282	283	-152	-77	-75
Narok	364	164	269	202	-200	-67	-133
T. Nzoia	364	146	241	227	-218	-102	-116
U. Gishu	364	198	273	264	-166	-79	-87
Baringo	364	114	236	162	-250	-88	-162
E.Marakwet	364	102	224	95	-262	-67	-195
Nandi	364	134	206	228	-230	-126	-104
W. Pokot	364	43	169	66	-321	-109	-212
Bungoma	364	181	349	204	-183	-19	-164
Busia	364	200	325	236	-164	-38	-126
Kakamega	364	177	284	224	-187	-64	-123
Total Deviations					6.438	2,033	4,405

Source: Unpublished data from Republic of Kenya,
Statistics Division, Ministry of Finance and Planning,
Annual Enumeration of Employees.

162

where the two factors work in opposite directions, for six of them the actual deviation from the national average is in the direction indicated by the "area effect".

Given the thirteen occupational classifications used by the Central Bureau of Statistics and comparing average earnings for each district with the national average, the "area effect" is clearly the major factor in the variation in earnings among districts. Even when account is taken of the relative importance of Nairobi and Mombasa and the significance of the "mix effect" in these districts, the contribution of the "area effect" to earnings differentials is still fifty percent.

Assuming a reasonable degree of similarity in skills between persons classified in an occupational category in the various districts, clearly these occupational labor markets are far from perfect, given the relative importance of the "area effect". More appropriate data to analyze the functioning of labor markets would involve knowing the distribution of earnings for each occupational description for each district. Lack of such information has necessitated the implicit assumption that all workers in a district similarly classified receive average wages for that job description.

The next exercise involved a search for the occupational categories which contribute most to the "area effect". Table 8.5 reports both the unweighted and the weighted coefficients of variation for the thirteen occupational categories for 1968. The weight used for each district was the proportion of an occupation's total employment attributable to the district.

The unweighted coefficients of variation demonstrate clearly that interdistrict variations in earnings for each occupational category are significant, ranging from fifty-seven percent for directors to thirty-three percent for bookkeepers.One suspects that with a much finer classification of occupations a large part of the interdistrict variation in earnings attributed to the "area effect" could be attributed to differences in the occupational mix.

However, as reported in Table 8.5, these occupations contribute only ten percent of Kenya's total modern, private-sector employment. Therefore their contribution to the weighted coefficients of variation for district average earnings reported in Table 8.2 would be negligible.

The weighted coefficients of variation for occupational earnings show a marked reduction from the unweighted coefficients for all categories except that of unskilled laborers. This is caused partly by the dominance of Nairobi and Mombasa which claim over

163

TABLE 8.5
Coefficients of Variation of Average Earnings Across
Districts for Thirteen Occupational Categories, 1968

| Occupation | Coefficients of Variation | | Percent of Total National Employment in Each Occupation |
	Unweighted (percent)	Weighted (percent)	
1. Directors and top level administrators	56.9	26.7	2.0
2. Professionals	56.5	37.0	0.9
3. Executives & Managers	34.7	20.6	1.8
4. Technicians, Foremen and Supervisors	42.3	33.3	2.7
5. Teachers	54.2	44.4	2.5
6. Secretaries, Stenographers & Typists	45.1	11.9	1.1
7. Clerks	38.1	21.5	3.5
8. Bookkeepers & Cashiers	33.2	16.0	1.0
9. Office Machine Operators	37.2	22.2	0.3
10. Technical Sales Representatives & Brokers	46.9	23.5	0.6
11. Shop Assistants	40.7	16.3	0.8
12. Miscellaneous Skilled & Semi-skilled	39.6	29.1	17.7
13. Unskilled Laborers	35.1	41.1	65.0
Total	55.5	59.8	100.0

Source: Unpublished data from Republic of Kenya,
Statistics Division, Ministry of Finance and Planning,
Annual Enumeration of Employees.

sixty percent of employment in all occupations except
teaching, miscellaneous skilled and semiskilled and
unskilled laborers.

Occupations classified as miscellaneous skilled
and semiskilled, and unskilled laborers are responsible for the largest representation in total employment, eighteen and sixty-five percent of total

employment respectively. The unskilled group, given
its relative size, is likely responsible for much of
the "area effect" we have reported in Table 8.4.

Yet it is to be expected that persons classified
as "unskilled laborers" would form a far more homogeneous group than any other occupational category.
If competitive forces are working and if the whole
of Kenya is viewed as one market for unskilled labor,
then small earnings differentials amongst persons in
this classification could be expected. Also, unskilled
labor has the widest representation of all occupations,
with only twenty-seven percent of the total located in
Nairobi and Mombasa. However, the relatively high
weighted coefficient of variation of average earnings
is a function of the very large average earnings of
unskilled employees in Nairobi (160) and Mombasa (192)
compared with the national average (100).

We are left then to speculate why, in an economy
where rate of growth of the labor force exceeds rate
of growth of modern-sector employment, and where the
large proportion of migrants and the overwhelming
majority of the unemployed and underemployed are
unskilled, there is such a wide variation in the
earnings of unskilled employees. In an earlier paper
the authors found in attempting to explain interindustry wage differences, a large variation for unskilled
earnings,[18] caused by variations in industry concentration, average industrial productivity, and the
amount of total industrial employment in Nairobi. The
first two variables attempt to measure industry's
"ability-to-pay", while the third can be explained
by the high cost of living in Nairobi.[19] Although
it was not possible to measure their influence, it is
conceivable that trade union pressure on private employ-
ers would make a greater impact in Nairobi and Mombasa
where such organizations are strongest. However, all
these forces remain inconsistent with the free workings
of a competitive labor market.

In a number of districts many of the forty-six industries were not represented so that any attempt to
calculate the industry-constant average district wage
would have given misleading results. Therefore the
"mix effect" was calculated as simply the rate constant
minus Kenyan average earnings (R - K) while the "area
effect" was calculated as the district actual minus
district rate-constant average earnings (D - R).

Earnings differences between the district and the
Kenya national average are much smaller here compared
with those derived from the private sector only. The
public sector's nationally determined pay scales appear
to act as a force for greater equality amongst

average district wages. In addition, average earnings
are much larger when the public sector is included,
since in many districts public servants and administrators are the only representatives of high-level
manpower.

Of the shs. 3,652 total difference between the
average for each district and Kenya average earnings,
with signs disregarded, thirty-nine percent was attributed to the "mix effect" and sixty-one percent to
the "area effect". In six of eighteen districts
where the two effects operate in the same direction
the "area effect" dominates, while in the remaining
sixteen districts where the two factors work in opposite directions, in thirteen the "area effect" dominates. (See Table 8.6).

How comparable the two-digit industries are across
districts remains open to question. Even with a finer
disaggregation of industrial activities it is likely
that many of the products from industries in Nairobi
and Mombasa are very different from similarly classified activities in other areas of Kenya. Nonetheless
we assert once again that a major contribution to interdistrict average earnings differentials is made by similarly classified industries paying different wages
in different districts of Kenya.[20]

The Determinants of Variation in Wage Levels Amongst Major Urban Centers

Given that most modern-sector activities are likely to be concentrated in urban areas, one factor which
would partly explain interdistrict average earning
differences would be the interdistrict distribution of
urban centers. Other factors would be the extent of
the differences in industrial and occupational composition of the towns as expressed by the "mix effect",
and the extent to which labor markets are segregated
from one another, as measured by the relative size of
the "area effect".

Following the example of Bell,

. . . wage data from the metropolitan area will be
employed since the area represents a classic labor
market in which spatial mobility of labor is high.
In addition, the spatial immobility of labor among
the markets creates a distinct regional dimension.[21]

Perhaps only Nairobi and Mombasa could be called metropolitan areas but the spatial separation of the other
towns would justify their being classed as distinct
labor markets. The degree of segregation of the eleven
labor markets can be determined by evidence of

166

TABLE 8.6
Analysis of Sources of Variation in Average Monthly
Earnings by District, in Shillings, in 1968. From
Information on Two-Digit Industries for Private
and Public Sector Activities

District	Average Earnings			Measures of Determinants of Variation in Earnings		
	K	D	R	Total	"Mix Effect"	"Area Effect"
Nairobi	394	702	562	+308	+168	+140
Kiambu	394	262	295	-132	-99	-33
Kirinyaga	394	348	416	-46	+22	-68
Murang'a	394	282	338	-112	-56	-56
Nyandarua	394	227	262	-167	-132	-35
Nyeri	394	355	409	-39	+15	-54
Kilifi	394	275	337	-119	-57	-62
Kwale	394	270	270	-124	-124	0
Lamu	394	390	483	-4	+89	-93
Mombasa	394	621	619	+227	+225	+2
Taita	394	224	329	-170	-65	-105
Tana River	394	354	477	-40	+83	-123
Embu	394	401	475	+7	+81	-74
Kitui	394	330	467	-64	+73	-137
Machakos	394	293	362	-101	-32	-69
Meru	394	271	378	-123	-16	-107
Kisii	394	309	442	-85	+48	-133
Kisumu	394	378	501	-16	+107	-123
Siaya	394	408	499	+14	+105	-91
S. Nyanza	394	323	485	-71	+91	-162
Kajiado	394	414	532	+20	+138	-118
Kericho	394	202	204	-192	-190	-2
Laikipia	394	204	271	-190	-123	-67
Nakuru	394	296	320	-98	-74	-24
Narok	394	329	468	-65	+74	-139
T. Nzoia	394	193	237	-201	-157	-44
U. Gishu	394	265	320	-129	-74	-55
Baringo	394	266	378	-128	-16	-112
E. Marakwet	394	278	414	-116	+20	-136
Nandi	394	170	184	-224	-210	-14
W. Pokot	394	196	326	-198	-68	-130
Bungoma	394	312	466	-82	+72	-154
Busia	394	373	465	-21	+71	-92
Kakamega	394	375	428	-19	+34	-53
Total Deviations				3,652	1,411	2,241

Source: Unpublished data from Republic of Kenya,
Statistics Division, Ministry of Finance and Planning,
Annual Enumeration of Employees.

different wages being paid within an occupational category, by a particular industry, among the various urban centers.

Table 8.7 presents the average earnings per worker relative to Nairobi, for the ten next-ranking urban centers. Nairobi is used as the reference standard because it is the capital city and exceeds by far the size of the other ten. Earnings relatives are based on total three-digit I.S.I.C. industry earnings which include earnings of casual workers. The one exception is 1972 which includes as well, a column of earnings relatives based on twelve occupational classifications. The final column excludes casual workers, so actual average town earnings exceed those of the other columns where casual employees are included.

TABLE 8.7
Average Earnings per Urban Worker Compared to Nairobi
1964 - 1972

Urban center	1964	1966	1968	1970	1972	1972*
Kisumu	65	61	60	60	73	69
Nakuru	70	69	65	64	77	81
Kericho	50	50	48	48	62	57
Eldoret	49	48	51	52	65	66
Kitale	50	50	47	46	61	60
Nanyuki	47	46	43	40	44	45
Nyeri	55	54	53	52	64	65
Thika	53	52	48	48	51	57
Mombasa	76	75	72	72	75	84
Malindi	49	49	53	51	56	54
Nairobi	100	100	100	100	100	100
Coefficient of Variation (%)	44.7	45.6	46.8	47.6	38.5	38.0

Source: Kenya, Statistics Division, Ministry of Finance and Planning, Employment and Earnings in the Modern Sector, Reports for 1964 - 1971. The 1972 data were in unpublished form from the same source.

*These average earnings relatives are based on the occupational classifications listed previously.

The detailed information for towns beginning in 1972 uses twelve occupational classifications, which are slightly different from those for earlier years, and also gives a three-digit industrial breakdown of

168

economic activities.

The average wage level in each town (T) is below that of Nairobi (N) throughout the nine-year period. In general, the extent of interurban wage disparity is less than that for the districts, and this has been declining over time, generally speaking. After 1970 there was a substantial fall in the coefficient of variation as all ten towns increased their earnings position relative to Nairobi.

The next step was to analyze the occupational and industrial wage structures for the towns for 1972.[22] Tables 8.8 and 8.9 present the results.

TABLE 8.8
Analysis of Sources of Variation in Average Monthly Earnings by Urban Centers in 1972 (in Shillings) from Information on Occupations for Public and Private Sector Activities

Urban Center	Average Earnings				Measures of Determinants of Variation in Earnings		
	N	T	R	O	Total	"Mix Effect"	"Area Effect"
Kisumu	784	541	678	604	-243	-85	-158
Nakuru	784	635	695	706	-149	-80	-69
Kericho	784	444	518	637	-340	-229	-111
Eldoret	784	515	621	636	-269	-142	-127
Kitale	784	470	606	626	-314	-167	-147
Nanyuki	784	355	527	588	-429	-245	-184
Nyeri	784	507	655	618	-277	-120	-157
Thika	784	448	557	637	-336	-208	-128
Mombasa	784	658	615	806	-126	-158	+32
Malindi	784	424	551	636	-360	-222	-138
Total Deviations					2,843	1,656	1,187

Source: Unpublished data from Kenya, Statistics Division, Ministry of Finance and Planning, Annual Enumeration of Employees.

Table 8.8 shows the occupation "mix effect" to be relatively more important than the "area effect" in all cases except Kisumu and Nyeri. Of the total deviations between the towns and Nairobi, fifty-eight percent is attributable to "mix effect" and forty-two percent to "area effect".

Table 8.9 shows the "area effect" to be relatively more important than the industry "mix effect" in all cases except Kitale and Malindi. Sixty percent of

169

TABLE 8.9

Analysis of Sources of Variation in Average Monthly
Earnings by Urban Centers in 1972 (in shillings) from
Information on Industries for Public and Private
Sector Activities

Urban Center	Average Earnings				Measures of Determinants of Variation in Earnings	
	N	T	R	Total	"Mix Effect"	"Area Effect"
Kisumu	825	602	748	-223	-77	-146
Nakuru	825	635	852	-190	+27	-217
Kericho	825	512	717	-313	-108	-205
Eldoret	825	537	708	-288	-117	-171
Kitale	825	503	582	-322	-243	-79
Nanyuki	825	363	595	-462	-230	-232
Nyeri	825	532	728	-293	-97	-196
Thika	825	420	708	-405	-117	-288
Mombasa	825	620	732	-205	-93	-112
Malindi	825	463	643	-362	-182	-180
Total Deviations				3,063	1,237	1,826

Source: Unpublished Data from Kenya, Statistics Division, Ministry of Finance and Planning, Annual Enumeration of Employees.

total deviations is attributable to the former and
forty percent to the latter.

The exercises reported in Table 8.8 and 8.9
suggest that Nairobi's relatively higher earnings per
worker are explained by a favorable occupational mix
and by similarly classified industries which pay more
in Nairobi than elsewhere. However a three-digit classification of an "industry" can encompass a wide spectrum of industrial activities. Possibly the more capital-intensive are located in Nairobi, requiring a higher
level of skilled labor. If so, the products and techniques of production are quite likely to be different
in Nairobi from other urban centers. This would explain the results obtained from occupational data showing higher skills in the Nairobi labor force, and might
account for its high average earnings because Nairobi
has a more advanced industrial structure.

Here, the "mix effect" was calculated as R - N
and the "area effect" as T - R since the data again did
not allow the calculation of an "industry-composition-
constant" average town wage.

As we might have predicted, the degree of labor market segmentation is much less between urban centers than between districts. For the unskilled, a reasonably homogeneous group, the degree of interurban income inequality is well below that for all workers across towns and for the unskilled across districts. The largest variation is in Malindi, where unskilled wages were sixty-nine percent of the Nairobi level in 1972. Two urban centers, Mombasa and Nakuru, reported average wage levels for the unskilled above the Nairobi level (116 and 106 percent respectively). The unweighted coefficient of variation for the ten towns, relative to Nairobi, was seventeen percent in 1968 and twenty-one percent in 1972. This indicates the interurban earnings differences are lowest in those parts of the labor market where the excess labor supply seeking employment is likely most pronounced and where the laborers involved are relatively more homogeneous.

Conclusions

This chapter has attempted to explain differences in earnings per worker among the districts and towns of Kenya and to bring some evidence to bear on the competitive functioning of labor markets in Kenya.

It was found that a major contributor to the interdistrict earnings differentials is the fact that similarly classified occupations and industries receive different remuneration in various districts. This is especially crucial for unskilled workers. Given a reasonable degree of homogeneity within each occupational classification, especially in the unskilled group, and the competitive forces working in an economy within a growing surplus of visibly unemployed, one might expect the intraoccupational, interdistrict earnings differentials to be relatively small, but this did not prove to be so.[23]

However analysis of interurban earnings differences showed that the occupational "mix effect" was more important, mainly because of the smaller variation in unskilled workers' wages between towns.

It is apparent that occupational and industrial structures are interdependent. We suspect that industry structure differences are much greater than our three-digit classification can discern, and that the large industrial base of Nairobi has attracted industries, some largely dominated by multinational corporations, which are capital-intensive in nature — requiring a labor force with a larger proportion of highly skilled workers — which was indeed our finding.

There is more interaction between towns in determination of wages, especially for unskilled workers,

171

than between districts. Given the requirements of
urban living perhaps these workers are more truly
homogeneous between towns than between districts,
which would help explain our results.

Because of lack of adequate time-series data it
proved impossible to examine our hypothesis regarding
the expected relative decline in the "area effects"
over time.

One writer has suggested that:

> The importance of mobility barriers is reflected
> in the magnitude of the interregional difference
> in wages for the same type of labour, after
> correcting for other sources of wage differences[24]

Certainly the Kenya population has been highly responsive to changing earnings and employment opportunities,
yet the "area effect" has remained very significant
especially at the district level. This suggests that
the simple competitive model of wage determination
needs to be amended to take account of other factors,
both economic and institutional. However, the Kenyan
experience is not unique, as borne out by the evidence
from Latin America where:

> . . . in spite of high rates of labour mobility
> (especially rural - urban) among regions and
> sectors in many countries, there is only scattered
> information to suggest that some differentials
> are narrowing.[25]

NOTES

1. International Labour Office, Employment, Incomes and Equality: A Strategy for Increasing Productive Employment in Kenya, (Geneva: ILO,1972).

2. At the turn of the century skilled workers
in U.S. manufacturing and construction earned twice
as much as the unskilled but, at the present time,
the differential has narrowed to less than 40 percent.
In European countries the differentials seem to be even
narrower. See Peter Gregory, "Wage Structures in Latin
America", Journal of Developing Areas 8 (June 1974),p.566.

3. After large regional inequalities open up in
the earlier stages of development, "convergence becomes
the rule, with the backward regions closing the development gap between themselves and the already industrialized areas. The expected result is that a stati-
stic describing regional inequality will trace out an
inverted "U" over the national growth path. See Jeffrey
G. Williamson, "Regional Inequality and the Process of
National Development", Economic Development and Cultural
Change 13(1965), p.9.

4. Gregory, op.cit., p. 557.

5. Edward F. Denison, "Comment", in *Regional Income: Studies in Income and Wealth*, Frank A. Hanna (ed.) (Princeton: National Bureau of Economic Research 1957), p. 163.

6. Gregory,.op.cit., p. 573.

7. Republic of Kenya, Statistics Division, Ministry of Finance and Planning, *Employment and Earnings, 1963-1967* (Nairobi: Government Printer, 1971), p.i.

8. William J. House and Henry Rempel, "The Determinants of and Changes in the Structure of Wages and Employment in the Manufacturing Sector of the Kenya Economy", *Journal of Development Economics* 3 (March 1976), pp. 83-98.

9. The seven northern districts: Garissa, Wajir, Mandera, Isiolo, Marsabit, Samburu and Turkana have been excluded because there is virtually no modern sector activity in this area other than government services.

10. Comparison of these results with the regional income differentials in twenty-four countries in various stages of development as reported by Williamson, op.cit., indicates that only Brazil had a coefficient of variation comparable in size to that of Kenya.

11. Denison, op.cit., p. 164.

12. The unweighted coefficient of variation is calculated as

$$\frac{\sqrt{\dfrac{1}{n-1} \sum_i (Y_i - \bar{Y})^2}}{\bar{Y}}$$ where Y_i is the average earnings

in the district i, $\bar{Y}$ is the Kenya average earnings and n is the number of districts. Each district carries equal weight so that the index measures the degree of inequality in earnings between the average man in each district, assuming he receives his district's average earnings, and the Kenya average. The weighted coefficient of variation is calculated as:

$$\frac{\sqrt{\sum_i (Y_i - \bar{Y})^2 \cdot \dfrac{e_i}{e}}}{\bar{Y}}$$ where e_i is total modern sector

employment in district i and e is total modern sector employment in Kenya. Here the index measures the degree of inequality amongst individuals' earnings and the national average, again assuming all persons in a particular district receive its average earnings.

173

13. These separate effects have been labelled the "mix effect" and the "area effect" respectively by Frederick W. Bell, "Relation of the Region, Industrial Mix and the Production Function to Metropolitan Wage Levels", Review of Economics and Statistics, 49 (August 1967), pp. 368-374.

14. Clearly, given this assumption, differences among occupational classifications are meant to describe differences in skills of workers which would be a function of age, education and other personal attributes of employees. We do not have any alternative means of measuring such differences in skills among employees.

15. This technique was used originally by Denison, op.cit. Subsequently it was adopted by House in analyzing earnings differences among the eight provinces of Kenya; William J. House, "Earnings per Worker Differentials in the Provinces of Kenya, 1967-1970", Journal of Developing Areas, 9 (July 1975), pp.359-376. For a list of the many shortcomings of the standardization technique see Richard Perlman, Labor Theory (New York: Wiley and Sons,1969), p.128.

16. The Rate Constant average district wage (Rd) is calculated as:

$$Rd = \frac{\sum_i eiwik}{\sum_i ei}$$

where ei = district employment in occupation or industry i,
and wik = average wage in occupation or industry i for Kenya.

The Occupation or Industry Constant average district wage (Od or Id) is calculated as:

$$Od \text{ or } Id = \frac{\sum_i eik\ wi}{\sum_i eik}$$

where eik = employment in industry i in Kenya; wi = average district wage in industry i.

17. The major contribution of the "mix effect" to the earnings differences comes from Nairobi and Mombasa where the majority of the professionals and executives are located.

18. House and Rempel, op.cit.

174

19. The cost-of-living difference is reflected partly in higher legal minimum wages for Nairobi and Mombasa. At the present time they are approximately sixteen percent higher than for the remainder of the country.

20. The occupational makeup of a particular industry's labor force will vary across districts which might partly explain this fact. With the available data it proved impossible to standardize for the occupational composition of industries across districts.

21. Bell, op.cit., p. 368.

22. Again this unpublished information gave a detailed breakdown of the industrial composition of each town and its occupational composition, but not of the occupational makeup of each industry in each town, so the two series were used as separate entities.

23. Considering human capital is created through on-the-job training which may result in varying levels of skill among those employees classified as unskilled. Again, this raises the issue of how reasonable it is to assume that the occupational categories, unskilled laborers in particular, are relatively homogeneous in their makeup.

24. Perlman, op.cit., p. 124.

25. Gregory, op.cit., p. 578.

9. Patterns of Spatial Interaction in Kenya

Wayne McKim

Introduction

An analysis of spatial interaction patterns can reveal the dynamic structure of the spatial organization of an area. Spatial interaction refers to the movement (or flow) of people, goods, and information between places. The existence and strength of linkages between places, the hierarchy of central places, and the extent of the hinterlands for various functions emerge most clearly from a comprehensive analysis and synthesis of information on the distribution of locational attributes, central place functions, and spatial interactions. Without spatial interaction data, the picture is incomplete. Surrogate measures for interaction such as the existence of lines of possible movement (roads, rail lines, telephone lines) are often used, in part because of the difficulty in obtaining flow data. A misleading picture may emerge when, for instance, two routes of similar capacity may actually carry vastly different volumes of traffic. This chapter will focus on the analysis of spatial interaction patterns, as one very important aspect of the spatial economy which frequently receives too little attention.

The purpose of this chapter is to present and analyze information on interaction flows in Kenya. Flow data are felt to be useful in identifying gaps in the urban hierarchy, locating underserved areas and delineating hinterlands at various levels of the hierarchy. Interaction patterns are an essential part of the broad picture of understanding the spatial organization of Kenya's economy.

The interaction data discussed in this chapter are bus/rail passenger movements, mail flows, and telephone calls collected in Kenya on a country-wide basis for 1969-70. Some major conclusions which can be drawn from the analysis of this flow data include:

1. Nairobi is more dominant in the communications network of Kenya than would be expected based on population figures, and is becoming more dominant over time.

2. Certain "underserved" areas of Kenya have such low levels of transportation and communication flows that they do not appear to participate in the spatial economy of the core of Kenya.

3. Relative position in the interaction hierarchy of the major and secondary central places of Kenya and their hinterlands indicate functional regions and may be useful for planning purposes.

The above are among the most important aspects of the spatial organization of Kenya which become apparent through the analysis of spatial interaction data.

Although relatively few studies have utilized more than one form of interaction data as part of a comprehensive approach to the understanding of the spatial organization of an area, several studies have examined patterns of one form of interaction. A few of these studies give an indication of the variety of interaction studies and the way in which interaction data has been used. Intercity telephone call patterns have been analyzed to determine urban hierarchies (Nystuen and Dacey[1] and Clayton[2]), to measure the effect of a political boundary (MacKay[3]), and to assess degrees of political integration (Soja[4,5]). Bus service routes were used by Green[6,7] to delineate central place hinterlands, and shopping trips are frequently used for the same purpose (see Berry[8] for several examples). Flows of goods within India were analyzed by Berry[9] and world trade movements were studies by Russett[10] and McConnell[11] to delineate major national and international trade regions. The studies of interaction in the above examples have yielded important information about the organization of space.

There have been fewer studies which combine more than one form of interaction or have tried to link the interactions with central place functions to gain a more comprehensive view of the spatial organization of an area. Smailes[12] examined the structure of the urban hierarchy in South Australia through the analysis of telephone traffic flows and shopping destination movements for the purchase of twenty-four selected goods. Board, Davies and Fair[13] mapped flows of telephone

177

calls, air passengers, and rail freight as part of a comprehensive study of the spatial organization of South Africa. At the local scale, Kimani and Taylor[14] included bus passenger movements and market-going behavior along with other attribute and functional data in their valuable study of development in Murang'a District, Kenya. Clark[15] employed factor analysis and canonical analysis to examine the relationship between formal and functional regions in Wales, using telephone calls as the interaction indicator while telephone directory listings were used to ascertain functions present in each of the telephone exchanges. Hirst[16] factor-analyzed telephone call data and compared the results with patterns of population potential and per-capita income for Tanzania. The value of these studies is in their holistic approach to the spatial organization of a study area by integrating interaction data with locational attributes and/or functional information.

Different forms of interaction data provide information about varying levels of spatial organization. Some types yield more information about the detailed local organization, while other interaction data such as telephone calls, are useful for gaining knowledge of regional or national patterns of spatial organization. The purpose of this chapter is to demonstrate the contributions that a variety of spatial interaction data can make in obtaining a clearer and more dynamic picture of the spatial structure of the Kenyan economy.

Rainfall Probability and Population Distribution

The understanding of the spatial organization of an area requires the analysis of many elements of the system. Two of the most basic elements are the physical environment and the people occupying that environment. The general population distribution of Kenya is closely related to the distribution of rainfall. The extremely uneven distribution of the population with concentrations in the better-watered areas of Kenya is striking. These population concentrations are mainly in the form of dispersed rural settlements.

Less than ten percent of the nearly eleven million Kenyans in 1969 lived in towns of greater than 5,000 people, with Nairobi containing well over one half of the town dwellers, and Mombasa another one quarter. The rural population is densest in areas north and south of Kisumu in western Kenya, along the eastern slopes of the Aberdare Range and Mount Kenya to the north and northeast of Nairobi, in the Machakos area east-southeast of Nairobi, and along the southern

coast. Most of Kenya is rather sparsely populated,
including some areas in the western highlands where
there is sufficient rain for agriculture. The pattern
of interactions should be studied with this population
distribution in mind. See Figure 9.1.

Bus and Railway Passenger Movements

Flows of bus and rail passengers are used as indicators of the number of people leaving their home areas
via public transportation and the orientation or direction in which they most often move. The possible number of origins and destinations for movement by bus and
the actual number of people who use public transportation in Kenya make movements by bus and rail one of the
most useful indicators of Kenyan spatial organization.
Almost all travel beyond the easy walking range of three
to five miles is by public transportation as there are
very few Kenyans able to afford their own car. There
was one car for every 200 persons in Kenya in 1969[17]
and many of these were owned by non-Africans or companies.
Private companies owning anywhere from one car to
a hundred buses provide public passenger service which
is licensed by the government. Each vehicle carrying
passengers for hire in Kenya must display a license
which indicates the passenger capacity, the route and
the timetable. The Kenya Government has generally
granted nearly every request for a bus license unless
an already-existing operator on a particular route
could demonstrate that further competition would not
be healthy due to a low demand along that route.
The capacity of buses moving along any given route
generally will not greatly exceed the demand for bus
service since the bus company would lose money and the
service would then be reduced or discontinued. There
is the possibility of a demand for bus service existing with no bus service present, due to lack of recognition of demand, lack of capital on the part of the
people who do recognize the demand, or such poor route
conditions that the service could not be profitable
and/or could not keep a timetable. The use of cars or
taxis has provided passenger service along some routes
where the demand is not great, as well as along main
routes where there is a demand for express service.
Licensed taxis having scheduled routes are included
with the bus data. In general, bus route capacity
should be a good indicator of the actual number of
people moving along each route. Based on sample surveys of bus occupancy in Kenya, approximately seventy-
five percent of seats are filled on average, subject
to many variables including route, time of year, and
weather.

FIGURE 9.1

Rainfall Probability and Population Distribution

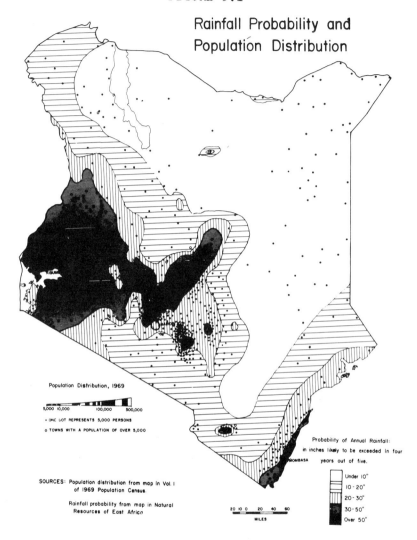

Population Distribution, 1969

5,000 10,000   100,000   500,000

• ONE LOT REPRESENTS 5,000 PERSONS

o TOWNS WITH A POPULATION OF OVER 5,000

SOURCES: Population distribution from map in Vol. I
of 1969 Population Census.

Rainfall probability from map in Natural
Resources of East Africa

Probability of Annual Rainfall:

in inches likely to be exceeded in four

years out of five.

Under 10"

10 - 20"

20 - 30"

30 - 50"

Over 50"

20 10 0   20   40   60

MILES

Figure 9.2 indicates the licensed bus passenger
capacity on the roadways of Kenya in 1969. The map
was prepared by collecting and organizing the information contained on copies of about 3,000 public transportation licenses issued for vehicles operated by an
estimated 1,000 bus companies.

Movements of people by bus are closely associated
with population density. The area of heaviest bus
usage is located in the area north of Nairobi to

FIGURE 9.2

BUS SERVICE IN SOUTHWESTERN KENYA

LICENSED CAPACITIES FOR 1969

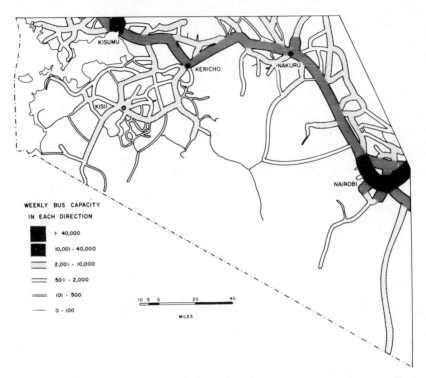

Nyeri, along the main Nairobi - Nyeri road, and up into the eastern slopes of the Aberdare range, with much of the traffic converging on Nairobi. Another area with especially dense traffic is to the north and northwest of Kisumu. Both these areas have dense-ly settled rural populations with many economic link-ages to nearby large centers.

In contrast to the two above-mentioned bus hinter-lands, the areas around Kisii and to the east of Mount Kenya between Embu and Meru are just as densely popu-lated, yet their bus traffic is lighter than would be expected when compared to population. The Kisii area and the Embu-Meru area are similar in many respects — ignored to a great extent in the infrastructure devel-opment of the colonial period, blessed with land suited for cash crops, low in inward- and outward-migration. If the recent improvement of the major and secondary

181

roads in these two areas is coupled with the stimulation of other infrastructure improvements and increasing economic demands on the part of the people, it is likely that the interregional flow of people, goods, and information throughout these areas will accelerate, greatly enhancing the economic contribution of these promising areas to the Kenyan economy.

The bus service map dramatically shows the lack of flow between the coastal bus hinterland and the rest of Kenya. There are heavy flows of bus passengers converging on Mombasa from the immediate north, northwest, and south but lack of a significant passenger flow from Mombasa to Nairobi is in strong contrast to the heavy passenger flow from the Nairobi bus region to the Kisumu bus region.

The areas with little or no bus service are also important to note. There are perhaps a million people in Kenya with virtually no bus service available, including vast areas of northern and northeastern Kenya, southern Narok District, and the northern coastal area between Lamu and Garissa. In addition to lack of bus service, these three large areas share widely dispersed, low-density populations, few and generally poor-quality seasonal roads, and a lack of economic, political, and social integration with the rest of Kenya.

Rail passenger flows are shown in Figure 9.3. Origin - destination information was obtained from the East African Railways and Harbours Administration records of all tickets sold during November and December 1969 and then dividing by nine to get approximate one-week average.

Rates for bus and rail passenger service in Kenya are distance-based and are similar. Railways generally carry far fewer passengers than do buses along the same routes, although certain rail routes have a much higher percentage of the passenger traffic than other routes. Frequency of service and condition of roads are contributing factors to this difference in preference for the use of rail passenger service as compared to buses.

In many areas of Kenya, good-quality roads have been constructed parallel to rail lines. The rail line from Nairobi to Nanyuki runs along the edge of a densely settled area with a population that is relatively active economically. The almost complete lack of rail passenger traffic can be explained by the fact that a paved road has existed parallel to this route for several years and bus service grew rapidly in response to the demand. Buses here generally move far more rapidly and there is a much better choice of schedule so that only in unusual circumstances will people ride on the train.

182

FIGURE 9.3

KENYA RAIL PASSENGER FLOWS-1969

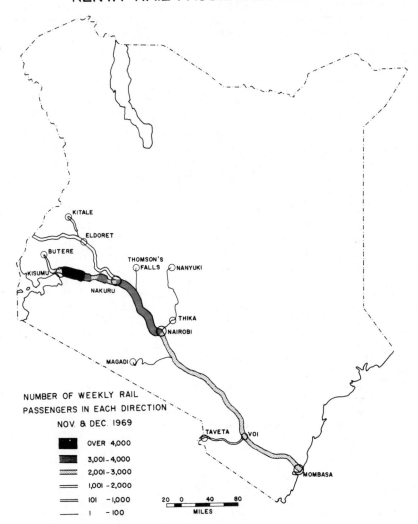

NUMBER OF WEEKLY RAIL
PASSENGERS IN EACH DIRECTION
NOV. & DEC. 1969

■	OVER 4,000
▨	3,001-4,000
▥	2,001-3,000
≡	1,001-2,000
=	101 -1,000
—	1 - 100

    20 0   40   80
    ─────────────
         MILES

    In the area east of Kisumu with a similar popu-
lation density and level of economic activity, the
rail passenger traffic is about one fifth to one
tenth of bus passenger traffic.   North of Nairobi
the bus passengers outnumbered the rail passengers
by about 2,000 to one.   Nairobi has nearly one half
of the urban population of Kenya (1969 population of
509,000)[18] yet the highest volume of rail passengers

183

is in the area east of Kisumu, a town with a 1969 population of 32,431. The generally poorer condition of
roads in the Kisumu area in 1969 was in part due to
the emphasis on road building in the white highlands
during the colonial period, with lower priority given
to areas where few European farmers lived.

Mail Flows

The postal service provides the major form of
long-distance personal communication in Kenya as it
does in most countries of the world. Kenyans posted
approximately 100 million pieces of mail in 1970[19]
(ten pieces per person) through the 350 post offices
and postal agencies throughout Kenya. The people of
Nairobi accounted for about one third of all mail sent
or about sixty-five pieces per person.

Information on mail flows was obtained by counting, according to destination, all of the mail sent
from forty selected centers for a one-week period in
1970. Orientation of the dominant mail flows from
these post offices is shown in Figure 9.4. The primate position of Nairobi within the Kenyan urban system is vividly portrayed by the fact that thirty-four
out of the forty centers have their largest flow to
Nairobi. Another pattern which emerges is that the
coast forms its own region, with Mombasa as the dominant center. There are few strong mail flows from
selected coastal centers to Nairobi. Four of the six
selected Kenya post offices which do not have their
dominant mail flows to Nairobi are located in the
coastal area. The role of Mombasa as a focus for the
coast is supported by the fact that of the eight coastal centers surveyed, three (Gede, Kinango and Voi)
had their largest mail flow to Mombasa.

Analysis of the second largest mail flow from each
of the forty centers is helpful in showing the emergence
of certain centers as regional nodes in the communications system. Centers which serve the role as regional
centers are Mombasa, Meru, Thika, Nyeri, Nakuru and
Kakamega. Other regional centers which would probably
become evident with a larger sample of post office
mail counts would include Kisumu, Kitale, and Machakos.
The patterns of mail interaction flows are, to some extent, a function of the centers which were chosen for
analysis, but the patterns which emerge serve to point
up some meaningful interrelations. In particular, the
dominant and/or second largest flows of mail can be used
as indicators of the orientation of many small centers
to larger centers, and therefore aid in the defining of
the hinterlands. In 1970 there were approximately 350
post offices and postal agencies and 150 telephone

FIGURE 9.4

ORIENTATION OF MAIL FLOWS
FROM 40 SELECTED KENYA CENTERS

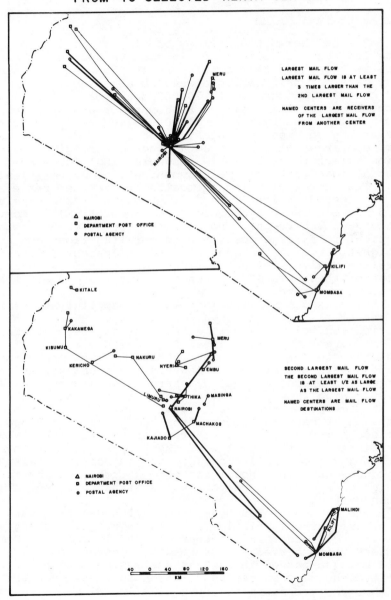

185

exchanges in Kenya. The amount and orientation of mail
flows from centers with no telephone service would
appear to be good indicators of future telephone service needs.

Telephone Call Flows

One of the most useful types of spatial interaction information indicating linkages between urban centers is telephone call origin-destination data. Basic
flow data for this analysis were obtained by sorting
and counting approximately 70,000 operator billing
tickets representing all of the operator-assisted telephone calls made by nearly 34,000 telephone subscribers
during the one week of August 17 to 23, 1969. Results
were compared with data from a nine-hour origin-destination telephone call sample conducted in 1963 by the
East African Posts and Telecommunications Corporation.[20]
The number of telephone calls between two centers
is considered indicative of the strength of an association between those two centers.[21] Theoretically, most
centers will have their nodal flows (or strongest association) to a larger center with more functions and at
a higher level in the central place hierarchy. Therefore the analysis of nodal flows can be used as an indicator of the hierarchy of central places and their spatial organization.
Figures 9.5 and 9.6 indicate the spatial structure
of the nodal flows in Kenya for 1963 and 1969 origin-
destination telephone call data. The general pattern
which emerges from both these figures is a series of
regional clusters of smaller centers most strongly associated with nearby larger centers. Nairobi serves the
largest of these regional clusters, covering an area in
1969 ranging from fifty miles south of Nairobi to the
north side of Mount Kenya, 150 miles north of Nairobi.
Other major centers evident from telephone call flows
include Mombasa, Kisumu, Eldoret and Nakuru. The 1969
data indicates that twelve of the fifteen largest towns
in Kenya and forty-five out of the 143 possible telephone
exchanges had their nodal flows to Nairobi, demonstrating
the primate position Nairobi holds within the Kenyan
urban system.
The 1963 and 1969 telephone call nodal flow patterns are markedly similar. A few significant changes,
however, did occur in an otherwise stable pattern. Some
centers which served as intermediate centers in 1963
were being bypassed in 1969 as smaller centers had
shifted their strongest association to larger centers
which were more distant. Specifically, Eldoret, Nanyuki,
Molo, Kericho,and Kisumu all lost nodal flows from at

186

FIGURE 9.5

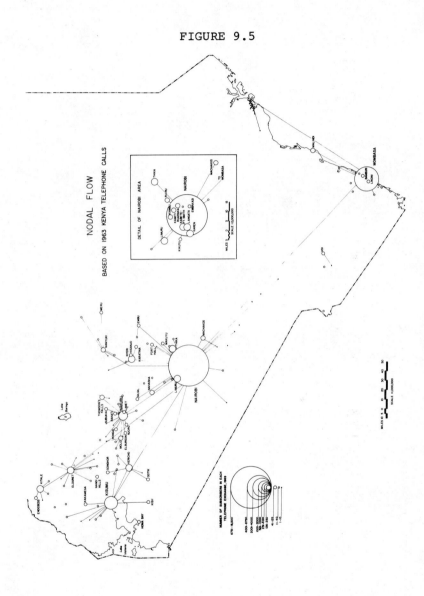

NODAL FLOW

BASED ON 1963 KENYA TELEPHONE CALLS

DETAIL OF NAIROBI AREA

NUMBER OF SUBSCRIBERS IN EACH
TELEPHONE EXCHANGE, 1963

187

FIGURE 9.6

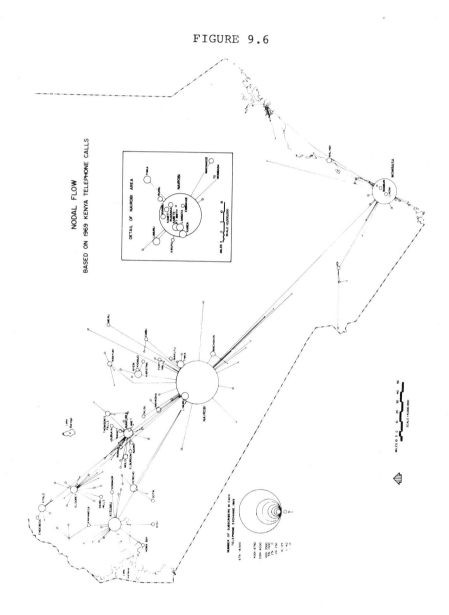

NODAL FLOW
BASED ON 1969 KENYA TELEPHONE CALLS

188

least one smaller center between 1963 and 1969. These
shifts seem to point toward the creation of a communications system even more strongly dominated by Nairobi.
    Telephone flow figures show that the Teita Hills
area which includes Voi and Mwatate, was not integrated
into the national communications system in 1963, and
that this situation had definitely changed by 1969. In
1963, Voi made twice as many calls to Mwatate as to
Mombasa, while in 1969, Voi made eight times as many
calls to Mombasa as to Mwatate. Also evident from the
data is the increasing strength of the association of
the Teita Hills area with Nairobi, which in a few years
could conceivably become the dominant receiver of Voi's
telephone calls.

Comparison of Flows

    The patterns of the three types of flows examined
in this chapter complement each other in such a way
that each flow pattern reveals more of the total spatial interaction picture. Differences in scale, cost,
users, and purposes of users all lead to the expectation that patterns would not be the same, and that the
examination of only one form of interaction would reveal an incomplete and perhaps misleading picture of
the spatial organization of Kenya.
    Bus passenger flows are especially useful in indi-
cating the local orientation of rural hinterlands and
the interconnections between even the smallest villages
and towns. Bus service is the most vital mode of interaction for most people in Kenya. In order to enter the
market economy it is frequently necessary for a producer
to move his own surpluses greater distances than can be
easily walked. Movement by bus may also be necessary
for communication with friends and relatives, particularly where population densities, the level of economic
development and literacy rates are all relatively low.
    The postal service provides the function of enabling
people to communicate socially and/or to conduct business over any distance at a very low cost. Mail flow
patterns can indicate the economic and social ties between places and may show center/hinterland patterns.
Telephone call flow patterns tend to illustrate urban
linkages and urban hierarchy even more strongly than
mail flows because of the more commercial nature of this
more costly mode of communication. Postal flow data
can potentially include many places which do not have
phone service.
    Bus and telephone services have rate structures
which increase with distance so that relative location is more important in these patterns, while relative size and importance of destination becomes more

relevant in the mail flows. By synthesizing the information gained from flow patterns and integrating it
with other information, conclusions can be drawn which
are helpful to understanding the spatial organization
of Kenya.

Synthesis and Conclusions

The spatial patterns of interactions in Kenya
make a meaningful contribution to the topics of urban
primacy, underserved areas, and functional regions —
especially when integrated with other spatial information. There are various methods of measuring whether
an urban system has a primate or dominant city, which
can lead to varying conclusions as to the degree of
primacy of Kenya's urban system. Underserved areas
are usually identified through the analysis of service
functions in central places, as is done in Kenya's
Regional Physical Development Plans.[22] Identification
of hinterlands and establishment of planning regions
have also been frequently accomplished without benefit
of interaction data. These topics will be briefly discussed with emphasis on the contributions that interaction data synthesized with locational information can
make to a more accurate understanding of Kenya's spatial organization.

Urban System Primacy in Kenya

Obudho in Chapter 5 considers this topic fully.
If an urban system contains one city which notably
dominates the others, that city is referred to as a
primate city, and the system is said to have a primate
city distribution. Some highly industrialized countries may have a primate city distribution (e.g.,
France), and most less-developed countries are expected to have a city distribution with one or two cities
functionally dominating the system.

One index widely used to measure the primacy of a
country is based on the ratio of the population of the
largest city to the combined population of the first
four cities. This primacy index has been applied to
data from the late 1950s for 104 countries.[23] In Kenya
57.5 percent of the population of the four largest
cities reside in the largest city, giving Kenya a rank
of 50th out of the 104 countries on the primacy index.
Comparable calculations indicate that Kenya is still in
the average category, although it is becoming slightly
more primate:

	Year		
	1948	1962	1969
Nairobi's population	118,976	266,794	509,286
4 largest cities	232,246	508,076	835,941
Primacy Index (largest city as percentage of the four largest)	51.2%	52.5%	60.9%

Another method of testing for primacy of an urban system is to examine the rank - size relationship of the population of many cities in the system.[24] The population of each city multiplied by its rank should be equal to the population of the largest city in the system in a normal rank - size distribution. Primacy is present if there are fewer cities of intermediate size than would be expected from the rank - size rule.

Table 9.1 illustrates the rank - size relationship of the ten largest towns of Kenya based on the data from the last three censuses. For 1969, Mombasa had approximately half the population of Nairobi, as would be expected in a nonprimate system. The other intermediate towns have a much smaller population compared to Nairobi, than would be expected in normal rank - size distribution, and even in relation to Mombasa, Nairobi is becoming more primate. The fourth-largest town had only one fifteenth of Nairobi's population and the tenth-largest had one fiftieth of Nairobi's population. By contrast, in the United States the tenth largest city has about one seventh as many people as the New York city metropolitan area and the twenty-fifth largest city has about one fifteenth the population of New York.

While population is often used to indicate the importance of cities in a system, primacy theoretically should be measured by the functional importance of a city in the urban system. A center of few administrative, commercial, or social functions mainly serving as an area of residence for agriculturalists is functionally less important than another center with fewer people all primarily engaged in commercial, administrative, and manufacturing functions. Long distance telephone calls in East Africa are usually made for commercial or administrative purposes, and therefore should be a good indicator of the functional importance of towns.

191

TABLE 9.1
Rank-Size and Primacy in Kenya

Town	Population (in thousands)			Fraction of Nairobi's Population			Theoretical Relationship with Largest Town		
	1948	1962	1969	1948	1962	1969	1949	1962	1969
1. Nairobi	119.0	266.8	509.3					1/2	1/2
2. Mombasa	84.7	179.6	247.1	1/1.4	1/1.5	1/2.1	1/2	1/3	1/3
3. Nakuru	17.6	38.2	47.2	1/6.8	1/7.0	1/11	1/3	1/4	1/4
4. Kisumu	10.9	23.5	32.4	1/11	1/11	1/16	1/4	1/6	1/5
5. Thika	4.4	13.9	18.4	1/27	1/19	1/28	1/7	1/5	1/6
6. Eldoret	8.2	19.6	18.2	1/15	1/14	1/28	1/5	1/7	1/7
7. Nanyuki	4.1	10.4	11.6	1/29	1/25	1/44	1/8	1/8	1/8
8. Kitale	6.3	9.3	11.6	1/19	1/29	1/44	1/6	1/13	1/9
9. Malindi		5.8	10.8		1/46	1/47		1/10	1/10
10. Kericho	3.2	7.7	10.1	1/37	1/35	1/50	1/9		

Sources: Republic of Kenya, Statistics Division, Ministry of Finance and Economic Planning, Statistical Abstract 1969 (Nairobi: Government Printer 1970), p. 15; and Republic of Kenya, Statistics Division, Ministry of Finance and Economic Planning, Kenya Population Census, 1969 (Nairobi: Government Printer, 1970), Vol. II, p. 1.

Table 9.2 indicates the number of telephone subscribers and a measure of the relative number of long-
distance (trunk) calls made or received for each of
the most important towns in Kenya. Nairobi has 3.68
times as many subscribers as Mombasa and eighteen times
as many as Kisumu, the second and third largest towns
respectively in terms of telephone subscribers. Nairobi
has nearly fifty-five percent of the telephones in the
entire country. This certainly would indicate that Nairobi holds a primate position in the telecommunications
network,and is a good indicator of its economic and administrative importance. Nairobi also dominates the
"participant percentage" measure although not to the
extent that it dominates the number of subscribers.
Because there are so many subscribers in Nairobi, people in Nairobi can reach more than half of the telephones in the country without calling long distance,
whereas people in smaller exchanges are almost limited
to making long distance calls. Even so, Nairobi is
clearly the dominant telephone exchange with each of
the towns having a smaller fraction of the calls as
compared to Nairobi than would be expected according
to their rank — the only exception being the third
largest town Nakuru which in 1969 had slightly more
calls than expected.
    The participant percentage is concerned with in-
teractions in a nondirected sense. When orientation
of the interactions is considered, Nairobi clearly
dominates the communications system of Kenya. As was
pointed out previously in description of the mail flows
and telephone calls, thirty-four out of forty post
offices sampled had their largest mail flow to Nairobi
and forty-five out of the total 143 possible exchanges
made Nairobi the most common destination of their telephone calls. This is in sharp contrast to a fully developed urban hierarchy which, according to classical
central place theory, would only have a few (three to
six) of the largest central places and a half dozen of
the smaller nearby central places with their strongest
functional associations to the largest city. Thus,
the orientation of the interaction flow gives the
strongest indication of the primateness of Nairobi in
Kenya's urban system, a degree of primacy not shown
in population statistics.

Underserved Areas

    A major step in the process of promoting economic
development and political stability is the identification of underserved areas — areas where a substantial
portion of the population does not receive the benefits from vital economic, social, and administrative

193

TABLE 9.2
Largest Kenya Telephone Exchanges, 1963 and 1969

Telephone Exchange	Telephone Subscribers*				Participant Percentage**		Ratio of Nairobi's Participant Percentage	
	1963	%	1969	%	1963	1969	1963	1969
Nairobi	12,649	50.8	18,515	54.7	47.0	48.6		
Mombasa	4,060	16.3	5,037	14.9	13.1	18.6	1/3.6	1/2.6
Nakuru	830	3.3	961	2.8	18.0	16.4	1/2.6	1/3.0
Kisumu	631	2.5	1,026	3.0	8.4	9.6	1/5.6	1/5.1
Nyeri	225	0.9	289	0.9	5.9	6.9	1/8.0	1/7.1
Eldoret	374	1.5	456	1.4	5.9	5.8	1/8.0	1/8.3
Nanyuki	209	0.8	224	0.7	3.7	3.8	1/13	1/13
Kericho	189	0.8	273	0.8	3.6	3.7	1/13	1/13
Kitale	242	1.0	278	0.8	3.7	3.5	1/13	1/14
Ruiru	115	0.5	132	0.4	4.1	3.4	1/11	1/14
Thika	217	0.9	410	1.2	2.9	3.4	1/16	1/14
Naivasha	135	0.5	160	0.5	4.0	3.0	1/12	1/16
Thompson's Falls	153	0.6	139	0.4	1.8	2.3	1/26	1/21
Molo	166	0.7	151	0.4	3.1	2.3	1/15	1/21
Machakos	83	0.3	139	0.4	1.9	2.1	1/24	1/22
Malindi	90	0.3	167	0.5	1.6	2.1	1/29	1/23
Kenya	24,916		33,824					

Source: East African Posts and Telecommunications Corporation, State of Exchange —
Kenya, Quarterly Reports, February 1964 and February 1970, Office of Regional
Director, Kenya.
*Participant percentage is defined as the percentage of total number of interexchange
telephone calls in which each exchange was a participant either as sender or receiver.

functions necessary for significant economic change.
In addition to information concerning population distribution, the location of service functions, and the
productive potential of the environment, the analysis
of interaction data provides further dimensions valuable for the delimitation of underserved areas. Since
interaction patterns indicate the strength and orientation of the flows of people, goods, and information,
they are necessary to show where links between regions
and between central places must be encouraged in order
to begin transformation of the economy of underserved
areas.

A synthesis of interaction and attribute data
points to the sparsity of at least some of the essential services and interregional linkages in major
parts or all of the well-populated districts of Lamu,
Meru, Kisii, Siaya, Elgeyo Marakwet, Baringo, Narok,
and Kajiado, as well as the more sparsely populated
districts in northern and northeastern Kenya. These
areas lack even the basic interaction mode of bus
service, as well as postal and telephone service.
Direct governmental effort in the form of the establishment of service functions and incentives for
entry into the cash economy are needed if these areas
are to become more integrated into the economy of
their surrounding regions.

An example from the above-mentioned underserved
areas is the Nyambeni Hills of Meru District, located
directly to the northeast of Meru. This is a functional region containing about 250,000 people, lying wholly within the hinterland of Meru Town. In this densely
populated area (213 people per sq. km. or 551 per sq.
mile in the highland areas in 1969), with good agricultural potential,[25] there are virtually no linkages to
the north, east or west. The only flows of people
from this area are to Meru Town by bus (since the densely populated areas range from ten to forty miles
from Meru Town), and the bus service was so inadequate
in 1970 that it could not carry the population of the
area to Meru even once a year. Analysis of market-going
behavior revealed that only three percent of the market
visits were outside the Nyambeni Hills and these, solely
to Meru Town.[26] In 1970 there was no telephone service,
few newspapers and radios, and very light postal flow
(three pieces of mail per 1,000 people per week) from
the four postal agencies. The most significant flow
of goods involved the cash coffee crop. Recent efforts
of the government to establish telephone service, extend
postal service, and upgrade roads in the Nyambeni Hills
for easier access to the core of Kenya should facilitate a transformation of this area. Encouragement of

complementary trade to areas in different environmental zones to the east, north, and west of the Nyambeni Hills should help strengthen the presently weak interregional linkages.

The coast of Kenya is a major region which is separate from the rest of Kenya politically, economically, and culturally. Lack of interregional flow is strongly evident in the mail, telephone, and passenger data analyzed. This lack of integration of the coast with the rest of the country is reinforced by the sparsity of transportation and communication linkages inland across a vast, nearly uninhabited area which lies interior to the coastal region. The difficulty of interaction between at least two potentially complementary areas could be reduced by developing an alternate route between the northern section of Kenya's coast and the highlands. An all-weather route between Kitui and Lamu could do much to stimulate economic development in areas which are essentially "end of the road" locations. At the same time, the economy of Kenya could become further developed with increasing interregional trade and a spreading-out of the accessibility to rural areas, particularly along the lower Tana River Valley.

Hierarchies, Hinterlands and Functional Regions

Information on service functions in the central places of Kenya was collected and organized in the Provincial Regional Physical Development Plans produced for each province of Kenya beteen 1967 and 1971, and provides a sound basis for one of the most detailed and comprehensive approaches to physical economic development planning anywhere in the world. The major goal of the planning is to spread economic development more equitably throughout rural and urban Kenya. Central place hierarchies and underserved areas were identified and growth centers selected, where future service functions would be encouraged in order to strengthen middle-level central places and eventually lead to a less primate urban system.

Although the amount of data and conclusions drawn in these Provincial Regional Physical Development Plans are remarkably valuable, the addition of origin-destination flow data would be helpful. Without flow data at the local level, the hinterlands of market centers and the orientation of smaller markets to medium- and larger-sized central places can only be roughly approximated. Centers may appear to be low on the hierarchy of central places because they do not have government functions, yet these centers may serve a large

196

population with a very active market, drawing people from a large surrounding area.

Development planning in Kenya uses the present district and provincial boundaries as a basis for planning. A major problem with this approach is that these administrative boundaries are based on ethnic group distributions, and are not functional economic regions. Planning is often rendered ineffective because the hinterlands of many central places are cut arbitrarily. With the present goal national integration, rather than separate development for each ethnic group, it would seem that boundaries reflecting functional organization would better suit national goals. A functional region is defined as an organized system of spatial interactions, oriented towards a center providing certain functions. The planning of functional regions based on hierarchies of central places and their hinterlands would be invaluable.

Figure 9.7 presents the top two levels of a proposed three-level set of planning regions for Kenya based on the functional region approach. Information used to construct these boundaries includes origin - destination data on telephone calls, mail flows, and rail passenger movements, bus routes and services, cattle routes to markets, physical features, and to a limited extent, current district boundaries. A third set of plans based on local central place hinterlands is very important for detailed location decisions in the planning process. It is believed that the resulting three levels of functionally based planning regions could serve as an efficient basis from which to plan and implement development projects.

FIGURE 9.7

PROPOSED PLANNING REGIONS FOR KENYA

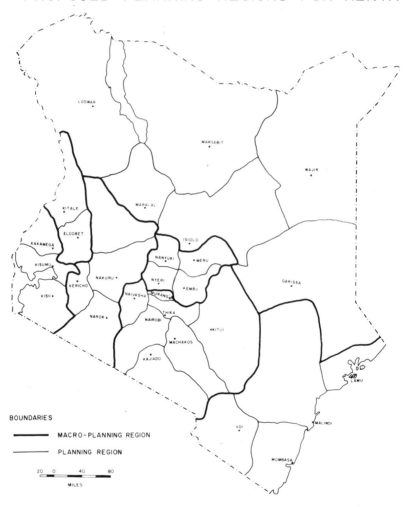

NOTES

1. J.D. Nystuen and M.F. Dacey, "A Graph Theory Interpretation of Nodal Regions", Papers and Proceedings of the Regional Science Association, 7, (1961), pp. 29-42.

2. Christopher Clayton, "Communication and Spatial Structure", Tijdschrift voor Econ. en Soc. Geografie, 65, (1974), pp. 221-227.

3. J.R. Mckay, "The Interactance Hypothesis and Boundaries in Canada: A Preliminary Study", The Canadian Geographer, XI, (1958), pp. 1-8.

4. Edward W. Soja, The Geography of Modernization in Kenya: A Spatial Analysis of Social, Economic, and Political Change (Syracuse, New York: Syracuse University Press, 1968), pp. 46-47.

5. Edward W. Soja, "Transaction Flows and National Unity: The Nigerian Case", in Expanding Horizons in African Studies, G.M. Carter and A. Paden (Evanston: Northwestern Press, 1969).

6. F.H.W. Green, "Urban Hinterlands in England and Wales: An Analysis of Bus Services", Geographical Journal, 116 (1950), pp. 68-88.

7. F.H.W. Green, "Urban Hinterlands: Fifteen Years On", Geographical Journal, 132, (1966), pp. 263-266.

8. Brian J.L. Berry, Geography of Market Centers and Retail Distribution (Englewood Cliffs: Prentice-Hall, 1967).

9. Brian J.L. Berry, Essays on Commodity Flows and the Spatial Structure of the Indian Economy (Chicago: University of Chicago, Department of Geography 1966).

10. B.M. Russett, "Delineating International Regions", in Quantitative International Politics: Insights and Evidence, J.D. Singer (New York: International Yearbook of Political Behaviour Research, 1967).

11. J.E. McConnell, "The Middle East: Competitive or Complementary?" Tijdschrift voor Econ. en Soc. Geografie, 58 (March - April 1967), pp. 82-93.

12. Peter J. Smailes, "Some Aspects of the South Australian Urban System", The Australian Geographer, XI, (1969), pp. 29-51.

13. C. Board, R.J. Davies and T.J.D. Fair, "The Structure of the South African Space Economy: An Integrated Approach", Regional Studies, 4, (1970), pp. 367-392.

14. S.M. Kimani and D.R.F. Taylor, Growth Centers and Rural Development (Thika, Kenya: Maxim Printers 1973).

15. D. Clark, "The Formal and Functional Structure of Wales", Annals of the Association of American Geographers, 63 (March 1973), pp. 71-84.

16. Michael A. Hirst, "Telephone Transactions, Regional Inequality and Urban Growth in East Africa", Tijdschrift voor econ. en Soc. Geografie, 66 (1975), pp. 277-293.

17. Republic of Kenya, Statistics Division, Ministry of Finance and Economic Planning, Statistical Abstract 1969 (Nairobi: Government Printer 1970), p.129.

18. Republic of Kenya, Statistics Division, Ministry of Finance and Economic Planning, Kenya Population Census 1969 (Nairobi: Government Printer 1970) Vol.1,p.1.

19. Republic of Kenya, Statistics Division, Ministry of Finance and Economic Planning, Statistical Abstract 1971 (Nairobi: Government Printer 1972), p.166.

20. This 1963 data was analyzed by Soja, Geography of Modernization in Kenya, pp.46-47.

21. Nystuen and Dacey, op.cit.

22. Republic of Kenya, Town Planning Department, Ministry of Lands and Settlement, Regional Physical Development Plans, for Central Province (1967), Coast Province (1970), Eastern Province (1960), North Eastern Province (1971), Nyanza Province (1970), Rift Valley Province (1971), Western Province (1970), (Nairobi: Government Printer).

23. Brian J.L. Berry, "The Organization of Population", in Atlas of Economic Development, ed. Norton Ginsberg (Chicago: University of Chicago Press 1969),p.36.

24. George K. Zipf, National Unity and Disunity (Bloomington, Indiana: Principia Press, 1941).

25. Frank E. Bernard, East of Mount Kenya: Meru Agriculture in Transition (Munich: Weltforum Verlag 1973).

26. L.J. Wood, "Spatial Interaciton and Partitions of Rural Market Space", Tijdschrift voor Econ. en Soc. Geografie, 65, (1974), p. 26.

200

10. Distance and Development in Kenya

Gary L. Gaile

Introduction

Distance is a major factor affecting development. Yet most studies of development, predominantly those by economists, do not explicitly consider the importance of this pervasive factor. Recent recognition of this factor by spatial planners has led to major concern for integrated spatial and social planning.

Kenya's development plans, with a major emphasis on growth center development, reflect comprehension of the importance of accessibility to central services and hence the relation of distance to development. It is the intent of this work to explicitly examine the relationship between distance and development both theoretically and in specific Kenyan cases so that the planning implications of these relationships can be considered.

Urban centers are concentrated areas for productive capability, for the provision of services, and for the adoption and diffusion of innovations. Hence, they are concentrated areas for development. This development is not restricted to those people inhabiting the urban center itself, but may also spread to all those with access to the center. Simply, the degree of accessibility or its cost is an inverse function of the distance from the urban center. Thus development may also be posited as inversely related to the distance from an urban center. The theoretical development surface is one of interlocking development cones,

The author wishes to express his gratitude to the Fulbright-Hays Program and the National Science Foundation for their support to the Institute for Development Studies, and the Department of Geography, University of Nairobi for their on-site assistance, and to Professors Wm.A.V. Clark, J. Friedmann, J. Huff and E. Soja of UCLA for their comments.

the apex of each being a growth center. Areas most
distant from a growth center are troughs of development. Where two proximate growth centers are linked
by a major transport artery, a ridge of development
may result from the intensified interaction and a
natural "growth path" may result. The unevenness of
the development surface depends on the size and spacing of growth centers. If the limited capital available for development is invested in a few large growth
centers, this efficiency-oriented investment will result in a development surface with a few high peaks of
development and a large portion of the surface (those
areas not easily accessible to major growth centers)
in troughs. If the development capital is more equitably distributed among smaller size growth centers
as well, the peaks will be less pronounced and there
will be less area in troughs. The choice in the size
and spacing of growth centers largely depends on the
weighting government planners attach to efficiency
and equality goals.

This study now turns to an analysis of the developmental and spatial aspects of Kenya's development
plans so that objectives of the plans may be critically evaluated, assessed, and related to distance.

The Government Plans

The two recent Development Plans for 1970-74 and
1974-78 were analyzed in detail in order to gain a
perspective of the Kenyan concept of development and
to distill out the spatial aspects of development as
put forth in the Plans. Whereas the Plans are extremely well-written for a newly independent nation, nonetheless for the task at hand, certain problems became
evident. Although many statements about government
objectives and aspects of development are made in
the Plans, no definition of development was found.

Specific statements in the Plans do yield some
useful bases from which development might be objec-
tively specified in the Kenyan context:

. . . The Government of Kenya defined its commitment to certain economic objectives. These included universal freedom from want, disease and exploitation; equal opportunities for advancement;
and high and growing per capita incomes, equitably distributed among the population.[1]

A similar statement is made in the most recent
Plan, the slight changes being that "individual freedom" is included and that "benefits" are to be equitably distributed instead of "incomes".[2]

The Kenyan government plans to achieve these efficiency - equality goals by a primary emphasis on rural development:

The Government plans to give new meaning to the phrase 'rural development': so that the principles of African socialism involving the equitable distribution of the benefits of prosperity can be given greater reality in a nation enjoying a higher level of general prosperity.[3]

The government further explicitly states that it will implement rural development through:

A raising of the levels of education and health in rural areas, an emphasis on the improvement of the secondary road system, higher expenditures on rural water supplies, an extension of electricity, rural amenity schemes and improvement of social services in rural areas . . . A fundamental objective of the Government related to rural development strategy is to secure a just distribution of the national income, both between different sectors and areas of the country and between individuals . . . the Government . . . will ensure that the standard of living of those with low incomes grows at a faster rate than the average.[4]

These statements from the 1970-74 Plan could result in a reasonably objective assessment of at least some aspects of development and a monitoring of the degree of implementation of infrastructural changes leading to development. A major difficulty, however, exists in that these emphases have been changed somewhat in the more recent 1974-78 Plan. An analysis of the two Plans indicates that the emphasis on rural development, while present, is substantially diminished in the more recent Plan. A shift towards increased planning for the urban and international sector is discerned by this author, including a new emphasis on the importance of the "informal sector" in the process of development. These shifts do not however greatly alter the basic objectives of the Plans. The shift seems to be such that efficiency - equality goals will be weighted with a stronger efficiency component.

Much of the policy put forth in the Plans has either explicit or implicit spatial components. Of specific interest is Kenya's commitment to a spatial investment strategy based on a hierarchy of growth centers. This spatial investment strategy has been proposed as a response to a variety of perceived needs:

203

First, it is important that the growth of the
urban population should be distributed over a
relatively large number of centres and not mainly concentrated on the two biggest towns, Nairobi and Mombasa. Severe problems would be posed,
for example, by the explosive growth of population in Nairobi implied by acceptance that the
bulk of the future urban population will be concentrated there. But even more important than
the need to avoid the negative consequences of
concentrating the growth of the urban population
in one place is the positive need to provide a
number of different focal points in different
parts of the country. Rural life cannot be complete without towns any more than towns can be
complete without access to the countryside, and
it will be an objective of government policy to
promote the growth of a number of towns to a
size where they are large enough to provide the
people of the surrounding districts with many of
the facilities and amenities available in a modern city. Work on the identification of centres
with high growth potential has been in progress
over the past two years and this Plan contains a
provisional list of towns and growth centres which
will provide the basic urban framework for the
future. New factories and other enterprises will
be grouped in the designated growth centres, and
thus act as a stimulus to the further growth of
output and employment, instead of being increasingly concentrated in Nairobi or scattered at
random around the countryside.[5]

That a growth center policy "completes" life for
both rural and urban dwellers is justified by the government through their statement of belief in the positive effects of the concept of spread:

The interdependence between rural and urban areas
grows in the process of development and with it
comes enhancement of the role of the town as the
producer of goods and services and the consumer
of agricultural production. This interaction
leads to cumulative self-sustaining growth.[6]

The result of Kenya's major spatial planning
effort has been the selection and classification of
1,682 proposed urban growth centers. Considering
that there were only forty-eight urban centers in 1969
with a population more than 2,000, the potential impact on the spatial reorganization of development of

204

such a major planning program is of considerable consequence.

A strict hierarchy has been imposed consisting of eleven principal towns, eighty-six urban centers, 150 rural centers, 420 market centers, and 1,015 local centers:

> The overall objective adopted in planning the network is to provide eventually one <u>Local Centre</u> for every 5,000 rural population, a <u>Market</u> Centre for every 15,000, a <u>Rural Centre</u> for every 40,000 and an <u>Urban Centre</u> for each 120,000.[7]

Further, each level of center is to be provided with a specific level of infrastructure.

Implementation of the Plans

Kenya's ambitious and comprehensive Plan cannot be implemented in a short time. Nonetheless, when considering the essentially redistributive or equality bases of growth center strategies, serious questions arise when the overall pattern of government expenditures in Kenya is considered:

> Government expenditure, like taxation, has a dual role: it can serve both to redistribute income and to stimulate growth (equality and efficiency). It has not been possible . . . to quantify the redistributive impact of government expenditure. On the basis of the limited evidence available, it does not seem to us that at present public expenditure does much to redistribute income in favour of the poorer members of society. The lion's share of public expenditure continues to go to urban areas. With some significant exceptions, the really backward parts of the country receive a very low share of government expenditure on social and economic services such as education, health, roads, and extension and training.[8]

The tendency of the government to continue to concentrate development in large urban areas and specifically in Nairobi can be demonstrated by a select few examples. The statutory minimum wage in the formal sector in Nairobi is approximately twice that of the wage in the rural sector.[9] Nairobi received 65.2 percent of National Housing Corporation housing expenditure in 1970 although its population comprises only

205

4.4 percent of the total population. The construction of industrial estates was proposed to aid the development of large growth centers throughout the country, yet the first such estate was constructed in Nairobi and a second has since been constructed there, the government claiming the original plan was "too ambitious". Between 1974 and 1978 five times more money was spent linking Mombasa and Nairobi with a 275 kV electrical transmission line than was spent for the entire rural electrification program. The amount of funding allocated for the pressing needs of rural water development is only half that allocated for Nairobi and Mombasa water development. These few selected examples are illustrative of the overall pattern of government expenditure and implementation with respect to the comprehensive national regional development strategy. In metaphoric summary, the government has constructed a spatial skeleton for national development yet the bones remain bare. Only the heart of the nation thrives.

The Theoretical Foundation of the Plans

Kenya's growth center strategy is essentially based on the concepts of Christaller's Central Place Theory.[10] Specifically, Kenya's spatial planners have apparently realized that a functional hierarchy as provided for by Central Place Theory is a useful space-forming concept which develops hierarchical linkages to facilitate interactions at all levels. Further, the centers are specifically designed and located to encourage the type of rural - urban interaction that is the foundation of the k = 3 marketing principle of Central Place Theory. In Table 10.1 a comparison of Kenya's planned urban structure and that described by Christaller for a "typical" central place system is shown.

As can readily be seen in Table 10.1, the proposed hierarchy of growth centers in Kenya does not precisely follow the Christaller model. Specifically, Kenya's centers have been designed to serve the population of rural areas without necessarily engendering a sizable increase in the center's own population, hence the low expected size of the center itself in comparison to the population of the region it serves. The espoused governmental interest in rural development has probably led to the designation and specification of the large number of local centers. These centers are distinguished from the noncenters only by the proposed infrastructure of elementary educational facilities and can largely be considered noncenters

206

for most noneducational planning purposes. What remains is a hierarchy of growth centers which roughly
does fit the central place theoretical distribution.

The Sites Analyzed

In order to examine Kenya's growth center strategy empirically and demonstrate the relationship
between distance and development, two regions were
selected for analysis, based on the availability of
suitable data and the existence of supportive research.
Murang'a is primarily an agricultural district
situated at the edge of Nairobi's extended hinterland.
Its population of about 500,000 live in a relatively
densely settled rural environment with densities aver-
aging 250 people per square kilometer. The district
is inhabited primarily by the Kikuyu ethnic group —
which group is dominant numerically, economically, and
politically in Kenya; and thus the district is well
integrated with the socioeconomic mainstream of the
nation. Much of the most productive land in the district was not in the former scheduled areas (the White
Highlands", restricted to colonial production), but in
the African reserves. This land came into intensive
cash crop farming under the Swynnerton Plan and in 1971
coffee production in the district accounted for more
than seventy percent of total crop value.
Physiographically, the district lies on a highland
volcanic plateau with pronounced ridge and valley topography. The rainfall is relatively abundant (approximately 120 centimeters annually), and reliable. The
equatorial location and altitude combine to provide a
moderate climate for the district throughout the year.
No known towns existed in the East African interior prior to the colonial administrations of the 1890s.
The two trading centers established under colonial administration — Maragua and Saba Saba — are still predominant centers, surpassed in importance only by
Murang'a/Makuyu which now serves as both the administrative center of the district and as a center serving
large local export cash crop estates. The current level
of urban development in the district is low and is restricted to these and several other small urban places.
The projected population of Murang'a/Makuyu for 1980 is
12,000 and for the next largest center in the district,
Murang'a, only 2,600.[11]
Nairobi is a classic primate city and its contin-
uance in this role seems inevitable. Currently a metropolis of more than one half million people, it is projected that continued growth will result in a population between 2.9 and 4.2 million people by the year
2000.

TABLE 10.1
A Comparison of the Typical Hierarchy of Christaller k=3 Central Place Theory
and the Explicit Hierarchy of Kenya's Growth Center Strategy 12

Christaller's k=3 Central Place Theory				Kenya's Growth Center Strategy			
Order of Center	Number of Centers	Typical Population of Centers	Typical Population of Region	Order of Center	Number of Centers	Typical Population of Centers	Typical Population of Region
7	486	1,000	3,500	7	1,015	< 200	5,000
6	162	2,000	11,000	6	420	<1,000	15,000
5	54	4,000	35,000	5	150	2-5,000	40,000
4	18	10,000	100,000	4	86	10,000	120,000
3	6	30,000	350,000	3	9	*50,000	*1,000,000
2	2	100,000	1,000,000	2	1	447,000	*1,000,000
1	1	500,000	3,500,000	1	1	1,098,000	*15,000,000

In 1964 the boundaries of the city were extended to enlarge the incorporated area from ninety to 690 square kilometers. The region covered by this study is a larger metropolitan region including much of Nairobi's periphery and covers 8,388 square kilometers. The region extends past the satellite cities of Limuru in the northwest, Thika in the northeast, and Machakos in the southwest.

Physiographically, much of Nairobi's land is relatively flat despite its mile-high situation near the rim of the tectonically active Rift Valley. The central city is edged by large tracts of flat plains, especially to the east in the Upper Athi Basin. To the north the flat land gives way to a dissected slope with a resultant parallel ridge and valley topography.

The economic base and internal structure of Nairobi are rooted in its colonial legacy. The Nairobi Master Plan for a Colonial Capital notes:

> In outward appearance the town is fixed in its western atmosphere, to which some variety will be given by Indian bazaars, a very English suburban belt, and a garden city tendency in the African townships . . . It will go ahead as a European-type town, that is, European in architecture, a little frigid, but efficient, tidy and progressive.[13]

Today the ethnic tripartition of the residential space of Nairobi remains clearly evident. The European section of upper-class housing to the northwest and west remains an area of high rents and land values. The Asian sector to the northeast still retains its ethnic identity. The African sectors to the east and south are swelling with migrants, and concerted efforts to construct low-cost housing cannot keep up with the demand from the migrant influx resulting in worsening slum conditions and the proliferation of squatter settlements. The planners' "garden city tendency" is becoming an exaggerated euphemism. It is projected that this residential segregation will continue to break down (as it has since independence), due largely to the continuing exodus of the European and Asian populations and the entry of Africans into the middle and upper socioeconomic classes. Thus the process of residential filtering has only recently begun.[14]

The Data Available

Time series data were not available for the case studies. Nonetheless, a significant set of data banks for the two regions of this case study is available and will allow limited testing of hypotheses and provide a base for further studies of a dynamic nature.

The delimitation of the Nairobi region is that initially developed by the Nairobi Urban Study Group (NUSG) in 1971. The area is approximately 120 km. by 95 km. in extent and is gridded into 233 square cells each measuring thirty-six square km.[15] Thirty-two variables per cell were coded from raw data and maps. These variables placed emphasis on demographic and infrastructural characteristics. Income data were not included. The thirty-two variables for each cell and the x-, y- coordinates of the center of each grid cell have been punched onto IBM computer cards and are available from the author.

The data for the analysis of the Murang'a District were collected by Kimani and Taylor and their field research team of fifty interviewers over a one-year period (June 1972 to August 1973). The data are catalogued on nine reels of computer tape at the University of Nairobi.[16] The data consist of ten files, nine of which are geocoded at district, divisional, locational, sublocational, and village or enumeration area levels. The original geocoding has been transformed into x-, y- coordinates for these analyses. Of specific interest to the study is file five which consists of interview responses from 5,141 farmers drawn from all over the district, and which includes individual-level income data.

Necessarily, the choice of data for analysis is strictly constrained by the pragmatic consideration of data availability. For the Nairobi region, the data available have a finely gridded spatial resolution, but this desirable aspect is overshadowed by the lack of certain variables which could more appropriately index development in the Kenyan context.

In order to put forth an example that may be more comprehensible to those not familiar with multivariate statistics, the analyses were run for only one variable — the infrastructure rating.[17] According to Johnson, " . . . one of the first objectives of a rural growth center program is to increase the degree of areal commercialization".[18] This variable was chosen since it places emphasis on commercialization.

For the Murang'a District the data available have a finely gridded spatial resolution and include income variables useful for determining a baseline pattern of economic wellbeing in the District. The cash income data included income from a variety of agricultural activities. This income was aggregated to yield total farm agricultural income for the 5,141 farms sampled in the District. Each farm has been assigned the

geocoding of the nearest village. The income and
demographic data for the farms were then aggregated
by village, resulting in 245 spatially distinct data
points within the District. From these data were
calculated three dependent variables:

Y_1 = annual income per farm worker

Y_2 = annual income per farm

Y_3 = annual income per cultivated acre

The x-, y- coordinates for each village were plotted
and encoded and the distance to Murang'a, the designated urban growth center, was calculated and encoded.

Hypotheses Tested: The Empirical Analyses

Specific hypotheses can be tested for the two
Kenya cases in order to assess the spatial pattern
of development around a growth center. The first
hypothesis to be tested is:

H1: Development is inversely related to distance
from a growth center.

Regression techniques were employed to determine
the relationship between distance from central Nairobi
and the level of the infrastructure index. The test
for hypothesis H1 resulted in clear rejection of the
hypothesis. The concentric, i.e. omnidirectional, hypothesis that development is inversely related to distance was not proven in this case. This hypothesis is
reconsidered and retested for this case when directional bias is taken into account in hypothesis H3.
The same regression techniques were employed on
the Murang'a District data to test the relationship
between the distance from the designated urban growth
center of Murang'a and the level of the three selected
income variables. The District is small enough so that
the furthest village was less than fifty km. from this
center. The results of the regression analyses in Table 10.2 indicate that a moderately strong relationship
did obtain between distance and the income variables.
Within the District, subareas around lower order
centers (with populations of less than 2,000) were
delimited and the distance from each center to the
villages within the subarea were calculated. Correlations which obtained when the dependent variables
were regressed against distance were either low or
insignificant. An analysis of scatter diagrams for

211

TABLE 10.2
Relationship Between Distance from the Growth Center
and Income Variables for Murang'a District

Dependent Variable	Correlation Coefficient	Regression Equation
Y_1	-0.45172	$Y_1 = 16203.8 - 16.098\ s$
Y_2	-0.46123	$Y_2 = 42848.0 - 35.271\ s$
Y_3	-0.43097	$Y_3 = 19035.7 - 21.290\ s$
$\log_n Y_1$	-0.49295	$\log_n Y_1 = 11.793 - 0.45807\ \log_n s$
$\log_n Y_2$	-0.50525	$\log_n Y_2 = 12.249 - 0.34551\ \log_n s$
$\log_n Y_3$	-0.51241	$\log_n Y_3 = 12.292 - 0.53530\ \log_n s$

Source: Based on the author's data.

these cases indicated that flat diagrams tended to
predominate — distance ceased to be a major explanatory variable at this lowest level of the urban hierarchy.
     The second hypothesis to be tested is:

     H2:   A modified development cone with an apex
           at the growth center exists.

In order to determine whether a modified development
cone does exist for the Nairobi region, the infrastructure index was analyzed using trend surface techniques.
Figure 10.1 shows the second order or quadratic trend
surface resultant. This surface displays marked concentricity largely due to the extrema limitations of
the quadratic form. Nonetheless, a definable development cone is clearly existant with an apex at the
city center, thus lending support to hypothesis H2.
The correlation coefficient for the surface is 0.341.
A large part of the variation unexplained by this surface is due to the expected extremely large residuals
at the city center itself.
     A third order or cubic trend surface is required
to illustrate directional variation and permits more
than one extrema, thus allowing specification of
"downward transitional areas". The third degree
polynomial trend surface of the infrastructure index

FIGURE 10.1

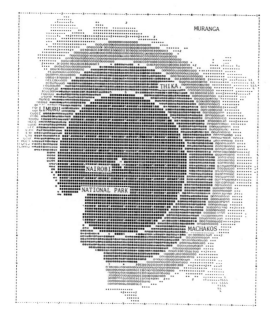

QUADRATIC TREND SURFACE
OF THE INFRASTRUCTURE
INDEX – NAIROBI REGION

FIGURE 10.2

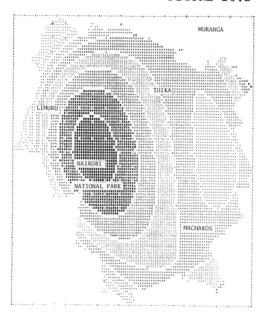

CUBIC TREND SURFACE
OF THE INFRASTRUCTURE
INDEX – NAIROBI REGION

for the Nairobi region is shown in Figure 10.2. Again,
a modified cone shape is evident, lending further support to hypothesis H2 and the general model. The correlation coefficient for this surface is 0.468. Again
a large part of the unexplained variation is due to
the large residuals at the city center itself.

The hypothesis H2 is further supported by an analysis of the Murang'a data. The a values in the regression equation are considerably higher than the mean
values for the dependent variables and are higher than
the a values which obtain for loosely-fitted regressions on lower-order centers.

The third hypothesis to be tested is:

> H3: The surface of the <u>development cone</u> is modi-
> fied along <u>directional axes</u>.

<u>Direction</u> has been shown to be a significant modi-
fier of an expected concentric process and it has thus
been incorporated into hypothesis H3. In the cubic
trend surface of Figure 10.2, directional bias is
clearly evident, with the surface being positively
distorted along the major transport axis which enters
the city from the southeast (the Nairobi-Mombasa Road)
and from the northwest. Sharp gradients are evident in
the direction of Nairobi National Park (the south and
southwest) and the African residential zone (the east).
In order to more rigorously test this hypothesis, the
data for Nairobi were assigned to sectors using a simple
radial method, employing twelve radials at 30° intervals and assigning each grid cell to a radial sector
depending upon the location of the grid cell's center.
The average number of grid cell points per radial sector is slightly less than twenty. Regression was again
employed to test hypothesis H1, that the infrastructure index was related to distance from the center,
but this test differs from the initial test of that
hypothesis in that each regression was restricted to
one directional sector. The resulting equations varied but were all significant. The correlation coefficient values are presented for each radial sector
in Table 10.3. The result indicates that <u>distance is
highly related to development when directional bias
is accounted for</u>, thus hypothesis H1 cannot be rejected. Table 10.3 shows the correlation coefficients
for regressions between the infrastructure rating and
distance from Nairobi to be significant and strong,
lending further support to hypothesis H1 when it is
modified for directional bias.

214

TABLE 10.3
Pearson Correlation Coefficients Relating Distance
and the Infrastructure Rating Along Radial Sectors -
The Nairobi Region

Sector Number	Pearson R
1 (north)	-0.70292
2	-0.61728
3	-0.59493
4 (east)	-0.52323
5	-0.51967
6	-0.59363
7 (south)	-0.74168
8	-0.90460
9	-0.89649
10 (west)	-0.91150
11	-0.75278
12	-0.69769

Source: Based on the author's data.

In order to more specifically test hypothesis H3,
that the surface of the development cone is modified
along directional axes, parameters from the regression equations relating the standardized infrastructure index and distance from Nairobi along each radial
sector were analyzed using the techniques of directional statistics. The simple linear regression
equation is:

$$\$ = \alpha + \beta s$$

where $\$$ is the standardized infrastructure index and
s is the Euclidean distance from Nairobi's center. In
this equation β represents the slope of the distance
decay line. In order to operationalize this parameter
for application of the directional statistics techniques each β was transformed into an integer quantity.[9]
Directional statistics were then calculated using the
midpoint direction of each sector and the β-transformed
frequencies. If the development cones were concentric
(nondirectionally biased), the circular variance,S_o,
would equal one. There would be no concentration about
any particular direction. The directional statistics
are used to test the hypothesis of uniformity:

$H_0 : \mu_o = 0,\ k = 0$ against $H_1 : \mu_o = 0,\ k=k \neq 0$

where μ_o is the circular mean direction of the population and k is a parameter related to the circular variance which is zero when the circular variance is one. Using a Rayleigh test for uniformity on the statistics calculated, the critical value for large n at the 0.01 level of significance is:

$$2n\bar{R}^2 > 9.210$$

where $2n\bar{R}^2$ is an approximation of the χ^2 distribution. For the radial sectoral data on transition for the Nairobi region the value of $2n\bar{R}^2 = 414.94775$. The hypothesis of uniformity is clearly rejected. There is significant evidence of directional bias in the distribution of the infrastructure index in the Nairobi region.

For the Murang'a District case, the town of Murang'a is not situated in the center of its District, but rather near its northeast boundary. Thus the distribution of the independent variable of distance from Murang'a town does not imply omnidirectionality (concentricity) since, given the spatial organization of the District, all but fifteen of the 245 villages fall to the west of a north-south axis through the town. Given the off-center location of the designated urban growth center within the region, hypothesis H3, referent to directional bias, cannot be tested.

The statistical testing of the remaining three hypotheses requires data in excess of the data limitations of this study. Nonetheless, the limited data available can be qualitatively analyzed in order to gain at least some elemental knowledge regarding these posited relationships.

The fourth hypothesis to be considered is:

H4:   The degree of development described by the surface of the development cone is modified by the hierarchy of urbanism.

A visual analysis of the map of residuals from the third order trend surface for the Nairobi region (see Figure 10.3) shows that cities of lower hierarchical orders (Thika, Machakos, and Limuru) within the Nairobi region do in fact display distinct positive residuals, thus tentatively supporting this hypothesis.[20] This hypothesis cannot be tested in the Murang'a District case due to the total absence of high order urban centers within the District.

FIGURE 10.3

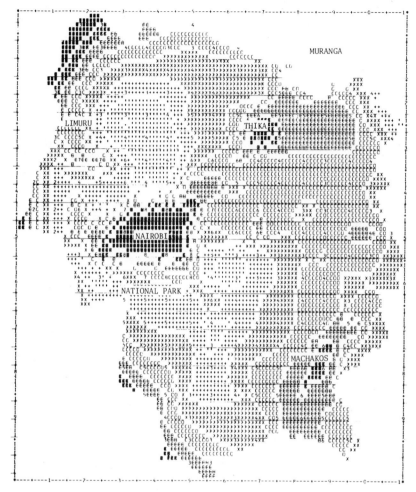

RESIDUALS FROM THE CUBIC TREND SURFACE – NAIROBI REGION

Of greater interest to the general model are the two remaining hypotheses:

H5: The radius of the base of the <u>development cone</u> does not change proportionally to urban size.

H6: The radius of the base of the <u>development cone</u> is a positive decreasing function of urban size.

In order to gain insight into this urban size relationship, subareas around two urban centers within the Nairobi region were analyzed separately and compared to Nairobi and Murang'a. Initially, thirty-eight grid cells around Thika and twenty-seven grid cells around Machakos were selected. These were divided into directional quadrats and the quadrat in the direction of Nairobi was deleted (in both cases these quadrats were bisected by a major transport artery). The remaining quadrats were analyzed using regression techniques in order to generate linear equations comparable to those generated for the Nairobi directional sectors. Although the strong distance decay relationship posited in hypothesis H1 obtains, the limited degrees of freedom prohibit statistical inference from being made.

The dependent variables used in the Murang'a District case study are of a more specific character than the transition index used in the Nairobi region case. Nonetheless, in order to facilitate comparison qualitatively between patterns depicted in the two regions, dependent variables for Murang'a were standardized. Although indices for the two regions are not strictly comparable, since they have been standardized they can be plotted on the same graph given that the distance variable has been scaled similarly.

The three urban centers in the Nairobi region are hierarchically stratified roughly by a factor of ten. According to the 1969 Census of Population, Nairobi's population was about 509,000; Thika's about 33,000; and Machakos' about 5,000. The population of Murang'a town is estimated at 6,000. As can be noted visually in Figure 10.4, the slopes of the standardized variable distance-decay curves are apparently related to urban size. The income gradient focused on Murang'a and the infrastructure index gradient focused on Machakos are considerably less steep than the infrastructure index gradients focused on the larger town of Thika and the largest town, Nairobi. The tendency for slope to increase (i.e. become steeper) with urban size provides preliminary evidence for the relationship posited in hypothesis H6. This suggests that smaller urban places may be more efficient in terms of extending transition to their hinterlands. The essentially flat scatter diagrams resultant from an analysis of income gradients around the smallest centers in Murang'a District may be considered as patterns expected from these hypothesized relationships.

218

FIGURE 10.4

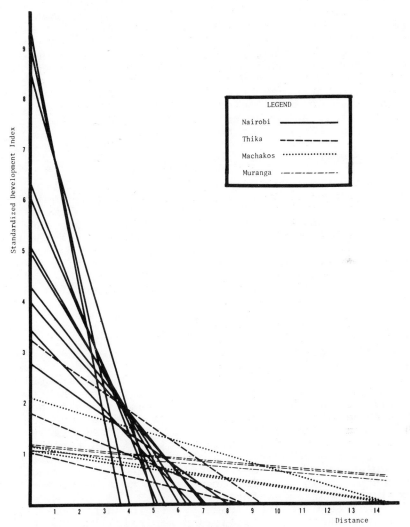

DEVELOPMENT DISTANCE DECAY CURVES FOR VARIOUS SIZED CITIES

Conclusions of the Testing:
Distance, Direction, Growth, and Size Effects

This preliminary study of examples from Kenya provides sufficient information to substantiate the posited inverse relationship between development and distance from a growth center in several empirical cases. Directional bias was shown to be a significant factor in one case where major transport arteries were present. Figure 10.4 indicates that a relationship between on-site growth and urban size obtained. Development patterns focused on small urban places have a distance decay curve less steep than those focused on larger urban places. The data upon which these inferences are based are of better quality and spatial resolution than can be found for most LDC's. Nonetheless, they lack sufficient quality and time depth to support true substantiation of the bases of the general model that has been proposed.

Reconsidering Kenya's Growth Center Strategy

This study provides a framework upon which an evaluation of Kenya's growth center strategy could be made and upon which alternative spatial investment strategies could be compared. This evaluation and comparison would require the refinement of all three aspects of the study: (1) development of a more precise and comprehensive model, (2) refinement of spatial analytical methodology, and (3) provision of a considerable data bank of relevant case-specific variables over time.

The description of the urban-focused development patterns found in the statistical analyses does provide some basis for speculation. Specifically, it is strongly suggested that in order to pursue the stated equality and rural development aspects of their development plans, the planners in Kenya should seriously consider refocusing their investment priorities towards smaller urban places. This suggestion is based on the preliminary evidence that district level growth centers and smaller local centers are less aspatially efficient but more spatially efficient (in terms of a less steep development - distance gradient). These speculations are in agreement with the policy suggestions of Kimani and Taylor relative to development policy in Murang'a District.[21]

Distance and development relationships have been demonstrated theoretically and empirically. These relationships are expected to vary with urban size. A continued effort towards the theoretical and empirical specification of these relationships would greatly improve the planner's ability to spatially allocate development capital in line with development goals.

220

NOTES

1. Republic of Kenya, Development Plan 1970-1974 (Nairobi: Government Printing Office, 1969), p.1.
2. Republic of Kenya, Development Plan 1974-1978 (Nairobi: Government Printing Office, 1974, p.1.
3. Republic of Kenya, Development Plan 1970-1974, p. 2.
4. Ibid.
5. Ibid., p. 15.
6. Republic of Kenya, Development Plan 1974-1978, p. 114.
7. Ibid., p. 120.
8. International Labour Office, Employment, Incomes and Equality: A Strategy for Increasing Productive Employment in Kenya (Geneva: International Labour Office, 1972).
9. Ibid., p. 77.
10. Walter Christaller, Central Places in Southern Germany, translated by C.W. Baskin (Englewood Cliffs, N.J.: Prentice-Hall, 1966).
11. For a more detailed geographical description of Murang'a District see S.M. Kimani and D.R.F. Taylor, Growth Centres and Rural Development in Kenya (Thika, · Kenya: 1973), pp. 8-11.
12. The left side of Table 10.3 is abstracted from Christaller, op.cit., p. 67.
13. Nairobi, Nairobi Master Plan for a Colonial Capital (London: Her Majesty's Stationery Office, 1948).
14. For a more detailed traditional geographical description of the Nairobi region see W.T.W. Morgan, ed., Nairobi: City and Region (Nairobi: Oxford University Press, 1967). A wealth of data and systematic observations can also be found in the volumes produced by the Nairobi Urban Study Group which are available from the Nairobi City Engineer's Office.
15. It is unfortunate for these and further spatial analyses that the fine-resolution grid was abandoned in the early stages of the NUSG study. Conversations with Mr. Lee of NUSG indicate that there is a possibility that the grid may be readopted in the near future.
16. The data are available from D.R.F. Taylor, Department of Geography, Carleton University, Ottawa, Canada K1S 5B6. I am very grateful to Mrs. Samson Kimani for her permission to use these data.
17. The use of principal components analysis to generate an index of development is not made here, since we feel its utility as an indexing technique to be overestimated, especially in dynamic cases.
18. E.A.J. Johnson, The Organization of Space in Developing Countries (Cambridge: Harvard University Press, 1970).

221

19. This was accomplished by rounding the value of -100β. The techniques of directional statistics are best demonstrated in K.V. Mardia, Statistics of Directional Data (London: Academic Press, 1972). They require that frequencies and not magnitudes be used. The result of the transformation yields a β value which can be interpreted as the frequency of the dependent variable decreasing by one unit for each one hundred units of the independent variable.

20. The residual map (Figure 10.3) displays differential values along the Nairobi - Thika axis which indicates that the development along this corridor is still quite disjointed. It is also evident that low values exist (as expected) in the hill country to the north and the plains to the southeast.

21. Kimani and Taylor, op.cit.

11. Housing Innovation in Kiambu District

R. A. Bullock

Introduction

In many parts of Africa today, marked changes
are taking place in house-types. While much interest
has been focused on events in the urban areas, the
housing revolution in rural areas has received surprisingly little attention. These changes affect
both building materials and form, and have been noted
in widely dispersed areas of the continent. Changes
in materials have often been attributed to a changing
resource base: for example abandonment of heavy wooden
walls in the earlier part of this century in Ethiopia
has been attributed to reduction of forest resources.[1]
More important in explaining modern changes seems to
be the factor of image and prestige. The adoption of
new roofing materials in the Ivory Coast, and of rectangular rather than circular plans in Nigeria have
both been attributed to status identification.[2] Similar trends can be seen in Kiambu District in Kenya.
This chapter examines the changes taking place in
Kiambu and explores the factors facilitating the
rapid change which has occurred since the institution
of land consolidation in the late 1950s.

Traditional Housing in Africa

African house types have been grouped into a
number of categories based primarily upon the basic
elements of plan, wall, and roof. This gives a broad
classification first into rectangular, circular, or
oval plans. Wall and roof variations lead to the
general distinction among those with circular plans,
between "beehive" and what have been termed "cylindrical", or "cone-on-cylinder".[3] Beehive houses are
those in which roof and wall form a continuous structural unit, as for instance in the Chencha or Sidamo
houses of Ethiopia.[4] In cone-on-cylinder houses,

the vertical walls are structurally separate from the
conical roofs which rest on them, as in the Gala and
Gurage house.[5]
    The Kikuyu house is of this cone-on-cylinder type.
It has been suggested that cone-on-cylinder houses ty-
pify the settled agricultural societies of Africa,
beehive types being more typical of nomadic pastoralists, hunters, and food gatherers.[6] While some have
associated house types with broad cultural groupings,
others suggest an environmental explanation for house
types and their distribution.[7] There is merit in both
viewpoints, for as Goldschmidt has commented, tribal
architecture " . . . is responsive as much to the inner environment of cultural presupposition and social
interaction as it is to the external environment of
wind and weather."[8]
    It is clear from the more detailed examination
of regional styles within similar environments or cultures that neither environments nor cultures alone
can explain the variety and distribution of house
types. Prussin's work in Ghana has eloquently demonstrated the variation among cultures within similar
environments, and Walton has shown how environmental
considerations have led to the occurrence of two house
types among the Ngoni of Fort Jameson in Zambia.[9] In
Kikuyuland, accounts and illustrations of housing in
journals of early European travellers demonstrate the
existence of two house types before the turn of the
century,[10] both of the cone-on-cylinder type. One
had substantial walls made of vertically placed adzed
planks, a building technique called "palisaded".[11]
This form was hardly known by the middle of the twentieth century and its demise is probably related to
the clearing of the forest. The other type was the
"wattle-and-daub" structure, consisting of a pole and
sapling framework covered in clay. This had become
the norm over most of Kikuyuland by the midtwentieth
century. During the last fifteen years however, it
has given way to a considerable variety of new forms
so that it now accounts for only a minority of all
houses in Kiambu district. The variety of these new
forms and the rapidity of their adoption clearly demonstrates the multiplicity of materials available and
willingly used when social and economic conditions
permit. Changes which have taken place show clear
spatial patterns of distribution related to development of the modern economy.

The Kikuyu Homeland

    The Kikuyu, a Bantu group, live in Central Kenya
on the eastern flanks of the Aberdare Mountains. Formed

by tertiary volcanic activity, the Abderares rise west-
wards above the plains to an elevation of some 14,000
feet (4,267.2 meters) on the eastern margin of the
Great Rift Valley. This elevation gives rise to a
marked increase in rainfall so that the slope is well
watered and deeply incised by numerous parallel streams.
In their natural condition the eastern flanks of the
range were heavily forested and the central sections
have for long been occupied by the agricultural Kikuyu
people. As long as the land lasted, they practised
shifting agriculture in the area now known as Murang'a
District. When population pressure on their resources
grew too great, they migrated northwards into Nyeri
District and southwards to Kiambu District, with which
area this study is concerned. Their range was restricted to the zone appropriate to the growing of their
main crops. The upper limit was set by declining tem-
perature and increasing rainfall where, in particular,
bananas failed to ripen, and a lower margin was set
by declining availability of moisture. A fringe of
land along this lower margin was used for grazing
their livestock, which were of great social importance. Kikuyu settlement then was restricted roughly
to areas lying between 5,500 and 7,000 feet (1,676.4
and 2,133.6 meters), where the mean annual rainfall
is about thirty-five to sixty inches (889 to 1,524
millimeters).
    Evidence suggests that by the second decade of
the nineteenth century, population pressure in Murang'a
District had reached such severe proportions that traditional religious constraints on the crossing of the
South Chania River were overcome and a southward migration developed into what is now Kiambu District. This
land was still forested and occupied by the Wandorobo
group of hunters and gatherers, from whom the land
was bought. Most of the Wandorobo were assimilated
into the Kikuyu tribe. This southward migration appears
to have reached the southernmost limits of land to
which the Kikuyu agricultural system was adapted just
prior to the advent of the colonial period in the 1880s.
Consequently there was little remaining potential for
the Kikuyu in this area to further exploit their
traditional strategy for coping with population pressure through extension of the agricultural frontier,
and it is likely that intensification of settlement
would have occurred naturally. The advent of colonial
government, however, insured a rapid increase in population density. Its policy of containing the African
population within reserves whose boundaries were essentially inflexible effectively blocked territorial expansion. The situation for the Kikuyu of Kiambu District was further aggravated by the alienation of

significant amounts of land for European settlement.
At the same time, and in the years following, medical
innovations had profound impact on mortality, particularly that of infants, so that there was a marked
rise in the rate of natural increase of the population, which now stands at about three percent per
annum. Apart from other effects, in Kiambu this
resulted in rapid depletion of the forest resource
so that materials for building the palisaded house
were rapidly exhausted.[12]

The bush-fellow system of agriculture had every-
where disappeared by 1940.[13] The growth in population
attributable to natural increase had been augmented
by immigration when the government repatriated "squatters" from the alienated lands. The viability of Kikuyu agriculture was further constrained by the traditional system of inheritance which created intense
fragmentation of agricultural lands within the confined
limits of the Kikuyu reserve, and by controls on their
growing of Kenya's main export crops, coffee, tea,and
pyrethrum. These and other issues led to the State of
Emergency in 1952.

During the first fifty years of this century, the
district had been subjected to differential development as a result of the operation of the modern economy. In the traditional period, north Kiambu had
been the favored part of the district, since for historical reasons farm sizes here were greatest.[14] In
the modern period, however, the situation was reversed.
The south, despite its much higher population densities and proportion of landless people, acquired a
favorable location by reason of its proximity to the
Nairobi market for agricultural produce. Moreover,
labor opportunities in the city provided opportunity
for many, including the landless. In the south too
proximity to European farms provided further opportunity for wage labor, particularly casual labor in connection with the coffee harvests.[15] Similarly, lower
parts of north Kiambu experienced development at an
earlier period than higher areas. Physical characteristics of the district played their part here.
The deeply dissected character of the terrain inhibited development of direct north-south routes due to
cost of bridging. Road distances between northern
areas, particularly the higher parts, and city markets
were thus greatly increased, with a corresponding
impact on cost of transporting produce to the city.
Furthermore, the isolation of the higher parts of the
north was enhanced by lack of through-routes over the
Aberdare Mountains. Consequently there was far less
contact with the modern economy in the north. The

greater farm size also meant that the subsistence economy remained viable for a longer period of time than in the south. With it, traditional values were preserved amongst a segment of the people, many of whom considered themselves guardians of tradition and superior in many ways to their less fortunate southern brethren. These circumstances contributed to the later adoption of modern housing in the north than in the south, and in higher areas later than in lower areas.

Following the declaration of the State of Emergency in 1952, the government adopted in 1953 a policy of "villagization", the concentration of the dispersed rural population into emergency villages similar to the strategic hamlets of Malaya and other disturbed areas. Having taken this major step in the dislocation of settlement, the government went further in 1955 when it committed itself to land consolidation which was to have marked impact on the whole fabric of the Kikuyu landscape.[16] The significance of this revolution for housing was fourfold. In the first place, when the population was resettled on the newly consolidated farms in 1959 and 1960, there was a great wave of new housing construction. Much of this new construction made use of more substantial materials than had been customary, and it was facilitated by bank loans which farmers could now raise for the first time against the security of their new title deeds. Secondly, the increased security of tenure which the new titles offered encouraged a greater investment than had previously appeared wise, particularly in housing and the planting of cash crops. Kiambu, alone among the districts of Kikuyuland, had traditionally acknowledged the practice of "restitution", whereby any descendent of an original landowner could reclaim land sold by his forebears if he could satisfactorily establish that the originally agreed price had never been paid in full. Since a farmer could never be sure that some stranger would not appear on the doorstep claiming restitution, it behooved him to minimize investment of any permanent kind. But with his new title deed and associated legislation restricting litigation over land ownership, this inhibition was removed. In the third place this increased security also led to the extension of agriculture and the clearing of large areas of wattle and eucalyptus woodland. This woodland had developed partly in response to traditional tenurial practices prohibiting foreclosure on a debtor's land as long as a crop stood on it. Thus long-maturing tree crops offered the best security under traditional law, particularly to the man who was away working in urban areas or in other employment distant from home. Provision of

227

secure titles removed this need and in the general
expansion of agriculture, large areas of this woodland
were cut. Much of the timber was sold as charcoal to
urban centers. Some was used for building. Finally,
the newly introduced cash crops of coffee, pyrethrum,
tea, and pineapples led to a much greater participation by Kikuyu farmers in the cash economy, resulting
in more ready availability of capital.

Diversification of Kiambu House Types

The years from 1956 to 1959 were spent preparing
the way for resettlement of the rural population on
newly consolidated land holdings under revised and
more secure forms of land tenure. The redispersal of
the population was accompanied by a marked diversifi-
cation of housing. The rapidity with which new forms
appeared arose from the extensive rebuilding which
necessarily accompanied resettlement of farmers on
their newly consolidated lands. It appeared to be
most pronounced close to Nairobi in those areas which
were most closely integrated into the city market,
where European influence had been greater, and where
the new elite congregated.
Whereas the circular daub-walled house continued
to be built, it was common only in new villages and
more isolated areas. But insofar as they were poor,
it may well be that the well-known conservatism of
the poor, rather than the fact of their poverty, was
more significant in their retention of the old icon.
In rural areas closer to town, amazing variety in
structures began to appear. The most marked change
was from the circular plan to rectangular. This
was not necessarily accompanied by any change in building materials, though it certainly facilitated the
use of a wider range of materials and techniques.
Thus stone came to be more widely though still sparsely used, and galvanized iron was introduced, not only
for roofing but also for walls.[17] Timber was more
commonly used than either of these. When the "palisade" technique was used, the plan might be either
circular or rectangular. Most commonly however,
planks were now laid horizontally on a rectangular
plan. Daub remained the most common wall material
whether the plan was circular or rectangular. Similarly, thatch remained the most common roofing material although it was clearly yielding to the flattened
kerosene tin. With this new range of choice open to
him, the Kikuyu now acquired a new status symbol. If
he had wealth, the farmer could construct his house
of stone or some less expensive though still innovative
material; if not, he could at least demonstrate

228

progressive attitudes by building in the new rectangular plan, if only in traditional materials. The
poor and the conservative still adhered to traditional materials and plans.

Enumeration of House Types

In order to examine these changes more closely,
an enumeration of houses was undertaken, using tran-
sects. Most roads follow ridge tops in a generally
NW-SE orientation. This offered the opportunity to
conveniently investigate the influence of isolation
on house types. These roads run through the main
areas of Kikuyu agriculture along ridge tops from the
coffee plantations of lower Kiambu to the margin of
the state forests some 2,000 feet (609.6 meters) higher, where most of them terminate. In the north, tran-
sects of over twenty miles (thirty-two kilometers)
are possible.
The method of data collection was simple. A prepared sheet was taken into the field, in the appropriate columns of which an assistant entered each house
enumerated. Only houses immediately beside the road
(as most are), were enumerated. In some areas land on
one side of the road was not open to settlement; in
others physiography precluded settlement on one side.
For this reason houses were counted only on the side
of the road, the north being used when necessary. In
this way a continuous transect was obtained. The
record was kept by one mile (1.6 km.) intervals, but
density of housing varied widely from one interval to
the next. The data were consequently smoothed by
three-mile (4.8 km.) intervals. Variation in totals
from one interval to the next was handled by using
percentages. The transect technique was least satisfactory in the south, for here the main area of Kikuyu
settlement is pinched between the former European-
settled areas, and only one suitably long transect
could be devised. There were also problems on this
one route (no. 7 in the figures) since it passed
alternately between areas of Kikuyu and former European occupation now settled by Kikuyu in various postindependence settlement schemes. This had a marked
effect on the distribution of housing quality.
Considerable experience of the area suggested that
interviews with householders concerning some of the
issues which might be involved would be difficult,
yielding questionable results. Questioning on attitudes, wealth, and so on, is sensitive at the best
of times, and particularly when posed by a foreigner.
For these and related reasons, no systematic interviews were attempted.

Field work was conducted in the months of March and July 1966, the break necessitated by the onset of rains which for a few months made the road impassable to all but four-wheel-drive vehicles. 2,200 houses were enumerated and classified. The survey was replicated in five days of July 1971, to test inferences drawn from the 1966 data concerning the order in which changes were taking place. As far as possible the same routes were used, but in one case a cross-valley route had been totally removed; in a second, a route had deteriorated to the point where it was not motorable. In these two cases, the closest parallel routes were used over a short section at the upper end of route two and at the lower end of route four (designated 2a and 4a in the figures for 1971). There is no reason to believe that this change resulted in markedly different results than would otherwise have been obtained except on route four. Here, the village of Mbari ya Igi was omitted from the 1971 transect and probably resulted in a smaller enumeration of traditional housing than might otherwise have been expected. In an attempt to fill out the data somewhat, an additional five routes were surveyed in 1971, but where comparisons over the time period are offered, they refer only to results for the original seven routes and their duplicates. The 1971 survey enumerated a total of 3,577 houses, of which 2,696 were on the original routes of 1966, or their equivalents.

A Classification of Kiambu Housing

The great significance of interior plans demonstrated in other parts of the world is not denied, and is perhaps of equal importance in modern Kiambu. In the desire to cover a fairly large area within a short time period however, exterior characteristics only were considered in the classification of modern housing.

A classification was developed using the easily distinguishable criteria of plan and building material (Table 11.1). The basic distinction made was between circular and rectangular plans, with no distinction as to details of plan. An interesting variation of the circular plan was first noted in the neighborhood of Limuru, where octagonal and some hexagonal houses occurred. These had shingle roofs, and it appeared that the octagonal shape might be an attempt to preserve the circular form while adopting improved roofing materials. This form was highly localized however, and was later found in another localized area near Ruiru, where octagonal houses had thatched roofs. The use here of thatch indicated that this plan was not necessarily an adaptation to new materials.

230

Their numbers were insignificant (amounting to no more than twenty in 1966) and they are believed to have resulted from the influence of a particular administrator. They have been treated as circular in the data. Rectangular plans appeared in great variety, and since this form was entirely new to the Kikuyu scene, there was no reason to suppose that folk preferences would be reflected in these differences in detail, which were not recorded. It may well be, of course, that after a period of experimentation one plan will be deemed more appropriate to social conditions than others. We might then expect new folk forms to emerge.

Wall materials used are stone, galvanized iron, wood and daub. Greatest variation is found in the treatment of wood. The old form of adzed timbers is used in some areas, usually set vertically and associated with circular plans. Milled planks are more common and are usually set horizontally in rectangular plans. These distinctions were not included in the classification. In higher areas, the local bamboo is frequently used in construction, sometimes plastered over with daub though often left exposed and arranged ornamentally in a herringbone pattern. Frequently also, bamboo walls are half covered with daub. Where the bamboo was completely covered, walls were classed as daub, but where only half covered, as wood.

There are also four types of roofing materials. The traditional thatch is giving way in order of preference to flattened kerosene tins, galvanized iron, and tile. Where a roof contained a mixture of materials, it was classed in the category of material lowest in the hierarchy of preference.

It is safe to say that a similar enumeration of house types prior to resettlement in 1959 would have revealed insignificant numbers of rectangular houses. General results of surveys however show that by 1966, just over half of all houses had rectangular plans, and by 1971 the figure was almost seventy percent (Table 11.1). Thus, paradoxically perhaps, the cultural symbol of the circular plan which had withstood the pressures of almost the entire colonial period, was reduced to insignificance in the first decade of independence.

Explanation for Change in Plan

In attempting to explain this dramatic change, it is tempting to postulate adoption of the idea from European immigrants, but such an explanation is too simplistic. Had this been so, we might have expected

231

TABLE 11.1
House Types along Seven Routes in Kiambu District, Classified by Plan and Material of Construction, 1966 and 1971

Wall Material	Tile		Iron[a]		Debi[b]		Thatch		Total
	Circular	Rectangular	Circular	Rectangular	Circular	Rectangular	Circular	Rectangular	
Roof Material and Plan, 1966									
Stone	–	5	–	28	–	–	–	–	33
Iron[a]	–	–	–	10	–	–	–	–	10
Wood	–	1	–	339	3	77	12	9	441
Daub	–	2	–	233	25	202	1,055	199	1,716
Total	–	8	–	610	28	279	1,067	208	2,200[c]
Roof Material and Plan, 1971									
Stone	–	17	–	85	–	–	–	–	102
Iron[a]	–	–	–	13	–	1	–	–	14
Wood	–	–	–	1,000	–	18	7	6	1,131
Daub	–	–	5	265	16	250	810	103	1,449
Total	–	17	5	1,363	16	369	817	109	2,696[d]

Source: Author survey
Notes: a= galvanized, corrugated; b= flattened kerosene tin;
c= 1,095 circular, 1,105 rectangular; d= 838 circular, 1,858 rectangular

232

the rectangular form to develop prominence at an earlier time. Many urban workers had experience of living
in rectangular structures. Had this been a form which
appealed to them, their frequent return to the rural
areas would have provided an adequate mechanism for
the rapid diffusion of the idea. The relatively short
lifespan of rural housing offered frequent opportunities for the adoption of new forms, but such opportunities were not seized. The converse argument is that
the rectangular form was generally rejected prior to
the 1960s because it was European. Yet the Kikuyu must
have been aware of a variety of African cultures in
which the rectangular form was the norm. Many who
worked on the coast would have experienced Swahili
ways; even many of those who had not travelled far
would have seen houses of Somalis and others who had
settled in small numbers in various parts of Kikuyuland. There was no reason therefore to reject the rectangular house as "non-African". The economic argument
against its adoption is also untenable, since it is
quite capable of construction in traditional materials.
This was demonstrated in the colonial period when many
European settlers built rectangular houses of daub and
thatch (though many also built a circular form, the
"rondavel"). A similar example was set earlier by
African groups, and the modern Kikuyu experience again
demonstrates the compatibility of the rectangular form
with traditional materials. We must therefore acknowledge that the adoption of the rectangular form is independent of cost of materials, for they need not be
changed. Clearly a careful systematic study is required
to identify individual perceptions of the issues; the
present study can only draw inferences for further
examination.

The argument that rejection of the rectangular
form through almost the whole colonial period was born
of a general rejection of all innovation is equally untenable, for the Kikuyu have been widely recognized as
innovators. Indeed, as Bascom and Herskovits noted,
" . . . the Kikuyu were so eager to adopt European ways
that, when frustrated in their desires, many resorted
to the violence of Mau Mau".[18] Rather than attempting
to explain the rejection of the rectangular, it is
perhaps more fruitful to ask why the circular form was
retained. Only the postulation of its place in the
culture as an icon seems satisfactory in explaining
its long retention in the face of alternative examples.
Primitive architecture strongly resists change, partly
because in relevant societies there are prescribed
ways of doing things;[19] and form itself becomes institutionalized. In such societies also, ostentation and
individualism are frowned upon, providing further

233

strong motives for following traditional ways. For
the Kikuyu then, adoption of the rectangular plan probably symbolizes a profound change in cultural values.
So the response of one old man, when asked why he was
not building a rectangular house, is significant:
"It is not our Kikuyu way", he said. This statement
reveals an ethnocentric viewpoint from which we can
see that observation of non-Kikuyu examples, whether
African or European, would be essentially irrelevant.
That such attitudes were indeed institutionalized is
demonstrated in the collective folk wisdom. One
proverb runs "Wega uumaga na mochie" (The quality of
a man is judged by his homestead).[20] This traditional
wisdom, however, is two-edged, for it can be used
equally by the conservative and the innovator to
cement his group identity; but initially it must be
seen as a force militating against innovation. The
reaction of the conservative against the more complex
modern house was further enhanced by the custom which
for ritual reasons required completion of a new house
in one day's work. Failure to respect that constraint
was traditionally believed to result in occupation of
the house by evil spirits, and consequent misfortune
to the occupant and his herd.[21] Moreover the more
modern house requiring the skills of craftsmen would
be anathema to those conservatives who still subscribed
to another old tenet: "Mochie ndwathagwo ne otawakire"
(A home is not ruled by one who has not built it).[22]
Those who build modern house forms must thus shed a
number of traditional constraints which would limit
their freedom of action, and must subscribe to a rather
different system than their traditions would teach.
With the development of more complex plans, the provision of extended facilities within the house, and the
utilization of new materials, it becomes at some point
impossible for the family to build a house within the
traditionally prescribed time period, or to build the
house by their own efforts, and new specialization of
skills develops. The point at which these positions
are reached will no doubt vary with the skills and
resources of each individual and the extent to which
he is willing and able to compromise his old values.
If economic constraints are assumed away, then the
potential complexity of housing is liable to increase
with willingness to abandon traditional time and labor
constraints. Economic wellbeing will facilitate such
change, but not cause it.

Retention of the traditional circular plan in
the postcolonial period is shown to have been greater
in the more remote parts of the district, particularly
in the north. This is related to both economic and

cultural factors. The advent of the modern economy
has resulted in a reevaluation of locational advantage
among participating farmers.[23] In terms of the traditional economy it was the northerners, possessed of
larger farms, who were best able to maintain their
traditional values and agricultural system; southerners
were forced in a variety of ways to an early compromise
of these values. Yet in the modern system the balance
has shifted increasingly in favor of the southerner
with his greater proximity to labor and produce markets
of the intrusive immigrant culture and its city. The
greater change in cultural values and attitudes which
had occurred in the south by the mid-1950s is best
demonstrated by the fact that private ownership of land
had come to be more widely recognized here than in the
north.[24] Though an examination of the Fragmentation
Registers compiled at the time of land consolidation
in 1956 has never been undertaken, it was the convic-
tion of the officers concerned that such an examination
would identify significant differences in levels of
private ownership between north and south. Examination
of the Register for Tinganga sublocation in the south
showed that among 851 landowners, fifty-four percent
(controlling seventy-five percent of the land) had en-
joyed private ownership prior to land consolidation,
which conferred it on all.[25] The extent of private ownership is significant because land was central to the
social structure. Rejection of traditional forms of
communal tenure implied most fundamentally a rejection
of the traditional hierarchy and its associated values.
Although it was the pressures of the modern economic
system which caused the change in values, it was these
changed values rather than economic influences in
supply of materials, which most significantly influenced the decision to adopt the rectangular plan.

Changes in Materials

        Although information was not collected in any
structured fashion, discussion indicated that among some
Kikuyu rebuilding homes in the 1960s, their order of
priority when changes in style were contemplated was
to change first the plan, secondly roof materials, and
finally wall materials. These attitudes are borne out
by data. For both 1966 and 1971 the numbers abandoning
circular plans exceeded those abandoning thatched roofs;
and similarly, abandonment of thatched roofs exceeded
that of daub walls. The adoption of changed roofing
materials was likely to precede a change in wall materials because of the ready availability of the ubiquitous
and cheap "debi" (kerosene tin). The debi was readily

available because of the extensive use of kerosene in
rural households, and cheap because its transport costs
had already been borne by the kerosene which it originally contained. Opened out, the debi yields a toler-
ably good roofing material although its life span is
short. More durable galvanized corrugated iron was
also becoming available at reasonable cost as a result
of redevelopment in the towns, providing a second-hand
supply. Most expensive of the new roofing materials
were tiles, and even in 1971 few houses had tile roofs
(see Table 11.1). A further factor inhibiting the adoption of tiles was their weight. They really require
stone walls, not only for weight reasons but because
only stone will match the tile in durability. Of
the few houses which in 1966 possessed tile roofs on
wooden and even on daub walls, none survived in 1971,
and there were no emulators. The choice of improved
roofing materials for the great majority of innovators
thus lay between debi and galvanized iron. The life
span of the easily corroded debi is much shorter than
that of galvanized iron. Although it is considered
preferable to thatch, debi lasts no longer and is regarded as a transitional material. For most people
adopting new roof materials, the rectangular plan is
prerequisite. A few however had retained the circular
plan while adopting new roofing materials. In such
cases debi was more common, being more flexible than
corrugated iron and more adaptable to circular structures. Nevertheless in 1971 a few circular houses
were found with iron roofs.
    In the adoption of new wall materials, prefer-
ence was clearly for some form of wood. Stone was very
costly, both the cost of labor in dressing it and
transportation; nor was it available on the second-hand
market. Galvanized iron was less costly, and indeed in
some places could be acquired more cheaply than some
forms of milled timber. There was however a strong dis-
inclination to use it. No single explanation for its
almost universal rejection can be given. Some people
were clearly aware of the discomfort of living in iron
structures which are not insulated, but there was also
some evidence of antipathy based on **aesthetics or on**
grounds of status: one man associated iron houses
with laborers' quarters, another with the use of iron
for building store sheds. Wood was plentifully available, much more durable than daub, with good insulation
properties, and also familiar to all.

The Diffusion of Innovation

    If we regard the circular house with thatched
roof and daub wall as having become "traditional" by

the late colonial period, then by 1966 there had been
a marked departure from tradition, for it now accounted for less than half of all houses enumerated (see
Table 11.1). By 1971 this figure had dropped to less
than one-third of all houses. Given the growing preference for rectangular structures, for iron roofs and
for wooden walls, it is not surprising that houses combining these elements should become the new norm. In
1971 such houses accounted for nearly forty percent of
all houses enumerated (Table 11.1). This new vernacu-
lar structure is most common in the southern parts of
the district, occurring with markedly less frequency
in the north.

The distribution of changes in house-type is
most easily analyzed through the study of retention
of the old forms. On both social and economic grounds,
traditional elements would be expected to occur with
greatest frequency in the north, and most particularly
in the highland areas. And this is indeed the case.
There is a marked decline in occurrence of "traditional" housing components as one moves from the northern
to southern routes (Figure 11.1). Not only were cultural constraints reduced at an earlier time in the
south, but economic factors were operative. With
greater access to the modern economy disposable income
was higher, so there was greater potential for investment in improved housing than in the north. Furthermore, being closer to the supply of modern building
materials, the transport element accounted for a lower
proportion of cost of modern housing in the south.
An additional factor here might be the higher land
values which enabled southern farmers to raise more
credit than their fellows to the north. The most obvious demonstration of this is in the distribution of
stone houses: in 1966 eighty percent of all stone houses
were on the macadamized section of route seven though
by 1971 the equivalent figure had dropped to forty
percent.

The tendency for retention of traditional forms
to be higher on the "southern" routes six and seven
than on route five requires some explanation. Both
routes run into relatively remote highland zones, and
one would expect the old forms to be retained. However
there are also large numbers of houses containing traditional elements even quite close to Nairobi. This
must be attributed to the high proportion of landless
and poor people in the southern parts of the district,
arising partly from congestion caused by alienation of
large amounts of land to European ownership in the
early colonial period, and partly from historical circumstances of Kikuyu migration into southern Kiambu.[26]

During land consolidation, therefore, more villages were created in the south and they tended to be larger than in the north. Consequently, longer sections of these routes run through villages where housing tends to be more traditional than elsewhere. At the same time, data for 1971 showed that on other southern routes less accessible than the macadamized routes six and seven retention of traditional elements was even higher; so it may be that in the south generally the retention of traditional elements may be greater than results for the improved routes six and seven suggest. Routes ten and eleven were of poor quality and difficult for motor transport even in the dry season, so it may be that accessibility per se is a significant factor influencing house types, particularly in the south. In the north, road quality is not nearly so variable as in the south, so that relative accessibility is more clearly a function solely of distance. The greater diversity not only in accessibility but also in socioeconomic status in the south may be expected to give rise to greater local variation in housing than is found in the north.

Analysis of data by individual route showed that in general the frequency of occurrence of traditional components increased with distance from the lower district margins (see Figures 11:2 and 11.3). Accessibility is the main factor though significant departures from the general trend can be observed. Where villages occur, there is a marked tendency for an increase in traditional housing. These villages were created during land consolidation and their residents are mainly the landless or nearly landless. It was also a design of land consolidation that smaller farms should be located close to villages. To the extent then that we may expect farm size to correlate with wealth, and economic factors to influence house type, we may expect more traditional housing in proximity to villages. A good example is the densely settled area round the village of Kiairie on route six (Figure 11.3). Conversely, the distribution of service centers accords with the occurrence of more modern housing. The most striking example is Githunguri on routes five and six (Figure 11.3). Githunguri has for long been one of the principal administrative centers of the district and this might be an important factor, though the same influence is found near even smaller centers such as Ngenya on route four (Figure 11.2). Precisely what factors are at work requires further investigation. It is conceivable that employment opportunities in Githunguri give rise to a market for improved rental housing. It is also possible that manipulation at the time of consolidation, or

238

FIGURE 11.1

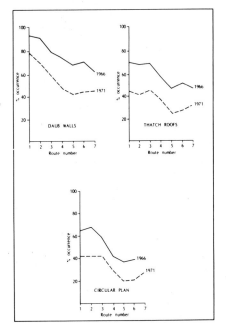

DISTRIBUTION OF "TRADITIONAL"
ELEMENTS IN KIAMBU HOUSING
BY ROUTE, 1966 AND 1971

FIGURE 11.2

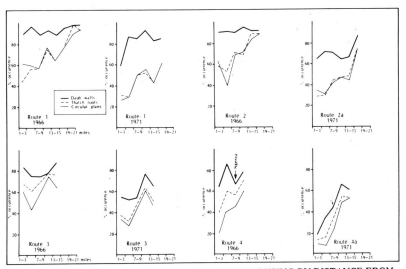

DISTRIBUTION OF "TRADITIONAL" ELEMENTS IN HOUSING BY DISTANCE FROM
LOWER DISTRICT MARGIN ALONG ROUTES 1–4a, 1966 AND 1971

239

FIGURE 11.3

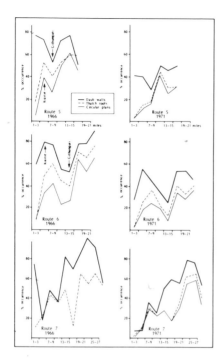

DISTRIBUTION OF "TRADITIONAL"
ELEMENTS IN HOUSING BY DISTANCE
FROM LOWER DISTRICT MARGIN
ALONG ROUTES 5–7, 1966 AND 1971

subsequent land transactions, have enabled wealthier
farmers to locate near trading centers. This influence was less marked in 1971 than in 1966, suggesting
that local variations are being eliminated relatively
quickly as modernization of housing diffuses over
the landscape.

It is appropriate now to look at some departures from the broad generalizations which have been
made, particularly with regard to conditions in the
southern parts of the district. It must be recognized
that the two main routes along which housing was enumerated in the south were unusual. Both had been important routes for many years. That section of route
seven south of Limuru, being the trunk road to Uganda,
had long been macadamized, and route six, the main
road to the administrative center of Githunguri, was
also macadamized at the time of the first survey.
They thus offered superior communications with the
city of Nairobi, and it is suggested that for this
reason the most expensive types of modern housing
were to be found along them; yet at the same time, in
contravention of the generalization that retention of

traditional forms tends to decline towards the south,
they had higher proportions of these forms than the
more northerly route five. If accessibility is a
factor predisposing to more modern housing, then we
should expect that results for these two routes would
be unrepresentative of the general situation in the
south: that traditional elements would be underenumer-
ated. In 1971 the survey was extended to three routes
which though short, were of considerably lower quality;
and it was found that indeed on routes eight, ten and
eleven, the retention of traditional elements was higher than results for routes six and seven would lead us
to expect. Despite the greater adoption of more modern housing in the south therefore, at the same time
there is also a greater retention of traditional forms.
This is attributable to the greater proportion of poor
in the south, a situation caused by two features of
the historical settlement of the area:
     First, the south had larger proportions of the
traditionally landless ahoi who had moved south in
the forefront of the nineteenth century migration into
Kiambu.[27] Consequently population densities under
normal circumstances would have been greater, and farm
sizes smaller. These effects were augmented by the
alienation of significant amounts of land to European
ownership in the early years of the twentieth century.
In combination, these forces resulted in not only
more landless people in the south, but smaller farm
sizes, a greater percentage of really small farms,
and more severe fragmentation of holdings. So although
a number of farmers had been able to profit by their
proximity to the Nairobi market, the disposable income
of a large sector of the population was still small.
These economic circumstances would explain higher
levels of use of traditional building materials. We
find however that the conservative circular plan was
also retained by higher proportions of householders
on these southerly routes. This would argue for the
proposition that there is a correlation between economic status and conservative attitudes; until there
is an investigation of this proposition however, we
cannot assert causality, though the inference is strong.
     Spatial patterns associated with these phenomena
(see Figure 11.4) suggest that modern economic factors
combine with traditional social factors to influence
decisions concerning modernization of housing. Conservative values in areas remote from modern foci tend
to preserve the old form, and the relative cost of
modern materials — highest in these same areas —
enhances those forces which inhibit modernization.
The patterns for 1966 and 1971 are broadly similar,
but clearly the north was developing as rapidly as

FIGURE 11.4

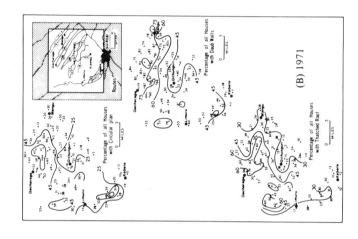

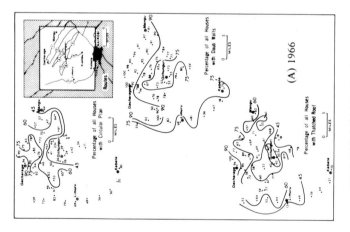

DISTRIBUTION OF "TRADITIONAL" ELEMENTS IN HOUSING, KIAMBU DISTRICT

242

the south during the period. In fact by 1971, traditional forms in the north had fallen to levels which
had typified the south five years earlier. Thus there
is a time lag between north and south, but no absolute
barrier to change, and it must be anticipated that
greater homogeneity in housing will develop.

Conclusion

First we have to be wary of a too-easy generalization of the character of traditional housing in
Africa, for evidence suggests that Kiambu is not the
only area in which traditional house-form and construction techniques were variable. It seems likely that
at least for the recent period (post-1880), variation
in these techniques in Kiambu was related to availability of resources. But it should be noted that if
the palisade construction was indeed the traditional
ideal, it was a form in which materials outlasted the
useful life of the structure.[28] (Periodic rebuilding
might be required variously by the rationale of a
shifting agricultural economy or for a variety of
ritualized social reasons.) That this was so gives
the lie to those who rationalize the traditional daub
structure's usage in terms of the designed structural
life of housing. It is indeed a paradox that as
development of a more stable settlement pattern enabled
longer use of the palisade structure, the simultaneous
reduction in availability of sturdy building materials
enforced in most areas the adoption of structures
with shorter life span.
When changes occurred in the availability of building materials, leading in the precolonial period to
the adoption of new construction methods, form was preserved in retention of the circular plan, in accordance
with the general hypothesis that form persists regardless of materials. However in the later modernizing
period evidence suggests that form tended to change
even when materials did not. This of course further
supports the general principle that form is to a large
extent independent of materials; but it also demonstrates that although form may be persistent, circumstances can arise in which very rapid change in form is
possible. Such rapid change has to be socially acceptable and there has to be a widely diffused knowledge
of the adaptive form. Another vital factor encouraging rapid change in Kiambu was the fragility and short
lifespan of housing, requiring fairly frequent rebuilding. Coupled with this, the redispersion of settlement out of the emergency villages when land consolidation was completed in 1959 resulted in a great wave

243

of new building. Land reform was causing great change
in the whole social and economic fabric, and the spirit
of reform was further strengthened by the promise of
early national independence. Such powerful forces in
combination kindled in many a spirit of rebirth in
which the receptivity to innovation was especially
strong.

The influence of European values cannot be underestimated. Fifty or sixty years of contact, direct
and indirect, could not but have profound impact on a
new generation now wishing to demonstrate its freedom
not only from colonial power, but also from at least
some of the strictures of traditional life. The most
powerful impact was undoubtedly experienced by those
in urban environments, planned and designed — at least
in their basics — in the British tradition. The impact of this urban experience on rural areas was
ensured by that system of selective male migration
which has so often been decried as one of the iniqui-
ties of the colonial period. Had the urban migrant divorced himself from rural origins, had he brought his
whole family to town,we might expect that the impact
of his experience on rural life would have been minimized. But that social and economic system whereby
he retained his rural associations provided a powerful
mechanism for the diffusion of innovation.

Proximity to diffusion foci is shown as an important influence on change in housing. If we were
dealing only with building materials, it might be
argued that the most important influence on the diffusion of innovation was transport cost — which no
doubt has had an impact. But the adoption of new
plans follows the same pattern as adoption of new
materials; and the two can be and frequently are
unrelated. That the areas where the rectangular plan
was earliest adopted are close to the city of Nairobi
or other centers of modernization, must be associated
with their importance as diffusion foci.

Finally, when changes in materials are considered
it is clear that roofing materials tend to be changed
in advance of wall materials. Of importance here is
the extensive use of kerosene, giving rise to the wide
availability of discarded containers, cheaply obtained
and readily used for roofing. Other forms of roofing
and wall materials are not so easily obtained, are
certainly not found as waste products from other enterprise, and involve considerably more expense. That
urban foci of innovation are also the most common
sources of these other new building materials, explains
the coincident pattern of adoption of new plans and
materials.

Though cost is clearly one relevant variable,
there are obviously others. Further research is required before it is too late, to elucidate the factors
involved. For example accessibility to materials in
terms of quality of communication is a possible factor.
This was obvious in the marked differences in frequency of occurrence of various materials between the two
adjacent routes ten and eleven as compared with route
seven, and route nine compared with route one.   Thus
while on route seven the macadamized trunk road to
Uganda, the occurrence of daub walls was on the order
of thirty percent in 1971, only one or two ridges away
where the road is barely passable even in dry season,
daub walls account for something like fifty-five percent of the total. Similarly on route nine, improved
to all-weather standards only in the late 1960s for
the extraction of tea, circular houses accounted for
only some twenty-five percent of the total — while
on a route a couple of ridges away they accounted for
fifty percent. This might be purely coincidental,
but that is doubtful and a phenomenon deserving of
investigation. The social attitudes of the people
also warrant examination and their effect on housing
decisions. It might be interesting to know if there
is any correlation between the occupant's age and
house type. In other words it would be nice to separate the socio- from the -economic in the determination
of house types among the Kikuyu. The distribution
of house types suggests some leads which should be
followed up not only for their contribution to an explanation of house types themselves, but for their
possible significance in the distribution of other
geographic patterns.

NOTES

1. N. Gebremedhin, "Some Traditional Types of
Housing in Ethiopia", in Shelter in Africa, P. Oliver
(ed.), (London: Bassie and Jenkins, 1971), p. 113.
2. U.S. Department of Housing and Urban Development, Division of International Affairs, Country Report
Series, Housing in the Ivory Coast (Washington, D.C.:
1966), p. 14; U.S. Department of Housing and Urban
Development, Division of International Affairs, Country Report Series, Housing in Nigeria (Washington, D.C.:
1964), p. 8. This question is also addressed in D.R.
Lee, "Factors Influencing Choice of House Type: a
Geographic Analysis from the Sudan", Professional Geographer, vol. 21 (1969), pp. 393-397. That attempts
may however be made to retain some traditional elements
is shown in D.R. Lee, "The Nubian House: Persistence of
a Cultural Tradition", Landscape, 18: 1 (1969),pp.36-39.

245

3. "Cylindrical" is the term used in S.D. Dodge, "House Types in Africa", Papers, Michigan Academy of Science, Arts and Letters, 10 (1929), p. 61. Similar structures are referred to as "cone-on-cylinder" in J. Walton, African Village (Pretoria: J.L van Schaik 1956), p. 228.

4. Gebremedhin, op.cit., pp. 117-119.

5. Ibid., pp. 114-116.

6. Walton, op.cit., p. 135.

7. P. Oliver, Shelter in Africa (London: Bassie and Jenkins, 1971), p. 18. However Oliver also recognizes the importance of cultural factors.

8. W. Goldschmidt, "Foreward", in Architecture in Northern Ghana: a Study of Forms and Functions, L. Prussin (ed.) (Berkeley: University of California Press, 1969), p. 1.

9. Walton, op.cit., p. 136.

10. Sources in which descriptions of traditional Kikuyu housing may be found are: J. Boyes, King of the Wakikuyu (London: Frank Cass & Co., 1968), p.83; C. Cagnolo, The Akikuyu: Their Customs, Traditions and Folklore (Nyeri: The Mission Printing School, 1933), pp. 53-55; R. Crawshay, "Kikuyu: Notes on the Country, People, Fauna and Flora", Geographical Journal, 20 (1902), p. 33; and J. Kenyatta, Facing Mount Kenya (New York: Vintage Books, 1962), pp.74-82.

11. F.B. Kniffen and H. Glassie, "Building in Wood in the Eastern United States: a Time-Place Perspective", Geographical Review, 56 (1966), p. 43. Diffusionists might care to consider the broader issues of how the Kikuyu practice relates to the spread of this "palisade" technique of construction. Perhaps herein might be another clue to the riddle of the Bantu expansion.

12. R.A. Bullock, "Subsistence to Cash: Economic Change in Rural Kiambu", Cahiers d'etudes Africaines, 56 (1975), pp. 699-714.

13. Anonymous, Land tenure file (Nairobi: Ministry of Agriculture Library).

14. Bullock, op.cit.

15. Ibid.

16. R.A. Bullock, "Landscape Change in Kiambu", East African Geographical Review, 3 (1965), pp.37-45.

17. The preference for galvanized iron has been noted for other areas in A. Rapoport, House Form and Culture, (Englewood Cliffs: Prentice-Hall 1969),p.22f.

18. W.R. Bascome and M.J. Herskovits (eds.), Continuity and Change in African Cultures (Chicago: University of Chicago Press 1962), p. 4.

19. Rapoport, op.cit., p.6.

20. Kenyatta, op.cit., p. 74.

21. Ibid., p. 76.

22. Cagnolo, op.cit., p. 218.
23. Bullock,"Subsistence to Cash ..", op.cit.,
24. Ibid.
25. R.A. Bullock, Land Consolidation in Kiambu, Kenya - a Study in Social and Agrarian Change, (M.A. thesis, Queen's University of Belfast, 1960), p.46.
26. Anonymous, op.cit.
27. Ibid.
28. Kenyatta has indicated that building materials might become family heirlooms, "sacred relics", to be used in the periodic rebuilding of the homestead. Kenyatta, op.cit., p.81f.

12. Spatial Variations in Oil Prices in Kenya—A Case of Peripheral Exploitation

Alan G. Ferguson

Introduction

The concern of the geographer with spatial aspects of economic development has become both more intensive and extensive during the past decade. The early descriptive-empiricist stage with its piecemeal and subjective appearance gave way to the spatial analysis approach by Soja,[1] Berry,[2] Taaffe, Morrill and Gould,[3] which stressed "modernization" and its quantitative measurement. While both approaches are still in evidence, an alternative view of the development process and its spatial ramifications is gaining ground. The approach stems from the center-periphery models of Myrdal,[4] Hirschman[5] and Friedmann[6] but is strongly influenced by the work of Marxist underdevelopment theorists such as Baran[7] and Frank.[8] Basically this approach, best summarized by Brookfield,[9,10], attacks conventional views on modernization as being prowestern and views the center-periphery relationships evident in many underdeveloped countries as exploitive rather than as necessary concomitants of economic growth. It is from this position that the present chapter is written.

[Despite the perpetual reemphasis of its commitment to rural development and regional equality, the Kenyan government has been unable to make significant inroads in a country where development was strongly polarized in the core urban and agricultural areas before independence, and where there is much evidence of continuing or increasing spatial concentration of

Grateful thanks to John Garling of the University of Sheffield and Dave Barker of Bedford College, University of London, for valuable assistance with the computer routine.

the artifacts of development.This has been discussed fully in several of the earlier chapters in this book. See,e.g.
Leys,[11] House and Rempel,[12] and Kinyanjui[13].

Domination of the major sectors of the Kenyan
economy by a few large firms, almost all wholly or
partially controlled from overseas, has aided the formation of monopolies, oligopolies and market-sharing
arrangements. The government's priority appears to
be the maintenance of a high national growth rate, a
priority outweighing most other considerations. Thus
there are minimal locational controls on industry in
Kenya and in the absence of strong material-oriented
location factors, industry and commerce are strongly
concentrated in Nairobi with secondary poles in Mombasa, Thika and Nakuru.[14]

Despite some isolated attempts at distributing
commerce and industry more evenly throughout the country, the pattern of strong concentration in the major
urban areas is a classic center-periphery feature,
strongly characteristic of a neocolonial economy.

The present study is an attempt to show, using
the example of the distribution of petroleum products,
how the core areas of Kenya actively exploit the peripheries. The Kenyan government is seen as partially
responsible for the existence of this situation since
the government has a large degree of financial and
fiscal control over the oil-refining industry in the
country and over the distribution of petroleum products.

Pricing Policies and Transport Mode

Mineral oil products in Kenya are obtained from
the refining of crude oil at the Changamwe oil refinery
in Mombasa. This is the sole supplier in Kenya of petroleum products, and is jointly owned by a consortium
of multinational oil companies with a fifty percent
shareholding by the Kenya government. Although fuel
oil and turbo fuel are the major refinery products by
volume, petrol (in two octanes), diesel and lighting
kerosene account for almost all the retail sales value.

With a single supply source and a free-on-board
(f.o.b.) transport pricing system, one would imagine
that spatial variations in the retail price of these
products would be a simple function of distance from
Mombasa. In the f.o.b. system the product is priced
at the supply source and the consumer bears the transport cost directly. This contrasts with the cost-
insurance-freight system (c.i.f.) where there is no
spatial variation in retail price, the distribution
costs being averaged out and added to the supply
source price.

The pricing system used for the retailing of petroleum products in Kenya is not however a true f.o.b.
system and price variations do not correspond exactly
to variations in distance from Mombasa. This is a
result of two factors: pricing policies and mode of
transport used in distribution. These are the only
factors involved, since there is little or no variation in the prices of different brands. The oil
companies form an effective cartel and although some
areas of Kenya are dominated by a particular company,
retail prices are set according to uniform principles.
The Kenya government in consultation with the oil companies fixes the retail price of the main products at
nine supply depots, which apart from Mombasa and
Kisumu are all located in the former White Highlands
area.* Prices fixed basically reflect cost of rail
transport from Mombasa even though many depots receive
part of their supply by road. All other retail outlets are supplied by road from these supply depots.
A standard charge for road distribution is also agreed
upon berween government and oil companies. This is
currently set at ninety cents per thousand liters per
kilometer — considerably higher than the actual cost
of road distribution. This cost is borne entirely
by the consumer.
    Retail prices therefore incorporate two different
distance effects:

    (a) distance from Mombasa

    (b) distance from nearest supply depot

    The pricing depots were established during the
colonial period with the aim of serving the white population whose vehicles and machinery formed the main
source of demand. The present distribution system
may therefore be considered somewhat anachronistic as
it continues to favor the former European areas. In
the most underdeveloped parts of Kenya prices of petroleum products tend to be extremely high with an atten-
dant rise in the cost of living induced by the strong
multiplier effect of high fuel prices. Perhaps more
important is evidence that supply depot prices do not
reflect actual transport costs, and that the richest
areas are being subsidized by the poorest.

Mapping Oil Price Variations

    Data were collected from three major oil compa-
nies, and consisted of prices of the four major

---

* Supply depots are located at Mombasa, Nairobi, Naro
Moru, Nanyuki, Gilgil, Nakuru, Londiani, Kisumu and
Eldoret.

petroleum products retailed in seventy-six outlets
throughout Kenya after the price rise of June 12, 1975.
A smaller data set consisting of thirty-nine points
was collected for three earlier price rises. A further price rise occurred in March 1976 but this simply
increased all retail prices by ten cents per liter
across the board. The price difference between any
two locations is the same for each of the four petroleum products since transport costs do not vary by
type of product. Relative differences are variable
however since the products have different values —
e.g., premium grade petrol is almost twice as expensive as kerosene.
    Figures 12.1(a) and (b) show the location of data
points for the two sets of observations. These correspond mainly to the main population concentrations in
Kenya, particularly the smaller data set where there
are few points outside Central, Nyanza and Western
Provinces. The effect of the irregular coverage of
the area is to increase the likelihood of interpolation errors in the sparsely inhabited areas in the
north of the country. Main population zones are however adequately covered by both data sets and the
larger one also includes several remote locations in
the north.
    [The maps produced from the data were drawn by
computer using a two-stage algorithm,[15] first over-
laying a regular grid on the map to estimate prices
at grid intersections using the six nearest data points,
and second interpolating isolines from these estimated
values.]
    Figure 12.2 shows an isodapane (price-contour)
map of premium petrol prices at June 12, 1975 measured
in cents above the Mombasa price. The effects of
transport mode and pricing policies are clearly shown.
Generally prices increase with distance from Mombasa,
but price increases are neither monotonic nor equal
in all directions. A corridor of relatively low prices
follows the railway to Nairobi, Eldoret and Kisumu.
Prices rise sharply on both sides of this corridor,
reflecting the higher cost of road distribution. The
Nairobi-Nakuru-Nanyuki area displays a price depression due to the low prices at Nairobi, Nakuru, Gilgil,
Nanyuki and Naro Moru. The map also shows a price
ridge between Nairobi and Mombasa. Despite their
situation on the railway, outlets at Sultan Hamud, Mtito
Andei and Voi are supplied by road from Nairobi or Mombasa, thereby incurring high prices (e.g. Mtito Andei,
half as far from Mombasa as Nairobi, pays a retail
price of twelve cents more per liter. Such anomalies
reflect the existence of backhauling and the delivery

251

FIGURE 12.1

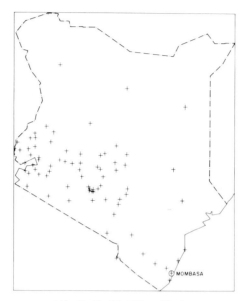

(A)   DATA POINTS   6/12/75

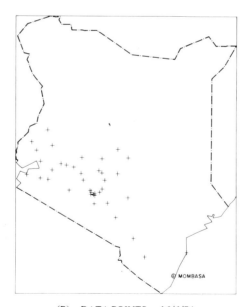

(B)   DATA POINTS   16/6/74

252

FIGURE 12.2

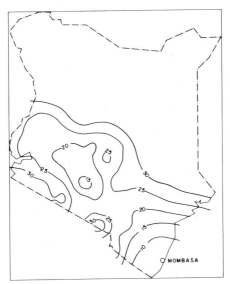

PREMIUM PETROL PRICES   6/12/75
IN CENTS ABOVE MOMBASA PRICE

of supplies by relatively expensive road haulage.
Physical barriers also play a role in distorting
simple straight-line distance effects. For example,
circuitous delivery routes result in "price peaks" in
the Meru-Embu, Kitui, Amboseli and Keekorok areas.

     Figure 12.3 presents the same information in an
isometric projection from the southeast. The low-
price corridor, peaks and depressions referred to
above are clearly shown. Nairobi is just hidden by
the price ridge at Mtito Andei. Figure 12.4 shows
the price of kerosene at June 12, 1975 relative to
the price at Mombasa. Kerosene is the cheapest of
the four products considered, so this map shows the
highest degree of relative variation. The pattern
of isodapanes is identical to that of Figure 12.2,
but the relative price differences are very high.
Kerosene is a widely used product in rural areas and
these differences are more significant for the average
mwananchi than the ones shown in Figure 12.2.

Modal Split and Price Discrimination

     Supply depots are located in the richest and most
productive areas of Kenya and are all supplied by rail
from Mombasa. However, variable amounts of petroleum

253

FIGURE 12.3

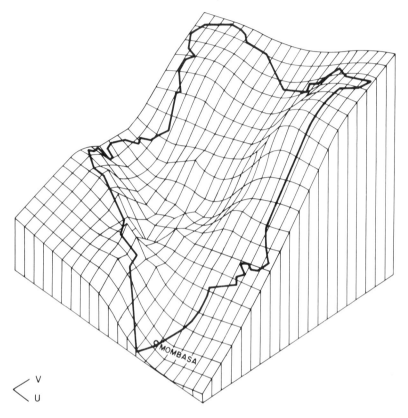

PREMIUM PETROL PRICES AT / 6/12/75 – ISOMETRIC PROJECTION

products are delivered to these depots by road. Exact
figures for road deliveries were "not available" from
the oil companies but one company stated that about
one third of its Nairobi supplies were shipped by
road. The method of pricing at the supply depots
"took both road and rail transport into consideration",
according to another oil company. However when we
examine retail price at supply depots we find that the
contribution to retail price made by road transport is
apparently very small indeed.

The cost of bulk transport to Nairobi from Mombasa by rail is shs. 13/60 per 100 kilos, which is
approximately twenty cents per thousand liters-per-
kilometer. This compares with the ninety cents-per-
thousand liters-per-kilometer levied by oil companies
for road deliveries.

FIGURE 12.4

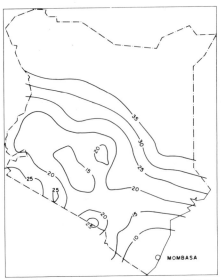

KEROSENE PRICES AS
PERCENTAGE ABOVE MOMBASA PRICE   6/12/75

   Figure 12.5 shows current retail prices of premium petrol at various points along the Mombasa-Kisumu
highway. The supply depots at·Mombasa, Nairobi, Gilgil, Nakuru, Londiani (just off the Nakuru-Kisumu
road), and Kisumu appear clearly as low-price locations
while other locations display local peaks in a generally rising trend. Except for the Molo-Kisumu section,
rail and road distances are approximately equal, and
when supply depots are linked to each other the result
is an almost-regular straight-line function. This
appears as the dashed line on Figure 12.5 and represents the price/distance relationship between Mombasa
the other supply depots. This can be calculated at
twenty-three cents per thousand liters-per-kilometer:
i.e., three cents above rail freight rate alone. Thus
it appears that road delivery costs figure to a very
small degree in pricing of fuel at supply depots even
though substantial amounts are delivered by road. We
may therefore logically conclude that petroleum products are sold at supply depot locations at a subsidized price since actual transport costs are not included. Alternatively, actual road transport costs are
far below the fixed rate of ninety cents and the oil
companies are choosing to make a lower rate of profit
on sales at supply depot areas. Thus, excess profits
to the oil companies are accumulated by pricing fuel

255

FIGURE 12.5

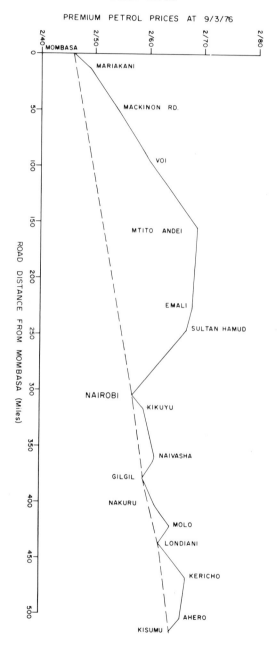

PREMIUM PETROL PRICES AT 9/3/76

256

fuel delivered by road from supply depots at well above actual cost, for the wholesale/retail price markup is in the region of five percent for all locations, which is not excessively high.

Thus we find that if price levied by oil companies for road transport from supply depots reflects actual cost involved, then fuel sold in supply depots is almost certainly priced below cost. Alternatively if prices at supply depot areas reflect actual transport costs then prices at nonsupply depot locations must be excessive. Investigation led to confirmation that this is the case and prices are indeed excessive. Although both oil companies and haulage contractors are very reluctant to reveal their pricing and distribution agreements, it appears that actual road transport costs are around twenty-five cents per thousand liters per kilometer. In other words, oil companies are making sixty-five cents per kilometer profit (less a small amount for handling charges) on every thousand liters of fuel delivered by road from the supply depots. The peripheral areas can therefore be seen to be suffering from price discrimination as a direct result of pricing policies set jointly by government and oil companies; and the more remote a retail outlet, the greater the penalty paid by the consumer. The motive behind this seems to be a cheap fuel policy for centers of industry and commerce, and provision of additional income to oil companies which may be used to offset additional costs incurred when unusually large amounts of fuel are shipped by road from Mombasa to the supply depots.

Increasing Spatial Disparities in Time

The position of peripheral areas vis-à-vis central areas is being constantly eroded by regularly increasing crude oil prices. And road transport costs are more affected by a price rise than rail transport costs, as more fuel is used per unit of volume/distance by road transportation. Small increases in crude oil prices may be absorbed by haulage companies, but eventually their prices (and therefore the government and oil companies' agreed price) must rise in order to maintain the same rate of profit.

In the four price rises to December 1975 there has been one adjustment each in rail and road haulage rates. The effects may be seen in Table 12.1 for prices in Mombasa, Nairobi (supplied by rail from Mombasa), and Kitui (supplied by road from Nairobi). Price disparity between Kitui and Mombasa was twenty-three cents per liter on June 16, 1974; and by December 12, 1975 this had risen to twenty-nine cents. During

257

the same period the difference between Nairobi and Mombasa had only risen from nine to eleven cents.[*]

TABLE 12.1
Premium Petrol Price Changes at Mombasa, Nairobi and Kitui

	Date of Price Change			
	16/6/74	20/2/75 [1]	14/6/75	6/12/75 [2]
Mombasa	1.83	1.93	2.17	2.36
Nairobi	1.92	2.03	2.27	2.47
Kitui	2.06	2.17	2.41	2.65

(Kshs. per liter)

Price Differences		(in cents)		
Mombasa-Nairobi	9	10	10	11
Nairobi-Kitui	14	14	14	18
Mombasa-Kitui	23	24	24	29

[1] Increase in rail freight rate
[2] Increase in road haulage rate

The effects of a rise in road haulage rates over the whole country can be seen by comparing Figure 12.2 with Figure 12.6 which shows premium prices in cents above the Mombasa price at June 16, 1974. The price contours in Figure 12.2 are much more closely aligned than in Figure 12.6, showing sharply rising prices in areas served predominantly by road transport. The position of particular isodapanes has also changed markedly. For example, the +15 cents price contour which enclosed a substantial part of southeast Kenya and the Nairobi-Eldoret-Nanyuki area in June 1974 has shrunk, to enclose only a small part of Coast Province and the immediate periurban area of Nairobi. Thus with increasing crude oil prices, spatial disparities in retail prices must continue to increase unless

[*] Since this research was completed there have been further price changes: pump prices as of October 1977 were as follows: Mombasa: 2.76, Nairobi: 2.89, Kitui: 3.07. (ed.note: prices have since increased even further).

FIGURE 12.6

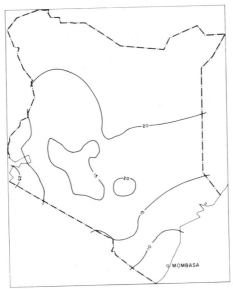

PREMIUM PETROL PRICES   16/6/74
IN CENTS ABOVE MOMBASA PRICE

there are changes in the present system of pricing
and distribution. The economic center of Kenya is
benefiting from these arrangements to the cost of the
periphery. This is seen as a backwash or polarization
effect in the models of Friedmann, Myrdal and Frank.
Transportation and distribution costs to the Kenyan
periphery are increased thereby hindering chances of
development under the present economic system. Since
these disparities result mainly from deliberate policy
decisions, it is in order to consider how the situation could be improved by alternative pricing and
distribution methods.

Alternative Pricing and Distribution Policies

c.i.f. Pricing

A change to a c.i.f. system of pricing would
average out all transport costs and give each product
a standard price throughout Kenya. The richer parts
of the country would then subsidize the poorer parts,
which would reverse the present situation and make
accounting procedures much easier. c.i.f. pricing is
however rejected by oil companies because prices would

259

be forced up in the Nairobi and Mombasa areas. This is deemed "politically unacceptable" by oil companies despite the fact that around two thirds of all retail sales are made in these two areas and resultant price rises would therefore be slight. By the oil companies' own evidence the urban political and economic elite of Kenya seem sufficiently powerful to resist even this modest regional equalization measure.

Price Zoning

In this system fixed retail prices would be established for broad regional zones. The remotest areas in each zone would therefore benefit from lower prices. This solution is favored by one oil company, and is certainly an improvement on the present system. However, unless a smaller number of zones is established, peripheral exploitation is still likely. In addition, price zoning tends to lead to boundary problems: for example the shadow effects of cheaper zones may affect retail outlets in nearby more expensive zones unless boundaries are carefully set. While price zoning is a more acceptable way of pricing than f.o.b., it is therefore less desirable than c.i.f. pricing.

Alternative Distribution Methods

There is a clear underuse of rail capacity and overuse of road haulage. The main justification for this by oil companies is the inefficiency of East African Railways but there are strong political pressures on oil companies to use privately-owned road haulage facilities. Apart from the inflationary effects of using road transport to shift supplies from Mombasa to supply depots, there are social costs which are not taken into account: e.g. the high rate of accidents involving oil tankers, and damage caused to the surface of the Mombasa-Nairobi Road. Even without substantially increasing the volume of oil products carried by rail, some of the worst anomalies of the present system could be removed: for example a small supply depot in the Kibwezi area supplied by rail would benefit a high-cost area of Eastern Province now served by road from Nairobi. The recommendation that all depots be supplied by rail is an obvious one but it is preempted by the current construction of the Mombasa-Nairobi pipeline. When the pipeline is fully operational all fuel will be carried from Mombasa to Nairobi by this method. The spare rail capacity is then intended to switch to the Nairobi-Kampala route, and

260

there should be sufficient excess rail capacity to
ensure that all depots in Kenya other than Nairobi
and Mombasa, are served exclusively by rail. The
pipeline will lower costs of transportation from
Mombasa to Nairobi, but prices are unlikely to be
reduced because of the high capital outlay involved
in the project.

Conclusions

Two main recommendations may be made in conclusion:
First, c.i.f. pricing should be used to equalize prices
throughout Kenya. This would result in a small price
increase in the most prosperous parts of the country
but would give substantial decreases in the poor,
remote areas. The application of c.i.f. pricing would
also include the removal of government oil companies'
road distribution charges which are far in excess of
actual costs incurred, and are the main source of
exploitation.
Second, road haulage must be used for fuel distribution only where no cheaper substitute transport
exists. By minimizing the use of road haulage, real
costs and social costs could also be minimized. Increasing use of rail transport could also include in-
stallation of some additional small storage depots at
intermediate points between existing depots.
Defence of the status quo is the argument that
minimization of costs in the main fuel-consumption
areas contributes to cost reduction in industry and
commerce. This argument however is circular, since
the beneficiaries of the arrangement are solely in
the same core areas. Those outside the modern sector
are little affected — and in any case any production
cost reduction at the center is countered by high
transportation costs to the periphery.
It is recognized that the argument, seen in center-
periphery terms, is only a partial one. A wider spectrum of industry needs to be examined to determine the
spatial effects of pricing policies. Some goods are
sold on a c.i.f. basis, equalizing prices throughout
Kenya, while others are sold at government-fixed prices
and therefore are also invariant. The price of cigarettes, beer, milk, maize meal and bread are such
examples. Many other products however are priced f.o.b.
and it seems probable that when their combined effects
are added to those of the distribution of oil refinery
products, the Kenyan periphery is placed in a very unfavorable position which must greatly hinder the desired goal: the more even spread of industrial and
commercial development resources.

The analysis and further study of the exact
nature of core-periphery differences in Kenya and
their effect in the retardation of regional equality
must provide urgent priorities in the research of
geographers and economists committed to the policy
of balanced growth in developing nations.

NOTES

1. Edward W. Soja, The Geography of Modernization in Kenya: A Spatial Analysis of Social, Economic and Political Change, (Syracuse: Syracuse
University Press, 1968).
2. Brian J.L. Berry, "Hierarchical Diffusion:
the Basis of Developmental Filtering and Spread in a
System of Growth Centres", in N. Hansen (ed.), Growth
Centers in Regional Economic Development, (New York:
Free Press, 1972) pp. 103-138.
3. E.J. Taaffe, R.L. Morrill and P.R. Gould,
Geographical Review, 53 (1963), pp. 503-529.
4. Gunnar Myrdal, Economic Theory and Underdeveloped Regions, (London: Methuen, 1957).
5. Albert O. Hirschman, The Strategy of Economic Development, (New Haven: Yale University Press, 1958).
6. John Friedmann, "A General Theory of Polarized
Development", in Hansen (ed.), Growth Centers in Regional Economic Development (New York: Free Press, 1972),
pp. 82-107.
7. Paul A. Baran, The Political Economy of
Growth, (New York: Monthly Review Press, 1957).
8. Andre G. Frank, Capitalism and Underdevelopment in Latin America, (New York: Monthly Review Press,
1969).
9. Harold C. Brookfield, "On One Geography and
a Third World", Institute of British Geographers,
Transactions 58 (1973), pp. 1-20.
10. Harold C. Brookfield, Interdependent Development, (London: Methuen, 1975).
11. Colin Leys, Underdevelopment in Kenya: The
Political Economy of Neo-Colonialism, (London: Heinne-
man, 1975).
12. William J. House & Henry Rempel, "An Analysis
of the Variation in Modern Sector Earnings Among the
Districts and Major Urban Centres in Kenya", Institute
for Development Studies Working Paper No. 243, University of Nairobi (1975), see also Chapter 8 in this
book.
13. Kabiru Kinyanjui, "The Distribution of Educational Resources and Opportunities in Kenya", Institute for Development Studies Discussion Paper No. 208,
University of Nairobi (1975).

14. Clay G. Wescott, "Industrial Location and Public Policy: the Case of Kenya's Textile Industry", Institute for Development Studies Working Paper No. 288, University of Nairobi (1976).

15. The contouring routine used is named CONJOB and was developed at the University of Manchester, U.,. computer center, where the data used in the present study was processed.

13. Meru District in the Kenyan Spatial Economy: 1890-1950

Frank E. Bernard

About 200 kilometers northeast of Nairobi lies Meru District, a large and diverse area stretching from the slopes of Mount Kenya northeastward to the Nyambeni Range and southeastward to the Low Eastern Plateau forelands and the Tana River (Figure 13.1). Before colonial rule, Meru participated actively in the broad patterns of East African spatial interaction. Beginning in 1908, the district became more and more divorced from the emerging economic nodes of Kenya Colony. Rough and rutted roads interrupted communication with Nairobi. White settler land alienation and politics hindered development. Instead of being an active region in the evolving spatial economy of Kenya, Meru languished in the shadow of the White Highlands and responded sluggishly to economic pulses.

This chapter argues that the course of recent change in Meru has been channeled by this experience of underdevelopment. Initially, the precolonial regional setting is briefly sketched as a backdrop to the stultifying impact of British overrule. The spatial structure imposed from 1908 to 1950 is then described, for it has clearly provided for better and for worse, the skeleton over which the flesh of a struggling modern economy has been stretched. Finally, consequent patterns of spatial organization are considered in detail. These demonstrate persuasively that the colonial experience rendered to Meru weakly developed external linkages to the wider Kenyan economy, an internal structure designed to suit the settlers and their allies, and an aimless ad-hoc pattern of development. To understand the opportunities and limitations facing Meru after 1950, one must reconstruct the detailed historical context of its spatial structure. In this reconstruction it will be possible to observe the impress of the colonial power on the course of development in modern Meru.

264

FIGURE 13.1

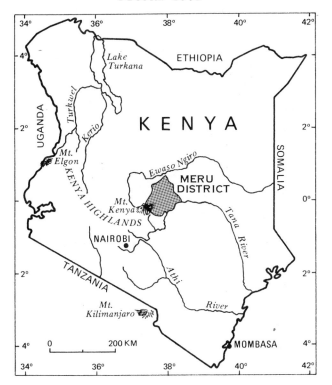

Precolonial Background

Spatial Interaction

Meru's situation in central Kenya in the late
nineteenth century has received little attention. The
common impression is that it was largely isolated, economically stagnant, and completely self sufficient.
Although detailed historical evidence is deficient,
there is little reason to believe these impressions.
The Meru were certainly participants in the broad patterns of East African history in the late precolonial
period and were affected in important ways by pulsations in this pattern.

In the northeast, for example, the Tigania and
Igembe subdivisions of Meru in the rich agricultural
highlands of the Nyambeni Range traded northward with
surrounding pastoral groups (Figure 13.2). The Meru
and Boran are said to have had a long-standing trade
involving foodstuffs from the highlands and livestock
and their products from the pastoral areas.[1] The same

265

FIGURE 13.2

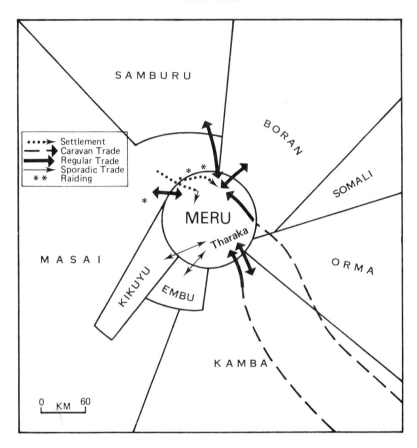

NINETEENTH CENTURY SPATIAL INTERACTION

was true of the Tigania Meru and their interaction
with Laikipia Masai. Though raids and skirmishes
between these groups punctuated a long-standing relationship, intermarriage, trade and settlement were
also characteristic. As in Kikuyuland to the south,
a Masai-Meru fusion had been taking place for at least
a generation.[2] In fact this was not uncommon elsewhere
in East Africa where Nilotic pastoralists and Bantu
agriculturalists were adjacent.[3] The technological
and ecological divergence of farming and pastoralism
thus fostered complementarity and cooperation.[4]

Another aspect of northeastern Meru's situation
was a link with the Kenya coast provided by Swahili
and Arab caravans. Sporadically, ivory expeditions

266

traversed the Nyambeni Range for restocking on the long journey northward to Lake Rudolf. In exchange for foodstuffs, salt, tobacco, and donkeys, the caravans offered wire, beads, cloth, and cowrie shells.[5] This trade brought an otherwise remote section of Kenya into contact with the Indian Ocean Basin.

Along the slopes of Mount Kenya, trade links reached north and south. Some trade apparently occurred between the Imenti Meru and the Masai and Samburu to the north. A small settlement of Masai completely surrounded by Imenti people, was encountered by Neumann in 1898.[6]

To the south, trade with the Embu and Kikuyu was likely much less important except during famines, being limited to exchange in a few agricultural goods and craft items. In some ways, despite their linguistic affinities, the Central Kenya Bantu interacted to a lesser degree than one would expect. Perhaps the similarity in lifestyles and their essential lack of complementarity made symbiosis unnecessary.

In lowland Meru though, Tharaka and Kamba traders carried on a lively interaction from at least the mid-nineteenth century.[7] Varied goods exchanged hands in this trade. Poison for hunting, ivory, honey, beeswax and livestock were traded by the Meru for various manufactured goods, cloth, beads, wire and shells. The vast Kamba economic empire of the 1840s, stretching from the coast to the Rift Valley, linked Meru to the Nyika peoples near the coast — especially in the exchange of ivory.

It is thus clear that situationally Meru participated in long-distance trade occurring in precolonial Kenya. Such spatial interaction had both local and regional effects on the traditional spatial economy of Meru, influencing food crop agriculture, miraa (Catha edulis) cultivation, animal husbandry, and distinctive economic activities such as hunting, beekeeping, salt collection, and crafts. The regional spatial economy at the coming of Europeans was neither stagnant nor isolated; nor was it totally self-sufficient.

Internally, the nine territorial subdivisions of Meru (Figure 13.3) also participated in intraregional contact and trade, particularly in specialized goods. Agricultural specialties engendering trade included miraa, honey and honey beer, salt, and tobacco, which all found their way across the district.[8] Crafts traded were iron goods, manufactured by blacksmith castes, clay pots, and palm basketry and mats. This continuous trade, as well as certain social and political institutions such as ritual brotherhood and the

FIGURE 13.3

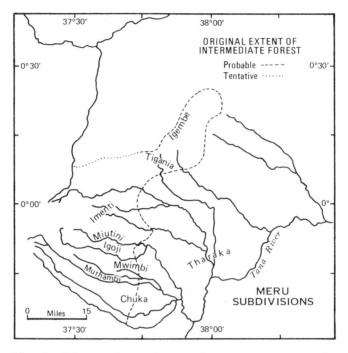

council of elders, brought various Meru subdivisions
together frequently. So also did raiding which was
part of a ritualized system of warfare common among
the Mount Kenya peoples.[9]
In light of this, the absence of an elaborate
system of markets is notable. Only in the Nyambenis
is there clear evidence that indigenous markets pre-
dated colonial times.[10] Here regular markets were
held in open places where women traded in crafts and
agricultural produce and men in livestock. Labor
division, regional specialization, and a functional
crafts industry certainly spurred market evolution in
the Nyambeni Range. Long distance trade was perhaps
also a catalyst of market development.[11] Yet elsewhere
along the wooded Mount Kenya slopes and in the dry
plains of Tharaka even peripheral markets apparently
did not emerge. To explain this contrast is to
require data never collected and perhaps forever
inaccessible. Even so, to characterize all or most
of Meru as having a totally self-contained and insular
economy is to ignore the spatial interaction which
clearly occurred both within and beyond Meruland.

268

Population and Settlement

Meru's physical geography, as perceived by its people, induced a complex interrelationship between man and land (Figure 13.4). By the late nineteenth century the vast majority of Meru people had settled on the slopes of Mount Kenya and the adjacent Nyambeni Range. These highland people were still moving upslope at first European contact, clearing the moist evergreen mountain forest as lineages expanded by fission, then became pioneers in new glades of misty virgin forest. Both their social structure and their environmental preferences brought a unique zonal system of settlement which in itself was firmly grounded in the district's mountainous landscape.

The highland Meru built dispersed extended family homesteads in the altitudes stretching from about 1,250 meters to about 1,850 meters. By any reckoning this is ideal tropical highland landscape for rain-fed, permanent arable farming. Equable temperatures, reliable rainfall, deep volcanic soils, ample surface water from Mount Kenya's glacial meltwaters, and the absence of malaria and trypanosomiasis all combined in Meru evaluation to provide highly favorable settlement conditions. Altitudes above and below this homestead zone were used for grazing and itinerant cultivation, but it was the broad, well-watered ridges and narrow valleys of the middle altitudes where most of the Meru people lived and conducted their livelihood in immediate precolonial times.

In the low-lying areas of Tharaka in eastern Meru by contrast, where physical gradients were much more gentle, zonal systems of land use and settlement did not evolve. The horizontal nature of these semiarid lowlands with their sandy, thin soils and huge water deficits seem to have created conditions for mobility. Temporary homesteads, widely dispersed over the landscape, and a system of shifting cultivation accompanied a much sparser population density. Hunting and gathering further reinforced the fluid spatial system of Tharaka. But the lowland people in their severe habitat had negotiated a reasonable arrangement between themselves, their technology, and the arid plains where they lived. An important clause in this arrangement was that population remain small and be dispersed over a vast region.

These brief sketches of highland and lowland Meru settlement point out the basic dissimilarity of the two respective traditional spatial structures. On the upland slopes of Mount Kenya and the Nyambeni Range people were concentrated in the middle altitudes.

269

FIGURE 13.4

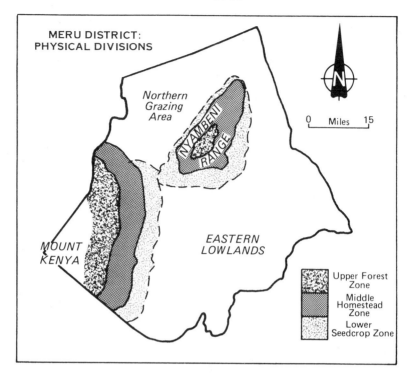

MERU DISTRICT:
PHYSICAL DIVISIONS

Northern
Grazing
Area

NYAMBENI RANGE

MOUNT KENYA

EASTERN
LOWLANDS

0   Miles   15

Upper Forest Zone

Middle Homestead Zone

Lower Seedcrop Zone

They went upslope for products of the forest, for
grazing, and for cultivating hardy grains. Downslope
they moved semiannually to cultivate seed crops on
the lower, hotter but still fertile and moist lower
volcanic slopes. This tiered spatial structure, most
prevalent along Mount Kenya's slopes, reflected a
sophisticated understanding of the diverse resource
base. Over the long term, the outcome was a reasonable
man-land balance. In the lowlands a system of shifting
cultivation and widely dispersed small settlements
corresponded to the exceptionally harsh living conditions of the area.

In the wake of the interloping colonial administration, as new and ultimately pervasive changes were
introduced to Meru, the structural dichotomy between
highland and lowland spatial systems was a most important traditional distinction. This structural differentiation became more inflexible and inequitable with
colonial action and inaction.

European Contact: 1895-1910

While the earliest European explorers were cross-ing Meru in the 1890s the British government, long en-tangled at both the coast and in Uganda, decided to connect the two by rail. The Uganda railroad, comple-ted in 1902, was the link by which the British would try to integrate the economy of eastern Africa with that of the rest of the British Empire.[12] This thin line of rail enabled Britain to extend its political hegemony over a vast area and its economic control over the raw materials flowing first from the Lake Victoria basin and later from the Kenya highlands. With the establishment of imperial overrule at the coast and along the rail line, the British moved to conquer or otherwise subdue local inhabitants, inject economic activities by which the colony would pay for itself, and create an economy which would insure a high rate of return on investment and a steady flow of commodities to the metropolis.[13]

At the site of a small railway camp some 480 kilo-meters from Mombasa, the headquarters of the Uganda Railway was established. This place of course was Nairobi. Because of the railway's central importance to East Africa, it was inevitable that its headquarters would also be the focal point for economic and politi-cal activities of the colony. Indeed, Nairobi became the capital of Kenya in 1901.

From this early focus the colonial administration began to move northward and eastward to bring the Kikuyu and Embu peoples under British control. Then in 1907, having established themselves securely in these areas, they marched into Meru with the imperial intent of surrounding Mount Kenya.[14] Meeting compara-tively little resistance in traversing the eastern Mount Kenya slopes, E.B. Horne and a garrison of the Third King's African Rifles pitched camp in the middle altitudes on Mount Kenya's slopes toward the northern limit of Meru settlement. This camp became the site of Meru Town.

The new district commissioner then moved south-ward to Chuka by a newly cut track along the ridges and ravines of the mountain and northeastward to Maua along the southeast slopes of the Nyambeni Range. The government met resistance only in low-lying Tharaka and this was decisively quelled with a punitive expe-dition in 1909.[15] The British thereby demarcated what they perceived to be an ethnic unit, encompassing all traditional subdivisions except Chuka which was administered as part of Embu District until 1933.

Meru was formally declared an administrative district in 1910. As such it became the primary unit of local government and the territory over which the British would try to implement their policy of indirect rule. In less than two years the foundations had thus been laid to manipulate the economy and organize the space of Meru.

On the heels of the colonial administration followed traders and missionaries. Indian and Swahili merchants served as agents for the introduction of a monetary economy, selling petty imported goods and trying to buy produce to export from the district. Encouraged by the colonial government, these interloping traders effectively hindered African participation in the local market economy. Missionaries from Italy and England brought Christianity, education, and health services — all of which were to have far-reaching impacts on the demography and social ecology of the area.

These then were the primary agencies at the interface of contact between colonial power and Meru peasantry. The government, though represented by only a handfull of administrators, was firmly established by 1910. In its efforts to extend its influence over the populace and encourage them to become fiscally responsible, the British introduced taxes, tried to legislate agricultural change, and attempted to develop an infrastructure to drain agricultural surplus from the district. Traders were encouraged to become established in Meru to foster acquisitive tendencies among the peasants, increasing their dependency on imported goods and instilling a greater desire to produce a surplus for cash. The previously well-established local precolonial trade was superseded by the imposition of these new agents of distribution. The missionaries increasingly reached into the very core of Meru value systems and social structures. Their influence cannot be underestimated in any historical analysis of change in Meru.[16] We will ultimately turn to a reconstruction of the spatial impacts of these agencies of change, but first we must consider the wider spatial system.

Kenya's Colonial Spatial System: 1920-1950

With the Crown Lands Ordinance of 1902 which effectively promoted European settlement in Kenya, and with the increasing flow of English exsoldier settlers after World War I, Kenya's rural space became rigidly partitioned. Land was classified as "scheduled", that is exclusively alienated for European settlement, and "reserve" (or native land unit), meant entirely for African habitation. Deriving from

272

this pattern of land classification two colonial socio-
economies evolved, a European subsystem and an African
subsystem.[17] The former was dominated by a small number of farmers, ranchers, and plantation owners (never
exceeding 3,500 families in this period), representatives of corporate enterprises linked to the British
empire and especially after 1920, colonial civil
servants and politicians, who responded to the Colonial Office, and the infinitesimally small semi-
autonomous white landed elite. The African subsystem
of course comprised the overwhelming majority of
people in Kenya, set apart in reserves or squatting
in the White Highlands, possessing no political and
little economic power, and being progressively encouraged to devote their labor and agricultural produce
to the colonial economy at low rates of return. Out
of these separate and unequal yet interconnected subsystems emerged the spatial structure of Kenya Colony.

This structure was characterized by a core area,
Nakuru to Nairobi and the White Highlands, which
received a relatively high level of investment and
progressively became better and better endowed with
physical infrastructure. At the peripheries were
African reserves which by comparison received little
or no infrastructural development but were still
expected to contribute to the colonial economic base.
African reserves closest to the core such as Kikuyu-
occupied Central Province, generally received innovations sooner than those farther from the core, and
thus felt the pulsations of change more rapidly and
more pervasively. But in Kenya as elsewhere in colonial Africa, there were substantial barriers to the
diffusion of innovations to the reserves, irrespective
of their location. In essence until well after World
War II, Kenyan space exhibited the commonly recognized
"islands of development" pattern — with the White
Highlands, a foreign enclave, standing above a sea of
traditionally organized space occupied by the African
peasantry in their segregated native land units.[18]

The Uganda Railroad and its branch lines established after World War I were the backbone of a
dendritic system meant to enhance the export-oriented
Kenya economy.[19]

European-occupied areas became heavily dependent
on this outward-thrusting system in which Nairobi and
Mombasa were the trading control centers drawing agricultural surpluses from the highlands.

The African subsystem was given only limited
access to these trading centers. Most of the native
land units in early and midcolonial days engaged in a
limited amount of horizontal trade, but only marginally

273

interacted with colonial urban places.[20] Indeed, the government organized a system of three classes of market centers which were largely independent of one another and certainly did not evolve to an intermeshed central place system.[21]

Meru in the Colonial Spatial System

In almost every sense Meru was peripheral to the emerging colonial spatial structure. Mount Kenya shielded the district from a number of influences which on the other side of the mountain reached deeply into Kikuyu life and landscape.[22] Accentuating Meru's remoteness was inaccessibility to the rail line. The veins of the dendritic system never stretched to Meru, although a branch line was built to Nanyuki in 1930, bringing rail transport to within ninety kilometers. This distance might as well have been twice as much, for between Meru and Nanyuki a vast immutable block of alienated land hindered interaction between Meru and Nyeri and Nanyuki. This block of European land caused virtually all flows west of Mount Kenya to move away from rather than toward Meru. Waves of change from Nanyuki thus rarely rippled to the eastern slopes of Mount Kenya. Meru was surprisingly isolated from changes occurring only a few kilometers away.
Motorable roads from Nairobi, Thika and Fort Hall through Embu to Meru were not constructed until the mid- to late 'twenties. Meant to serve as feeders to the railways, these earth roads were to draw out laborers and facilitate more effective administration. The southbound feeder road from Meru Town traversing the rough terrain of Mount Kenya was not always open. Often hopelessly severed by acts of nature, Meru's southward connectivity to the Kenya core was thus significantly poorer than distance alone would suggest.[23] Poor roads hampered efforts to develop a commercial, export-oriented "native economy". It is no exaggeration to say that Meru's interaction southward in the 1920s and 1930s was insignificant compared to precolonial times when Swahili and Kamba traders forged links to the wider region.
Whereas the Kikuyu, Kipsigis, Gusii and others by virtue of their location, were drawn into a vortex of change by producing foodstuffs for the colonial economy, attempts to foster the same in Meru failed. In the 1920s for example, Meru was designated the supply base for the Northern Frontier Province. This northward hinterland never really took shape however, and except for a brief resurgence in government interest in 1928 which was an utter failure, trade northward

274

waned into oblivion during the hard years of the
depression.[24] After this Meru's hinterland to the
north never reached much beyond the boundaries of
the district. In effect the imposition of colonial
rule had thus almost totally squelched previous
interaction between Meru's agricultural highlands
and the semiarid pastoral lands to the north and
west.

If Meru's remoteness and its weak linkages to
the economic nodes of the colony suppressed development, so also did lack of capital and a poorly supported administration. This was especially true for
agriculture, the supposed focus of colonial development. Resources of the Ministry of Agriculture which
throughout most of the colonial period were comparatively meager, were almost totally encumbered in
developing the European, rather than the African
sector of the economy.[25] Both staff and equipment
were thus difficult to obtain for remote African
reserves such as Meru. For the first twenty-five
years of colonial rule except for one year, there
was no agricultural officer at government headquarters
in Meru and almost no junior staff in the field. As
a measure of the poverty of agricultural extension,
after twenty-five years of colonial rule only four
African agricultural instructors had been trained
for the entire district.[26]

This same low level of capitalization was characteristic of other agricultural ventures, the provision
of health facilities, and market development. Meru
District was consistently short of funds for such
capital development; but this was not uncommon in this
period throughout the colony. Van Zwanenberg and King
note corresponding capital shortages even in the White
Highlands, for industrial infrastructural development,
marketing and distribution, banking and credit, before
World War II.[27] The entire colony was merely a poor
extension of the British metropolis throughout most
of the first forty years of colonial rule. The centralized state, the administrative machinery and the
infrastructure primarily were meant to improve conditions for the white settler minority — but even they
were often economically hard pressed.[28]

Evolution of Meru's Spatial Structure

Marked spatial inequities were characteristic of
the internal space of Meru during the early decades
of the colonial period. Imposition of alien rule
over the political space of Meru, introduction of a
contrived system of markets, construction of a rudimen-
tary infrastructure, and intrusion into the agricultural

275

economy greatly altered traditional spatial organization and promoted new accessibility patterns. Some areas became situationally endowed relative to the new structure; others became marginal. Still others more remote yet, were cast into a perpetual condition of underdevelopment. It is to these differences that we now direct our attention.

The Government: Political Space

Early administrative interest focused on establishing a system of local government based on the principle of indirect rule, enhancing communications across the district, ensuring security, promoting agricultural change, and raising tax revenues. The desire to give impetus to agricultural production of course was linked to forces mentioned above, namely the metropolitan demand for agricultural raw materials and the need to support the colony itself.[29]

In facing these tasks the government created structures for extending their influence over the Meru peasantry. The district headquarters at Meru and the Chuka substation were foci of the political infrastructure from 1913 to 1940. These were later augmented by district offices in Nkubu and Maua (Figure 13.5). In remoter areas, rest camps and houses were visited periodically to give the impression of ubiquitous government presence. To implement their decisions and to communicate them to the Meru people, the government depended upon a system of chiefs and subchiefs throughout the district. As government servants, these chiefs became estranged from their traditional base of support (which in Meru was largely fabricated by the colonial government) as their ties to the alien power increased. They presided over sublocations and locations which themselves were artificial administrative units based only partially on traditional political subdivisions. By fixing the boundaries of these local political units, the colonial government effectively inhibited interethnic migration and contact, and for a time certainly reduced the degree of spatial interaction across the district.

Tax laws were written in the early colonial years to raise revenues and stimulate market participation among the peasantry. A hut tax established in 1910 was initially resisted by the Meru, but within a decade government enforcement began to oblige people to comply. Shortly afterwards a poll tax was imposed.

To create opportunities for peasants to earn cash for these taxes, the government attempted to promote wage employment. In Kenya this was accomplished by recruiting manual labor for government projects, by

276

FIGURE 13.5

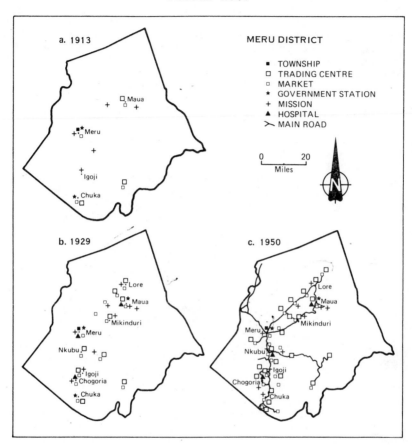

MARKETS, MISSIONS, GOVERNMENT STATIONS, AND ROADS 1913–1950

creating incentives for labor migration to towns and European farms and ranches, and by promoting the market principle wherever possible so that surpluses of local produce could be sold to generate tax revenues.

Labor migration was not a popular means of raising taxes among the Meru. Comparatively few workers left the district for towns and plantations. On the other hand, the government did try to invest its meager resources in market and road development as a means of broadening Meru's tax base. Since markets were based almost entirely upon the sale of surplus foodstuffs and livestock, the government's efforts naturally began to affect traditional agriculture. At

various times Europeans introduced new crops, tried
to diffuse new tools and techniques, and made efforts
to increase lands under cultivation. These policies
were discriminatively imposed, favoring the areas near
government offices and with best accessibility to
market. The induced market system and its linking
roads thus became the nodes and networks around
which colonial development was planned.

The Market System

Wild fluctuations in market development in Meru
in the first forty colonial years were the result of
Kenya's mercurial economy as well as the difficulty
of imposing a supposedly outward-thrusting market
system in an area with little connectivity to the
colonial economy. The location of markets further
indicates aspects of locational discrimination and
regional underdevelopment.

Three kinds of market place were recognized,
each forming a rung in a simple trading hierarchy
contrived by the colonial government. At the lowest
level native markets served as open places of barter,
operating on one or two days a week and dealing primarily with trade in food products. Trading centers
were at the second level. Often located at the site
of a native market, trading centers exchanged local
and manufactured goods in permanent shops. Finally
Meru Town, the only township in the district, was
the wholesale and retail center with the widest range
of goods and services, and the bulking center for
produce leaving the district.

The design of this system was theoretically intermeshed, but in actual fact as there was very limited
horizontal interaction in the system among Meru peasants, and retail and wholesale trade was concentrated
in the hands of a few Indian, Goan and Swahili traders,
flows from one level of the hierarchy to the next were
modest at best. Moreover, interstices between market
places were vast, leaving large populated areas entirely deprived of market opportunities.

The basic structure became fixed early in colonial times with the establishment of a market bazaar
in Meru Town in 1911 (Figure 13.5). By 1913 nine
shops were being operated in Meru by Indians, and
twenty-five resident Swahili merchants formed the
nucleus of a Swahili village at the edge of town.
Elsewhere in the district were government-initiated
native markets and trading centers in several highland places such as Maua and Chuka.[30]

The system continued to expand into the middle
and late 'twenties. By 1925, Meru Town included

278

twenty-one plots operated by Indians and twenty-nine by Swahilis.[31] Trading centers had also been opened by this time at Tigania, south Imenti, Igoji, and Mwimbi, and nine native markets were functioning primarily in highland locations.

A view of these markets at the end of the 'twenties shows the maximum reach of the system before the depression (Figure 13.5). Notably at this time market location correlates spatially with zones of highest agricultural potential. In other words, the contrived market system and the former highland homestead zone almost perfectly correlate. While it is true that this reflects attempts by the colonial government to concentrate their energies in the zone of highest population density and agricultural potential, it is also clear that market places were located near government stations and missions. European preferences thus largely determined the emerging nodes in the colonial spatial system.

Still, in 1929 much of the district was miles from the nearest market, and surely less than half the people at that time ever traded at a government market place. Especially notable amongst those regions beyond the reach of the market system is the Nyambeni Range, which with the exception of Maua, was isolated and only weakly within the colonial economic sphere. The same may be said of Tigania and almost all the eastern lowlands, where Tharaka life continued in its traditional way.

Market distribution at the end of the period shows recovery from the depression and expansion in the 1940s (Figure 13.5). Again, new market places were almost exclusively located in the densely settled areas above the 1,400-meter contour on Mount Kenya. By 1950 some nodal development had occurred in places where administrative offices or missions were located. Examples are Meru Town-Kaaga, Nkubu, Igoji, Chogoria, and Chuka. In the Nyambenis, despite concerted attempts to draw Tigania and Igembe into the market place, by comparison to Mount Kenya fewer than half as many markets and trading centers had been established. This lag is certainly best explained by the poor roads between Meru Town and the Range. Similarly to an even greater extent the eastern lowlands still had few markets and interacted weakly with the rest of Meru District.

Urban development — if it can be called that — was limited to Meru Town, which even in 1950 was a small administrative center of less than 2,000 people with a tiny government hospital, a few resident Asian and Swahili traders, European administrators, and about forty-five shops. Land use within the town was

279

segregated, with administrative functions at the site of the original boma; European residents in a small neighborhood overlooking the club, golf course and Anglican church; the Swahili town in a lower area adjacent to the two rutted, muddy main streets.

Roads

In the absence of any other form of transport, the road system (and motor-driven vehicles from 1918) were meant to link together the market places, enhance the flow of migrant laborers, and enable produce from rural areas to reach the market. In actual fact the road system was maintained primarily for colonial government communication and for mission work. The colonial administration was concerned mainly with administrative order and tax collection. In these efforts it had all it could do to develop and maintain major links between places, and into and out of the district. Little capital was available to expand the network especially along the Mount Kenya slopes where rugged topography hindered construction. Moreover as was the case in all Kenyan native land units, even the best district roads were subject to landslides, washouts, severe gullying, and bridge failures. To say that Meru roads were rough in this period by no means does justice to the scabrous texture of these rutted tracks.

Three such roads, all constructed between 1910 and 1920, provided the only connectivity between Meru places. Even in 1950 the network of roads linked only the major markets, administrative posts and missions, leaving a large proportion of the densely settled area without motorable roads and providing virtually no connection to the more sparsely populated eastern and northeastern areas (Figure 13.5).

Missions

Three Christian missions became established within twelve years of imposition of colonial rule. Italian Roman Catholic missionaries of the Consolata Order initially penetrated the district from the north and west, curiously bypassing Meru Town to set up their first mission at Mojwa. Later they founded other stations at Nkubu, Meru Town, Lare and Tigania in the Nyambenis and Egoji and Chuka in southern Meru.

Among the Protestants the district was subdivided by the Church of Scotland and the English Methodist Mission Society. As an extension of the Kikuyu mission field, the Church of Scotland station in Chogoria was established in 1922. It became a center for

proselytization and health services in southern Meru
but never attracted administrative functions. In
like fashion the Methodist Mission Society at Kaaga,
eight kilometers northeast of the Meru boma, served
as the core of Methodist outreach throughout northern
Meru.

Mission stations established in this early time
continued to be the nuclei of mission activity throughout the period (Figure 13.5). As with other Europeans,
the missionaries' desire to live in cooler altitudes
and their antipathy for lowlands is reflected in the
distribution of their stations. The Methodists had
in fact come to Meru specifically to escape the fatal
consequences of malaria which had debilitated their
staff at the coast for fifty years.[32]

The missions faced difficult years initially,
meeting resistance in their attempts to convert, heal,
and educate. However by the early 1940s their efforts
began to attract Meru people to churches, hospitals,
and schools. In some areas such as Maua, Kaaga, and
Chogoria, the mission station had by 1950 become a
node for several interrelated activities: primary
and intermediate education, teachers training, voca-
tional centers, health care, etc. The Kaaga and
Chogoria missions even provided sites for the first
experimental coffee grown in the district, and were
ultimately instrumental in convincing the government
that coffee would succeed in the district — but not
until after 1950.

Of more importance to the eventual spatial structure of the district was mission impact upon the traditional demography of Meru. As Greeley has recently
shown, mission influence on family life in southern
Meru inadvertently undermined a number of values and
practices limiting family size.[33] The introduction
of scientific medicine and health practices through
mission hospitals reduced mortality. Higher birth
rates and lower death rates thus laid the foundations
for an unprecedented population expansion which has
continued to the present. By 1950, population pressure was already beginning to produce ecostress all
along the Mount Kenya and Nyambeni slopes.

Agricultural Change

Development in the native land units was virtually
synonymous with agricultural development. Colonial
administrators insisted that they were thoroughly
dedicated to agricultural change. At the same time
their dedication had severely defined limits: limits
imposed by fluctuating markets, inaccessibility, and
especially the political economy of the colony. A

281

brief look at colonial efforts to alter the Meru agricultural economy will serve to highlight processes of underdevelopment.

The motive for changing agriculture as mentioned above, was to expand agricultural production in order to raise tax revenues and produce agricultural raw materials for export. In this effort, new and improved varieties of food crops were introduced and lands under cultivation were increased. These innovations were generally received with indifference and resistance and had an extremely variable effect on district revenues. On more than one occasion farmers were left with unmarketable produce yielding no income.

In the government's program to develop new and better varieties of food crops, only a few plants had any significant impact on the spatial economy of the district. The adoption of maize must certainly be considered a major change.[34] Pre-European maize in Meru was small, low-yielding and not widely cultivated. New varieties introduced in the first decade of colonial rule began to diffuse rapidly, so that by the late 1940s maize had become widely cultivated and was one of the most important crops exported from the district. Even more important, in most highland areas maize was competing strongly with millet and sorghum as the staple grain. This change, certainly the most important of the early period, established the basis of a new staple food economy and altered an entire complex of practices associated with traditional staples. The adoption of maize also inadvertently reduced the protein content of Meru diets and further accentuated the importance of the homestead zone of the district.[35]

Though not as pervasive as maize, a number of other new or improved food crops also diffused across highland Meru. These included new varieties of beans, cassava, sweet potatoes, and Colocasia, all of which were distributed free by the government in the 1930s.[36] On the other hand white potatoes and green peas came to be widely grown, largely without encouragement of the colonial government.[37]

Yet for every successful food crop brought to highland Meru there was at least one failure. Wheat, red flint maize, groundnuts, buckwheat, Boston beans, linseed, and coriander are examples of crops which never took hold.

In the lowlying areas rice, simsim, and groundnuts were tried but ultimately were unsuccessful.[38] A primary economic shortcoming inherited from these failures was the tenacious retention of all traditions of the lowland agricultural system throughout the period in spite of changing spatial, economic, and political patterns in the district.

Perhaps more representative of abortive measures to change agriculture were commercial farming ventures, the program to force expansion of lands under cultivation, faltering irrigation schemes, cash crop underdevelopment, and interference with the system of animal husbandry. In each of these instances an orderly progression toward well-defined goals was lacking. Each project seemed to be divorced spatially and economically from the district economy. In no case did the colonial government consider the consequences of their actions upon the Meru people.[39]

Of the attempts to introduce European-managed commercial farms, notable among failures in the late 1920s was a dairy industry in Imenti which neglected to incorporate the transhumance pastoral pattern of the people.[40] Similarly several vegetable schemes collapsed after World War II when the unusual market demand of that time diminished.[41] Rice in the lower lands of Imenti and Tigania was promoted by European managers between 1923 and 1936 to be sold to the northern frontier market which, we have observed, never materialized. Moreover rice was disliked by the Meru and was unsuited to the ecologic conditions of the sites where it was tried. Sizable investments in hulling equipment thus gathered dust and collected rust in the wake of yet another fruitless commercial venture. In this early period rice never spread beyond the trial sites.

The farm irrigation and expansion campaigns of the 'teens, 'twenties and 'thirties provide other case studies of underdevelopment. In 1918, a year of severe drought, the district commissioner initiated an ambitious program of irrigation to reduce risk of drought in subsequent years.[42] While this may have provided temporary relief, the campaign ceased in better years. This "stop and go" pattern of change had no enduring value to the peasants affected by dry weather conditions. Under similar circumstances in 1929 irrigation was reemployed, but once again persisted only as long as the famine.[43]

The successful adoption of the steel hoe (jembe) after 1929 made government campaigns to increase lands under cultivation possible. The rationale, of course, was that more food crop acreage would lead to more tax revenues. In 1935 at the will of the colonial administration, the Local Native Council of Meru ordered all families to increase their plots by one quarter of an acre.[44] Predictably, production surpassed market demand and farmers were caught with unmarketable surpluses. Potatoes for example were buried and burned in 1935 and vegetables in that year

rotted in market stalls.[45] In view of the collapse
of the northern market and Meru's poor roads and faltering market system, failure of the colonial administration to foresee such consequences suggests palpable
callousness. In the short term it left such distaste
for market participation in Meru that the district
fell far behind others in monetization and capital
accumulation.

Resistance to the introduction and diffusion of
cash crops to the native reserves was a well-known
white settler attitude in colonial Kenya. As van
Zwanenberg and King note, it was not merely a case of
disinterest, indeed there was perverse and sustained
discrimination against allowing "native incursion"
into cash crop markets.[46] European planters believed
that such competition would deflate the quality and
price of Kenyan products on world markets.[47] European
prejudice and attitude thus blocked attempts to help
farmers develop export crops such as coffee, tea,
pyrethrum, sisal, wheat, and sugar, all of which might
have measurably altered the course of modernization.
The small plantations of coffee at Chogoria and Kaaga
in 1935 and at Chuka in 1947 were only minor exceptions to the rule for in these places, expansion was
rigidly controlled and production limited to only
14.40 tons by 1948-1949.[48]

It is true that cotton was heavily promoted as
a cash crop in 1936-1937 but in no way did this
compete with the European sector. Cotton was considered a low-esteem, low return venture unworthy of
European interest.[49] In a characteristic gesture
reflecting the doctrine of white supremacy, cotton
became an acceptable African cash crop.

Much of the area planned for cotton in Meru was
unfortunately poorly suited to its cultivation and
in spite of a substantial cotton campaign, by the
early 1940s cotton faded from the Meru scene, yet not
without a residue of acrimony. As the introduction
of cotton had partly been compelled, many Meru
detested the crop. In 1940, the district commissioner
wrote that " . . . the Meru loathe the very name of
cotton."[50] These negative attitudes persisted, hindering reintroduction of the crop in the 1960s.

Finally, the impact of colonial policies on
animal husbandry had similarly unexpected and negative
consequences. British decisions to alter traditional
exchange and ceremonial practices involving livestock
had the effect of dramatically increasing herd size
in Meru. Livestock could no longer be used in pay-
ment of court fines. Traditional oaths, repugnant to
Europeans, were eliminated thereby prolonging the
lives of thousands of goats and sheep each year. Other

herd-culling customs were eliminated for health
reasons, and cattle raiding and unimpeded movement
between districts were severely curtailed. Furthermore, cattle diseases were continually being reduced
by innoculation, spraying and dipping; and lack of
market opportunities inhibited reduction of the herd
through sales or auctions.[51]
By the middle 'twenties officials were beginning
to note that by continuing these policies the colonial
government was actually contributing to overstocking.[52]
Degradation of the plant cover and soil erosion became
prevalent. And subsequent efforts to reduce herds
largely failed in Meru as elsewhere.[53] Compulsory
culling was met with resistance, overgrazing and
burning of grasslands continued, and herd sizes
increased.
A salient lesson from these faltering examples
of agricultural change is that what was perceived as
development in most instances became just the opposite.
The intrusion of the colonial government into the agricultural economy actually took little account of pre-
existing ecologic, social and economic balances —
and eventually made life worse for the peasantry. This
insensitivity to the gestalt of traditional life was
compounded by the myth of pseudoscientific racism.
It was precisely these attitudes which engendered so
much hatred of colonialism. The poverty of administration in native areas, the absence of any redeeming
purpose in agricultural development, and the blatant
denigration of traditional institutions and lifeways
all made mockery of any promises to bring significant
change to Meru agriculture between 1908 and 1950.

Conclusion

Meru's colonial experience yielded problems and
material constraints to its development after 1950.
The inherited spatial economy was designed — and
poorly at that — for the convenience of a colonial
power that demonstrated little understanding of Meru
life. Land tenure reform, improvement in the food
crop economy, and introduction of cash crops, all of
which came after 1950, required substantial reconstruction of the spatial framework of the district — a
reconstruction necessarily based on major policy
revisions. In other words the infrastructure of the
colonial years was hardly sufficient to propel Meru
into the modern period.
Among the most serious external spatial problems
to be overcome were the poor linkages between Meru
and the south and west. Improved communications southward have been and continue to be inhibited by the

difficult topography between Meru and Embu. Although infrastructurally well developed and well connected to Nairobi, the Timau-Nanyuki area persisted as an obstacle to the free movement of people, goods and ideas. Even today this tract of large-scale farms hinders Meru development to some extent. While it is true that the region can now be traversed on a modern tarmac road from Nanyuki to Meru, it is also true that extension, research,and marketing facilities available to the large-scale farms do not extend deeply into Meru.

The colonial power also prevented Meru from entering markets beyond the region. This resulted in a low level of monetization, and caused the district to lag behind similar yet less-well-endowed areas of Kenya. To say that Meru was weakly tied to the national economy during the period in question is to understate the situation. Remoteness from the national economy was surely an inherited constraint which to this day has not been entirely overcome.

Pastoral and agricultural interaction was also substantially reduced in colonial times. The symbiosis of interdependence between herders and farmers at the edge of Meru waned in the early colonial period and was later actively discouraged. Eventually Meru interaction with the surrounding lowlands virtually ceased, and the spatial economy turned further inward. Similarly the pastoral areas within Meru were forgotten in colonial planning up to 1950. In comparison to the highlands, they received no attention and were consequently underdeveloped in terms of basic infrastructure and services.

The colonial promotion of food crops instead of cash crops was especially disadvantageous to Meru. Remote from major markets and inaccessible from all directions, the district farmers simply were not able to capitalize on opportunities to enter the market. Even when cash crops were promoted after 1950, Meru's basically poor connectivity to Kenya's spatial economy retarded development. Thus an exceedingly rich, high-potential agricultural district in the 1950s contributed remarkably little to the colonial economy, and in the 1960s was still at the periphery in independent Kenya.[54]

Internally too the district inherited a number of spatial economic weaknesses. Notable among these were poor infrastructure and consequent low level of spatial interaction, weak nodal development and an incomplete central place system, dramatic inequalities between highland and lowland and between Mount Kenya and the Nyambeni Range, lack of regional specialization, and virtual absence of secondary and tertiary economic activity. These elements as earlier described

286

relegated the region to a state of underdevelopment which to some degree persists today. For example, in 1976 the district could claim only two tarmac roads extending over less than 120 kilometers.

Of gravest consequence to modern spatial economy is the prevailing dichotomy of highland and lowland. Early and late colonial and postindependence attention has been obsessively focused on medium and upper altitudes. As we have seen, this pattern had its roots in European missionary and administration preference and prejudice. The rift between advantaged high- and medium-potential areas on the one hand and low-lying areas on the other has intensified, creating economic and social as well as technological problems. On all points the lowlands lose out.

The implication of such spatial inequities is that while economic development is being promoted in favored areas, a large region is acting parasitically to mitigate overall growth. As Millikan and Hapgood have written, "Concentrating resources on the more promising regions and individuals may result in increasing rather than reducing the disparities between the more and less fortunate."[55] In this way the inherited spatial disparities are carried forward, actually prolonging a legacy of underdevelopment. If the benefits of modernization are to be diffused equitably, such disparities must be minimized; yet minimization of differences is only possible if the course of underdevelopment is understood in an historical context, and subsequent plans formulated to break out of the cycle of regional and national dependency.

NOTES

1. Bernardo Bernardi, The Mugwe: A Failing Prophet (London: Oxford University 1959), pp. 4, 162.
2. cf. Godfrey Muriuki, A History of the Kikuyu 1500-1900 (London: Oxford University, 1974).
3. B.G. McIntosh, "The Eastern Bantu People", in Zamani: A Survey of East African History, B.A. Ogot and J.A. Kieran (eds.) (Nairobi: East African Publishing House 1968), p. 211.
4. J.E.G. Sutton, "The Settlement of East Africa", in ibid., p. 73, and R.M.A. van Zwanenberg and Anne King, An Economic History of Kenya and Uganda 1800-1970 (Nairobi: East African Literature Bureau 1975), p. 148.
5. H.R. Tate, "Journal to the Rendile Country, British East Africa", Geographical Journal, XXIII (1904), p. 223 and A.H. Neumann, Elephant Hunting in East Equatorial Africa (London: Rowland Ward 1898), pp. 8,80.

6. Neumann, Elephant Hunting, p. 128.
7. J.L. Krapf, Travels, Researches, and Missionary Labours During Eighteen Years Residence in Eastern Africa (London: Trubner, 1860), pp. 256-257.
8. W.A. Chanler, Through Jungle and Desert: Travels in Eastern Africa (London: Macmillan, 1896), pp. 189-190, 343; Neumann, Elephant Hunting, pp.32-33; Alfred Arkell-Hardwick, An Ivory Trader in North Kenia (London: Longmans Green, 1903), p. 124; and Bernardi, The Mugwe, pp. 100-101.
9. Jeffrey Fadiman, Mountain Warriors: The Pre-Colonial Meru of Mt. Kenya, Papers in International Studies, Africa Series, No. 12 (Athens: Ohio University, 1976).
10. Chanler, Through Jungle and Desert, p. 239.
11. B.W. Hodder, "Some Comments on the Origins of Traditional Markets in Africa South of the Sahara", Transactions, Institute of British Geographers, XXXVI (1965), pp. 97-105, and Charles Good, Market Development in Traditionally Marketless Societies: A Perspective on East Africa, Papers in International Studies, Africa Series, No. 12 (Athens: Ohio University, 1971).
12. van Zwanenberg and King, Economic History, p. 184.
13. Ibid., p. 186.
14. D.A. Low, "British East Africa: The Establishment of British Rule 1895-1912", in History of East Africa, ed. V. Harlow and E.M. Chilver (Oxford: Clarendon, 1965), II, pp. 24-26.
15. H. Moyse-Bartlett, The King's African Rifles (Aldershot: Gale and Polden, 1956), p. 206.
16. Roland Oliver, The Missionary Factor in East Africa (London: Longmans, 1967).
17. Edward W. Soja, The Geography of Modernization in Kenya (Syracuse: Syracuse University Press, 1968), pp. 101-106.
18. Ibid., 23.
19. E.A.J. Johnson, The Organization of Space in Developing Countries (Cambridge: Harvard University Press, 1970), pp. 83-92.
20. Ibid., p. 85.
21. P.A. Memon, "Some Geographical Aspects of the History of Urban Development in Kenya", in Hadith 5: Economic and Social History of East Africa, ed. Bethwell A. Ogot (Nairobi: East African Literature Bureau, 1975), pp. 128-153.
22. Soja, Geography of Modernization, p. 24.
23. Ibid., pp. 97-99.
24. C.C. Wrigley, "Kenya: The Patterns of Economic Life: 1902-1945", in History of East Africa, II, pp. 210-264.
25. van Zwanenberg and King, Economic History, pp. 33-43.

26. Meru District Agricultural Department, Annual Report, 1928, Ministry of Agriculture, Nairobi, p.1.

27. van Zwanenberg and King, Economic History, pp. 123-144, 201-226, 275-298.

28. E.A. Brett, Colonialism and Underdevelopment in East Africa (London: Heinemann, 1973).

29. C.M. Elliott, "Agriculture and Economic Development in Africa: Theory and Experience 1880-1914", in Agrarian Change and Economic Development, E.L. Jones and S.J. Woolf eds., (London: Methuen, 1969), pp.123-150.

30. Meru District Commissioner, Annual Report 1912/13, National Archives, Nairobi, pp. 29-30 (hereafter M.D.C.).

31. M.D.C., Annual Report, 1925, p. 8.

32. A.J. Hopkins, Trail Blazers and Road Makers, (London: Henry Hooks, n.d.), p. 111.

33. Edward H. Greeley, "Family Planning in Southern Meru: The Background to Successful Male Acceptance", (Nairobi: Bureau of Educational Research, University of Nairobi, Staff Paper 1975). Mimeographed.

34. Eric S. Clayton, Agrarian Development in Peasant Economies: Some Lessons from Kenya (New York: Praeger, 1966), pp. 237-238.

35. M.D.C., Annual Report, 1949, p. 2.

36. M.D.C., Annual Report, 1935, pp. 14-16; M.D.C., Annual Report, p. 26.

37. M.D.C., Annual Report, 1914/15, p. 2; M.D.C., Annual Report, 1915/16, p. 28.

38. M.D.C., Annual Report, 1924, p. 11; M.D.C., Annual Report, 1927, p. 17; M.D.C. Annual Report, 1928, p. 3; M.D.C., Annual Report, 1936, p. 16; M.D.C., Annual Report, 1939, p. 50.

39. An interesting commentary on the disintegrating effects of colonial decision-making in Meru may be found in H.E. Lambert, "Disintegration and Reintegration in the Meru Tribe", (Nairobi: National Archives, 1939). Typewritten.

40. M.D.C., Annual Report, 1911/12, p. 6.

41. M.D.C., Annual Report, 1940, p. 35.

42. M.D.C., Annual Report, 1918/19, pp. 1-3.

43. M.D.C., Annual Report, 1929, 5-6.

44. M.D.C., Annual Report, 1935, p. 21.

45. Ibid., p. 2.

46. van Zwanenberg and King, Economic History, p. 40.

47. Wrigley, "Kenya: Patterns of Economic Life", pp. 210-214.

48. Meru District Agricultural Department, Annual Report, 1961, Ministry of Agriculture, Nairobi, Appendix II, p. 7.

49. van Zwanenberg and King, Economic History, p. 40.

50. M.D.C., Annual Report, 1940, p. 36.

51. M.D.C., Annual Report, 1934, pp. 34-35.

52. Ibid., p. 35; M.D.C., Annual Report, 1938, p. 34.

53. van Zwanenberg and King, Economic History, pp. 97-102.

54. Soja, Geography of Modernization, p. 85.

55. Max F. Millikan and David Hapgood, No Easy Harvest: The Dilemma of Agriculture in Developing Countries (Boston: Little Brown, 1967), p. 25.

Bibliography

Abiodun, Josephine Olu. "Urban Hierarchy in a Developing Country." Economic Geography 43:4 (October 1967).

Acquaah-Harrison, R. Rural Urban Disparities: Spatial Dimensions of Development Strategies. Toronto: 1975.

Ahmad, Qazi. Indian Cities: Characteristics and Correlates. Chicago: University of Chicago Press, Research Paper 102 (1965).

Alonso, W. "The Form of Cities in Developing Countries". Papers and Proceedings of the Regional Science Association XIII (1974).

Andersen, Kaj Blegrad. African Traditional Architecture: A Study of the Housing and Settlement Patterns of Rural Kenya. Nairobi: Oxford University Press.(1977).

Anonymous. Land Tenure File. Nairobi: Ministry of Agriculture Library.

Arkel-Hardwick, Alfred. An Ivory Trader in North Kenia. London: Longmans Green (1903).

Bailly, A.S. "Les théories de l'organisation de l'espace urbain". L'Espace géographique, Regions - Environnement. T. II, No. 2 (1973).

Baran, Paul A. The Political Economy of Growth. New York: Monthly Review Press (1957).

Bascom, W.R. and M.J. Herkovits (eds.), Continuity and Change in African Cultures. Chicago: University of Chicago Press. (1962).

Bawden, M.J. "Downtown Through Time". Economic Geography 47 (1971).

Bernard, Frank E. East of Mount Kenya: Meru Agriculture in Transition. Munich: Weltforum Verlag. (1973).

Bernardi, Bernardo. The Mugwe: A Failing Prophet. London: Oxford University. (1959).

Bell, Frederick W. "Relation of the Region, Industrial Mix and the Production Function to Metropolitan Wage Levels." Review of Economics and Statistics 49. (August 1967).

Berry, Brian J.L. Commercial Structure and Commercial Blight. University of Chicago, Department of Geography Research Paper No. 85, 1963.

Berry, Brian J.L. Essays on Commodity Flows and the Spatial Structure of the Indian Economy. Chicago: University of Chicago Department of Geography. (1966).

Berry, Brian J.L. Geography of Market Centers and Retail Distribution. Englewood Cliffs, New Jersey: Prentice-Hall (1967).

293

Berry, Brian J.L. "Hierarchical Diffusion: the Basis of Developmental Filtering and Spread in a System of Growth Centers". Growth Centers in Regional Economic Development. Niles Hansen (ed.) New York: Free Press. (1972).

Berry, Brian J.L. "Latent Structure of the American Urban Systems with International Comparisons". in Brian J.L. Berry (ed.) City Classification Handbook: Methods and Applications. New York: Wiley-Interscience. (1972).

Berry, Brian J.L. "The Organisation of Population". Atlas of Economic Development. Norton Ginsberg (ed.) Chicago: University of Chicago Press. (1961).

Berry, Brian J.L. "Relationships between Regional and Economic Development and the Urban System: the Case of Chile". Tijdschrift voor Economische en sociale Geografie 60:5. (1969).

Blacker, J.C. "Demography". East Africa: Its Peoples and Resources. Nairobi: Oxford University Press (1972).

Bohnert, J.E. and P.E. Mattingly. "Delimitation of C.B.D. Through Time". Economic Geography 40. (1964).

Boyes, J. King of the Wakikuyu. London: Frank Cass and Co. (1968).

Board, C.; R.J. Davies and T.J.D. Fair. "The Structure of the South African Space Economy: an Integrated Approach." Regional Studies 4. (1970).

Brett, E.A. Colonialism and Underdevelopment in East Africa: The Politics of Economic Change 1919-1939. New York: NOK Publications. (1973).

Brookfield, Harold C. Interdependent Development. London: Methuen (1975).

Brookfield, Harold C. "On One Geography and a Third World". Transactions of Institute of British Geographers. 58 (1973).

Buchanan, Colin and Partners. Programmes of Urban Studies. Nairobi: East African Engineering Consultants, Final Draft Monograph, 1970.

Bullock, R.A. "Landscape Change in Kiambu". East African Geographical Review. Vol. 3, 1965.

Bullock, R.A. Land Consolidation in Kiambu, Kenya - A Study in Social and Agrarian Change. Queen's University of Belfast, unpublished M.A. thesis (1960).

Bullock, R.A. "Subsistence to Cash: Economic Change in Rural Kiambu". Cahiers d'Etudes Africaines. 56. (1975).

Burgess, E.W. "The Growth of the City". Proceedings of the American Sociological Society 18. (1923).

Bunker, Raymond. Town and Country or City and Region? Melbourne: Melbourne University (1971).

Cagnolo, C. The Akikuyu: Their Customs, Traditions and Folklore. Nyeri: The Mission Printing School. (1933).

Carruthers, W.I. "Service Centers in Greater London" Town Planning Review. (1962).

Chanler, W.A. Through Jungle and Desert: Travels in East Africa. (London: Macmillan 1896).

Christaller, Walter. Central Places in Southern Germany. Translated by C.W. Baskin. Englewood Cliffs, New Jersey: Prentice-Hall (1966).

Clark, D. "The Formal and Functional Structure of Wales". Annals of the Association of American Geographers (63). (March 1973).

Clark, D., W.K.D. Davies and R.J. Johnston. "The Application of Factor Analysis in Human Geography." The Statistician. R 3(1974).

Clark, Paul G. "Towards More Comprehensive Planning in East Africa". East African Economics Review 10:2 (December 1963).

Clayton, Christopher. "Communication and Spatial Structure". Tijdschrift voor Econ. en Soc. Geografie. 65 (1974).

Clayton, Eric S. Agrarian Development in Peasant Economies: Some Lessons from Kenya. (New York: Praeger, 1966).

Colbatch, H. personal communication to the author.

Crawshay, R. "Kikuyu: Notes on the Country, People, Fauna and Flora." Geographical Journal 20 (1902).

Cochran, W.G. Statistical Methods. Ames, Iowa: Iowa State University Press (1967).

Curry, L. "Central Places in the Random Spatial Economy". Journal of Regional Science (1967).

Curzon, Lord Curzon of Keddleston. Frontiers. Oxford: Clarendon Press (1907).

Dacey, M.F. "A Probability Model for Central Place Locations". Annals of the Association of American Geographers. 56.

Davies, R.J. and D.S. Rajah. "The Durban C.B.D.: Boundary Delimitation and Racial Dualism". The East African Geographical Journal. 47 (December 1965).

Davies, R.L. "Effects of Consumer Income Differences on the Business Provisions of Small Shopping Centres". Urban Studies 5 (1968).

Davis, D.H. Land Use in Central Capetown: A Study in Urban Geography. Capetown: Longmans, 1965.

Davis, J.T. "Development of the Small-Farm Sector in Kenya, 1954-1972". The Canadian Geographer Vol. XXL, 1 (Spring 1977).

de Blij, H.J. Dar-es-Salaam: A Study in Urban Geography. Evanston: Northwestern University Press (1962).

de Blij, Harm J. "Functional Structure and Central Business District of Laurenco Marques, Mozambique". Economic Geography 38 (1962).

de Blij, Harm J. Mombasa: An African City. Chicago: Northwestern University Press (1968).

Denison, Edward F. "Comment". Regional Income Studies in Income and Wealth. Frank A. Hanna (ed.) Princeton: National Bureau of Economic Research (1957).

Diamond, D.R. "The Central Business District of Glasgow". Proceedings of the International Geographical Union Symposium in Urban Geography. Lund Studies in Human Geography Series B, No.24 (1962).

Dodge, S.D. "House Types in Africa". Papers Michigan Academy of Sciences Arts and Letters 10. (1929).

Eastwell, J.A.N. "Kenya 2000: A Study of Increasing Population Pressure in a Developing Country: Planning Possibilities in an Ecologic-Economic Perspective. M.Sc. thesis. University of Toronto (1973).

Elliott, C.M. "Agriculture and Economic Development in Africa: Theory and Experience 1880-1914". Agrarian Change and Economic Development. London" Methuen, 1969.

El-Shakhs, Salah. "Development, Primacy and Systems of Cities". Journal of Developing Areas XII (1972).

El-Shakhs, Salah and R.A. Obudho. Urbanization, National Development and Regional Planning in Africa. New York: Praeger, 1974.

Fadiman, Jeffrey. Mountain Warriors: The Pre-Colonial Meru of Mount Kenya, Papers in International Studies, Africa Series, No. 12. Athens: Ohio University, 1976.

Fair, T.J. "A Regional Approach to Economic Development in Kenya". South African Geographical Journal. Vol. 45, 1963.

Fearn, Hugh. An African Economy: An Economic Study of Development of the Nyanza Province of Kenya 1903-1953. London: Oxford University Press, 1961.

Frank, Andre B. Capitalism and Underdevelopment in Latin America. New York: Monthly Review Press, 1969.

Friedmann,John. "A General Theory of Polarized Development". Growth Centers in Regional Economic Development. New York: The Free Press, 1972.

Friedmann, John. Urbanization, Planning, and National Development. Beverley Hills: Sage Publications, 1973.

Friedmann, John and M. Douglass. "Agropolitan Development: Towards a New Strategy for Regional Planning in Asia". UNCRD, Growth Pole Strategy and Regional Development Planning in Asia. Nagoya, Japan.

Friedmann, John and C. Weaver. Territory and Function: The Evolution of Regional Planning. London: Edward Arnold, 1979.

Gaile, Gary. The Spatial Reorganization of Development around Growth Centers. UCLA: Ph.D. Thesis 1976.

Gambini, Raymond. A Computer Program for Calculating Lines of Equilibrium Between Multiple Centers of Attraction. Lawrence, Kansas: Center for Regional Studies, University of Kansas, 1966.

Gambini, Raymond; David L. Huff and George F. Jenks. "Geometric Properties of Market Areas". Papers of the Regional Science Association. 20 (1968).

Garner, B.J. "The Internal Structure of Retail Nucleations". Northwestern University Studies in Geography No. 12 (1966).

Garner, B.J. "A Review of Murphy's "The Central Business District'". The Canadian Geographer 17 (1973).

Garrison, W.L. et al. Studies of Highway Development and Geographic Change. Washington, D.C. (1959).

Gebremedhin, N. "Some Traditional Types of Housing in Ethiopia". Shelter in Africa. London: Bassie and Jenkins, 1971.

Georgulas, Nikos. An Approach to Urban Analysis for East African Towns with Particular Reference to the African Population. Syracuse, New York: Maxwell Graduate School of Citizenship and Public Affairs Occasional Paper 4. Program of East African Studies.(1963).

Gilbert, A.G., D.E. Goodman. "Regional Income Disparities and Economic Development: A Critique". Development Planning and Spatial Structure. London: Wiley, 1976.

Gitao, T.K. "Location of Industry and Policies for Location in Kenya". The Role of Urban and Regional Planning in National Development for East Africa. Kampala: Milton Obote Foundation, 1970.

Goldschmidt, W. "Foreward". Architecture in Northern Ghana: A Study of Forms and Functions. Berkeley: University of California Press, 1969.

Good, Charles. Market Development in Traditionally Marketless Societies: A Perspective on East Africa. Papers in International Studies, Africa Series No. 12. Athens: Ohio University, 1971.

Gould, Peter R. "Research Strategies for Rural Spatial Planning. Canadian Journal of African Studies 3.1. (Winter 1969).

297

Greeley, Edward H. "Family Planning in Southern
Meru: The Background to Successful Male Accep-
tance". Nairobi: Bureau of Educational Research.
University of Nairobi Staff Paper. 1975. Mimeo.
Green, F.H.W. "Urban Hinterlands in England and
Wales: An Analysis of Bus Services". Geographi-
cal Journal 116 (1950).
Green, F.H.W. "Urban Hinterlands: Fifteen Years On".
Geographical Journal 132 (1966).
Gregory, Peter. "Wage Structures in Latin America".
Journal of Developing Areas 8 (1974).
Hadden, Jeffrey K. and Edgar F. Borgatta. American
Cities: Their Social Characteristics. Chicago:
Rand McNally, 1965.
Halliman, D. and W.T.W. Morgan. "The City of Nairobi".
Nairobi City and Region. Nairobi: Oxford Uni-
versity Press, 1967.
Hamadan, G. "The Growth and Functional Structure of
Khartoum". Geographical Review 50 (1960).
Hapgood, David and Max F. Millikan. No Easy Harvest:
The Dilemma of Agriculture in Developing Coun-
tries. Boston: Little Brown, 1967.
Harris, C.D. and E.L. Ullman. "The Nature of Cities".
Annals of American Acedemy of Political and Soc-
ial Science. 242 (1945).
Hartman. "The Central Business District: A Study
in Urban Geography". Economic Geography 26 (1950).
Harttenstein, W. and G. Staack. "Land Use in the
Urban Core". Urban Core and Inner City. Leiden:
E.J. Brill, 1967.
Harwitz, M. "On Improving the Lot of the Poorest:
Economic Plans in Kenya". African Studies Review.
Vol. XXI, No. 3, 1978.
Hill, M.F. "Planters Progress, Coffee Board of Kenya".
Nairobi: East African Standard, 1956.
Hirschman, Albert O. The Strategy of Economic Devel-
opment. New Haven, Connecticut: Yale University
Press, 1958.
Hirst, Michael A. "Telephone Transactions, Regional
Inequality and Urban Growth in East Africa".
Tijdschrift voor Econ. en Soc. Geografie 66 (1975).
Hodder, B.W. "Some Comments on the Origins of Tra-
ditional Markets in Africa South of the Sahara".
Transactions Institute of British Geographers
XXXVI (1965).
Hodge, Gerald. "Developing Regional Statistics for
Policy Purposes: The Prediction of Trade Centre
Viability in Saskatchewan". Papers on Regional
Statistical Studies. Toronto: University of
Toronto, 1966.
Hopkins, A.J. Trail Blazers and Road Makers. London:
Henry Hooks, n.d.

Horton, F.E. "Locational Factors as Determinants Consumer Attraction to Retail Firms". Annals of the Association of American Geographers 58 (1968).

House, William. "Earnings per Worker Differentials in the Provinces of Kenya 1962-1970". Journal of Developing Areas 9 (July 1975).

House, William J. and Henry Rempel. "An Analysis of the Variation in Modern Sector Earnings Among the Districts and Major Urban Centers in Kenya". Institute for Development Studies Working Paper No. 243. Nairobi: University of Nairobi, 1975.

House, William J. and Henry Rempel. "The Determinants of and Changes in the Structure of Wages and Employment in the Manufacturing Sector of the Kenya Economy". Journal of Development Economics 3 (March 1976).

Hoyt, Homer. "Classification and Significant Characteristics of Shopping Centers". Readings in Urban Geography. Chicago: University of Chicago Press, 1959.

Hoyt, Homer. One Hundred Years of Land Values in Chicago. Chicago: University of Chicago Press, 1933.

Hoyt, Homer. The Structures of Residential Neighborhoods in American Cities. Washington: U.S. Federal Housing Administration, 1939.

Huff, David L. "The Delineation of a National System of Planning Regions on the Basis of Urban Spheres of Influence". Regional Studies, Vol. 7, 1973.

Illeris, Sven. "Hierarchies of Functional Regions: Theoretical Models and Empirical Evidence from Denmark". Geographic Perspectives on Urban Systems with Integrated Readings. Englewood Cliffs, New Jersey: Prentice-Hall, 1970.

International Labour Organization. Employment, Incomes and Inequality: A Strategy for Increasing Productive Employment in Kenya. Geneva: ILO, 1972

Ivanicka, K. "Problems Connected with Research in Regions in Czechoslovakia. Function and Forming of Regions". Acta Geographia, Universatatin Comunen Economico Geographica Nr 8. Bratislavie, 1968.

Jefferson, Mark. "The Law of Primate City". Geographical Review XXIX (1939).

Johnson, E.A.J. The Organization of Space in Developing Countries. Cambridge, Mass.: Harvard University Press, 1970.

Johnson, G.E. and Whitelaw, W.E. "Urban-Rural Income Transfers in Kenya: An Estimated Remittances Function". Economic Development and Cultural

Exchange. Vol. 22, No. 3. 1974.
Keeble, L. Principles and Practice of Town and Country Planning. London: Gazette, 1969.
Kelly, E.J. "Retail Structure of Urban Economy". Traffic Quarterly 9 (1955).
Kenya, Republic of. Development Plan 1970-1974. Nairobi: Government Printer, (1969).
Ibid., Development Plan 1974-1978 (1974).
Ibid., Statistics Division, Ministry of Finance and Economic Planning, Statistical Abstract 1969. Nairobi: Government Printer (1970).
Ibid., Employment and Earnings 1963-1967 (1971)
Ibid., Kenya Population Census, 1969 (Vol. 1), 1970
Ibid., Statistical Abstract 1971 (1972).
Kenya, Republic of. Town Planning Department, Ministry of Lands and Settlement. Regional Physical Development Plans for Central Province (1967), Coast Province (1970), Eastern Province (1960), North Eastern Province (1971), Nyanza Province (1970), Rift Valley Province (1971), Western Province (1970). Nairobi: Govt. Printer.
Kenya, Republic of. U.N. Conference on the Human Environment. A Case Study: Urbanization and Environment in Kenya. Nairobi: Government Printer, 1971.
Kenyatta, Jomo. Facing Mount Kenya. New York: Vintage Books, 1962.
Khan, F.K. and A. Salehuddin. "The City Center of Chittagong". Oriental Geographer 11 (1967).
Kimani, Samson M. "Spatial Structure of Land Values in Nairobi, Kenya". Tijdschrift voor Economische en Sociale Geografie Vol. 63:2 (1972).
Kimani, Samson M., "The Structure of Land Ownership in Nairobi". Journal of Eastern African Research and Development Vol. 2:2 (1972).
Kimani, S.M. and D.R.F. Taylor. Growth Centers and Rural Development. Thika, Kenya: Maxim Printer, 1973.
King, Anne (R.M.A. van Zwanenberg and A. King. An Economic History of Kenya and Uganda 1800-1970. Nairobi: East African Literature Bureau, 1975.
King, Leslie J. "Cross-Sectional Analysis of Canadian Urban Dimensions: 1951 and 1961". Canadian Geographer 10:4 (1966).
Kinyanjui, Kabiru. "The Distribution of Educational Resources and Opportunities in Kenya". Institute for Development Studies Discussion Paper No.208. Nairobi: University of Nairobi, 1975.
Kniffen, F.B. and H. Glassie. "Building in Wood in the Eastern United States: a Time-Place Perspective". Geographical Review 56 (1966).

Krapf, J.L., Travels, Researches, and Missionary Labours During Eighteen Years Residence in Eastern Africa. London: Trubner, 1860.

Lambert, H.E. Interesting commentary on disintegrating effects of colonial decisionmaking in Meru in "Disintegration and Reintegration in the Meru Tribe". Nairobi: National Archives 1939.

Langdon, S. "Multi-National Corporations, Taste Transfer and Underdevelopment: A Case Study from Kenya. Review of African Political Economy No. 2, 1975.

Larimore, Ann E. "The Africanization of Colonial Cities in East Africa". East Lakes Geographers. 5. (December 1969).

Lee, D.R. "Factors Influencing Choice of House Type: A Geographic Analysis from the Sudan". Professional Geographer 21 (1969).

Lee, D.R. "The Nubian House: Persistence of Cultural Tradition". Landscape. 18:1. (1969).

Levine, R.A. "Wealth and Power in Gusiiland". Markets in Africa. Evanston, Illinois: Northwestern University Press, 1962.

Leys, Colin. Underdevelopment in Kenya: The Political Economy of Neo-Colonialism 1964-1971. Berkeley: University of California Press, 1974.

Lo, F.C. and Salih, K. "Rural-Urban Relations and Regional Development Planning". Paper read to 3rd. biennial meeting, Association of Development Research and Training Institutes of Asia and the Pacific. Goa, India: September 1977.

Lo, F.C., Salih, K. and Douglass, M. Uneven Development, Rural-Urban Transformation and Regional Development Alternatives in Asia. UNCRD. Nagoya, Japan, 1978.

Logan, A. "The Pattern of Service Centers in Warringah Shire". Sydney: Sydney University Planning Research Center, 1968.

Low, D.A. "British East Africa: The Establishment of British Rule 1895 to 1912". History of East Africa. Oxford: Clarendon, 1965.

Mabogunje, Akin L. "The Evolution and Analysis of the Retail Structure of Lagos, Nigeria". Economic Geography 55 (1964).

Mabogunje, Akin L. "Urbanization in Nigeria: A Constraint on Economic Development". Economic Development and Cultural Change. 13.4 (July 1965).

Majid, R. "The CBD of Dacca, Delimitation and Internal Structure". Oriental Geographer 14 (1970).

Mardia, K.V. Statistics of Directional Data. London: Academic Press, 1972.

Mascarenhas, A. "Land Use in Dar es Salaam". Tanzania in Maps. New York: Africana Publishing Corporation, 1972.

McConnell, J.E. "The Middle East: Competitive or
Complementary?". Tijdschrift voor Econ. en Soc.
Geografie 58. March-April, 1967.

McIntosh, B.G. "The East Bantu People". In Zamani:
A Survey of East African History. Nairobi: East
African Publishing House, 1968.

McKay, J.R. "The Interactance Hypothesis and Boundaries in Canada: A Preliminary Study". The Canadian Geographer XI. (1958).

McNulty, Michael. "Urban Structure and Development:
the Urban Systems of Ghana". Journal of Developing Areas 3:2 (January 1969).

McRae, D.J. "MIKCA: A FORTRAN IV Iterative K-Means
Cluster Analysis Program". Behavioral Science
10:4 (1971).

Memon, P.A. "Some Geographical Aspects of the History
of Urban Development in Kenya". Hadith 5: Economic and Social History of East Africa. Nairobi:
East African Literature Bureau, 1975.

Meru District Agricultural Department. Annual Report,
1961. Ministry of Agriculture, Nairobi, Appendix
II.

Meru District Commissioner, Annual Report 1911-12.
National Archives, Nairobi.

Ibid., 1912-13.
Ibid., 1914-15.
Ibid., 1915-16.
Ibid., 1918-19.
Ibid., 1925.
Ibid., 1927.
Ibid., 1929.
Ibid., 1924.
Ibid., 1934.
Ibid., 1935.
Ibid., 1938.
Ibid., 1940.
Ibid., 1949.
Ibid., 1928.
Ibid., 1936.
Ibid., 1939.

Millikan, Max F. and David Hapgood. No Easy Harvest:
The Dilemma of Agriculture in Developing Countries.
Boston: Little Brown, 1967.

Morgan, W.T.W. Nairobi: City and Region. Nairobi:
Oxford University Press, 1967.

Morgan, W.T.W. "The White Highlands of Kenya". Geographical Journal 129:2 (June 1963).

Morgan, W.T.W. "Urbanization in Kenya: Origins and
Trends". Transactions. Institute of British
Geographers No. 46 (March 1969).

Moser, C.A. and Wolf Scott. British Towns: A Statistical Study of Their Social and Economic Differences.

Moyse-Bartlett, H. The King's African Rifles. Alder-
    shot: Gale and Polden,(1956).
Muriuki, Godfrey. A History of the Kikuyu 1500 to
    1900. London: Oxford University, 1974.
Murphy, Raymond. The American City: An Urban Geogra-
    phy. New York: McGraw-Hill 1966.
Murphy, R.E. The Central Business District. Chicago:
    Aldine Press, 1972.
Murphy, R.E. and J.E. Vance Jr. "Delimiting the CBD".
    Economic Geography Vol. 30 (1954).
Myrdal, Gunnar. Economic Theory and Underdeveloped
    Regions. London: Methuen, 1957.
Nairobi. Nairobi Master Plan for a Colonial Capital.
    London. Her Majesty's Stationery Office, 1948.
National Christian Council of Kenya. Who Controls
    Industry of Kenya. Nairobi: East African Publi-
    shing House, 1968.
Neumann, A.H. Elephant Hunting in East Equatorial
    Africa. London: Rowland Ward, 1898.
Nystuen, J.D. and M.F. Dacey. "A Graphe Theory Inter-
    pretation of Nodal Regions". Papers and Procee-
    dings of the Regional Science Association 7 (1961).
Obudho, R.A. Development of Urbanization in Kenya:
    A Spatial Analysis and Implications for Regional
    Development Strategy. New Brunswick, New Jersey:
    Unpublished Ph.D. Thesis, 1974.
Obudho, R.A. The Nature of Kenya's Urban Hierarchy:
    Implications for Regional Planning Strategy.
    Nairobi: East African Publishing House, 1978.
Obudho, R.A. Urbanization and Development Planning
    in Kenya. Nairobi: Kenya Literature Bureau, 1979.
Obudho, R.A. "Urbanization and Regional Planning in
    Western Kenya". Urbanization, National Develop-
    ment and Regional Planning in Africa. New York:
    Praeger, 1974.
Obudho, R.A. "Urbanization and Development in Kenya:
    an Historical Appreciation". African Urban Notes.
    1:3 (Fall 1975).
Obudho, R.A. "Spatial Dimension and Demographic Dy-
    namics of Kenya's Urban Subsystems". Pan African
    Journal IX:2.
Obudho, R.A. and Peter P. Waller. Periodic Markets,
    Urbanization and Regional Planning: A Case Study
    from Western Kenya. Westport, Connecticut:
    Greenwood Press, 1976.
Ogendo, R.B. "The Significance of Industrial Zoning
    to Rural Industrial Development in Kenya: A
    Study of the Facts and Methodology". Cahiers
    d'études Africaines, 7 (1947).
Oliver, P. Shelter in Africa. London: Bassie and
    Jenkins, 1971.
Oliver, Roland. The Missionary Factor in East Africa.

London: Longmans, 1967.

Ominde, S.H. The Population of Kenya, Tanzania and Uganda. Nairobi: Heinemann Educational Books, 1975.

Perlman, Richard. Labor Theory. New York: Wiley and Sons, 1969.

Porter, Philip W. Review of The Geography of Modernization in Kenya. Geographic Analysis, 1973.Vol.5.

Pred, Allan. "Behaviour and Location: Foundations for a Geographic and Dynamic Location Theory". Land Studies in Geography. Lund: University of Lund, Series B No. 27, 1967.

Proudfoot, M.J. "City Retail Structure". Economic Geography 13 (1937).

Rapaport, A. House Form and Culture. Englewood Cliffs, New Hersey: Prentice-Hall, 1969.

Ratcliff, R.V. "Internal Arrangement of Land Uses". Urban Land Economics.

Rees, P.H. "Factorial Ecology: An Extended Definition Survey and Critique of the Field". Economic Geography 47:No. 2 Supplement (1971).

Rempel, Henry. "The Rural to Urban Migrant in Kenya". African Urban Notes VI (Spring 1971).

Rempel, Henry and William J. Whitehouse. The Kenyan Employment Problem. Nairobi: Oxford University Press, 1978.

Rondinelli, D.A., and K. Ruddle. Urbanisation and Rural Development. New York: Praeger, 1978.

Rummel, R.J. Applied Factor Analysis. Evanston: Northwestern University Press, 1970.

Russett, B.M. "Delineating International Regions". Quantitative International Politics: Insights and Evidence. New York: International Yearbook of Political Behavior Research, 1967.

Sachs, I. Environment and Development - A New Rationale for Domestic Policy Formulation and International Cooperation Strategies. Environment Canada and CIDA. Ottawa, 1977.

Safier, M. On the Political Economy of Resource Allocationffor Planning. Makerere Institute of Social Research, 1969.

Scott, P. "The Australian CBD". Economic Geography 30 (1955).

Scott, Peter. Geography and Retailing. London: Hotchingson, 1970.

Secomski, Kasimierz. "Modern Factors in Development Policy of Metropolitan Areas". Urban and Social Economics in Market and Planned Economies: Policy Planning and Development. New York: Praeger, 1974.

Seers, D. "The New Meaning of Development". International Development Review, Vol. XIX, 3. (1977-3).

304

Smailes, A.E.   "The Central Business District of
     Cities". Geographical Review, 45 (1955).
Smailes, Peter J. "Some Aspects of the South Austra-
     lian Urban System". The Australian Geographer,
     XI, 1969.
Smout, M.A.H. "The Hierarchy of Central Places in
     Natal". Tijdschrift voor Economische en Social
     Geografie, 61:1, 1970.
Smith, Robert H.T.   "The Functions of Australian
     Towns". Tijdschrift voor Economische en Sociale
     Geografie, 56:3 (1965).
Soja, Edward W. The Geography of Modernization in
     Kenya: A Spatial Analysis of Social, Economic
     and Political Change. Syracuse Geographical
     Series No. 2. Syracuse: Syracuse University Press
     1968.
Soja, Edward W. The Political Organization of Space.
     Washington, D.C.: Association of American Geo-
     graphers Resource Paper No. 2,1971.
Soja, Edward W. "Rural-Urban Interaction". Canadian
     Journal of African Studies, 3:1 (Winter 1969).
Soja, Edward W. Social Justice and the City. Baltimore:
     Johns Hopkins University Press, 1973.
Soja, Edward W. "Transaction Flows and National Unity:
     The Nigerian Case". Expanding Horizons in African
     Studies. Evanston: Northwestern Press 1969.
Soja, Edward W. and Richard J. Tobin. "The Geography
     of Modernization: Paths, Patterns and Processes
     of Spatial Change in Developing Countries".
     A Policy Approach to the Study of Political Dev-
     elopment and Change. New York: The Free Press,1974.
Soja, Edward W. and C. Weaver. "Urbanisation and Un-
     derdevelopment in East Africa". Urbanisation and
     Counter-Urbanisation. New York: Sage, 1978.
Sommer, John W. "Spatial Aspects of Urbanization an
     Political Integration in the Sudan". Urbaniza-
     tion, National Development and Regional Planning
     in Africa. New York: Praeger, 1974.
Stohr, W., D.R.F. Taylor. Development from Above or
     Below? A Radical Reappraisal of Spatial Planning
     in Developing Countries. London: Wiley. Forth-
     coming.
Stohr, W., F. Todtling. "Spatial Equity - Some Anti-
     theses to Current Regional Development Doctrine".
     Paper read to the IGU Commission on Regional
     Aspects of Development. Dushambe, U.S.S.R.:
     July 1976.
Sutton, J.E.G. "The Settlement of East Africa". Zamini:
     A Survey of East African History. Nairobi: East
     African Publishing House, 1968.
Taafe, E.J., R.L. Morrill and P.R. Gould. Geographi-
     cal Review 53 (1963).

Tate, H.R. "Journal to the Rendile Country, British East Africa". Geographical Journal, XXIII (1904).

Taylor, D.R.F. Development of Central Places in the Coast Province of Kenya. Ottawa: Department of Geography, Carleton University, 1974.

Taylor, D.R.F. "The Role of the Smaller Urban Place in Development: A Case Study of Kenya". Urbanization, National Development and Regional Planning in Africa. New York: Praeger, 1974.

Taylor, D.R.F. "Spatial Organisation and Rural Development". Freedom and Change: Essays in Honour of Lester B. Pearson. Toronto: McClelland and Stewart, 1975.

Taylor, D.R.F. "Growth Centres and Rural Development in Africa". Regional Development and Planning: International Perspectives. Leiden: Sithoff, 1975.

Taylor, D.R.F. "Regional Studies, Social Systems and Regional Policy in Africa, An Appraisal". Paper read to the European Regional Science Congress, Krakow: August 1977.

Thomas, E.N. "Some Comments on the Functional Bases of Small Iowa Towns". Iowa Business Digest, 1960.

Thorpe, D. and G.A. Nader. "Customer Movement and Shopping Center Study: A Study of a Central Place System in Northern Durham". Regional Studies, 1, 1967.

Tiwari, R.C. C.B.D. Delimitation in Developing Countries: A Case Study of Nairobi, Kenya. Paper read at the 4th Annual Conference, The Canadian Association of African Studies. Halifax, 1974.

U.S. Department of Housing and Urban Development, Division of International Affairs. Housing in the Ivory Coast. Washington, D.C.: Government Printer, 1966.

Ibid., Housing in Nigeria. Washington, D.C.: Government Printer, 1964.

van Zwandenberg, R.M.A. and Anne King. An Economic History of Kenya and Uganda 1800-1970. Nairobi: East African Literature Bureau, 1975.

Vukovich, A. Population and Employment. Nairobi: Draft paper Technical Appendix No. 1, 1971.

Waller, P.O. et al. Basic Features of Regional Planning in the Region of Kisumu (Kenya). Berlin: Deutches Institut fur Entwicklungspolitik, 1960.

Walton, J. African Village. Pretoria: J.L. van Schaik. 1956.

Weaver, C. "Regional Theory and Regionalism: Towards Rethinking the Regional Question". Comparative Urbanisation Studies. School of Architecture and Urban Planning, University of California. Los Angeles, 1978.

Weinand, Herbert E. "Some Spatial Aspects of Economic Development in Nigeria". Journal of Developing Areas, 7:2 (January 1973).

Weiss, S.F. The Central Business District in Transi-
tion. Research Paper No. 1, City and Regional
Studies,University of North Carolina. North
Carolina: Chapel Hill, 1957.

Wescott, Clay G. "Industrial Location and Public
Policy, the Case of Kenya's Textile Industry".
Institute for Development Studies Working Paper
288. University of Nairobi, 1976.

Whitelaw, W.E., and G.E. Johnson. "Urban-Rural Income
Transfers in Kenya: An Estimated Remittances
Function". Economic Development and Cultural
Exchange. Vol. 22, No. 3, 1974.

Williamson, Jeffrey G. "Regional Inequality and the
Process of National Development". Economic Development and Cultural Change, 13. 1965.

Wood, Leslie J. "Spatial Interaction and Partitions
of Rural Market Space". Tijdschrift voor Econ.
en Soc. Geografie 65 (1974).

Wrigley, C.C. "Kenya: The Patterns of Economic Life:
1902-1945". History of East Africa, II.

Yeates, M. An Introduction to Quantitative Analysis
in Human Geography. Toronto: McGraw Hill, 1974.

Zipf, George K. National Unity and Disunity. Bloomington, Indiana: Principia Press, 1941.

About the Authors

Frank E. Bernard is currently Professor of Geography
and Chairman of the Department of Geography, University of Ohio. His current research is on rural population in Kenya and is supported by a Rockefeller Foundation Grant. He is author of East of Mount Kenya:
Meru Agriculture in Transition, Humanities Press 1972.
        Professor Bernard holds an M.A. and Ph.D. in
geography from the University of Wisconsin at Madison.

R.A. Bullock is an Associate Professor in the Department of Geography at the University of Waterloo, Waterloo, Ontario. He has published a number of works on
Kiambu, the principal of which are: "Landscape changes
in Kiambu", East African Geographical Review 3 (1965),
37-45; "Subsistence to cash: economic change in rural
Kiambu", Cahiers d'Etudes Africaines, 56 (1974) 699-
714; Ndeiya, Kikuyu frontier: the Kenya land problem
in microcosm, University of Waterloo, Department of
Geography Publication Series No. 6, (1975) 144 pp.
        Professor Bullock holds a B.A. and M.A. from the
Queen's University of Belfast, and a Ph.D. from the
University of London.

Alan Ferguson has been a Lecturer in Geography at the
University of Nairobi since 1973. Dr. Ferguson has
published articles in several different fields of
human geography. He has contributed to the Journal of
Tropical Geography, Institute of British Geographers
Transactions, AREA, Tropical Geographical Medicine
and other learned journals.
        Dr. Ferguson's main research interests are in
medical geography, underdevelopment theory, spatial
perception and quantitative applications.
        Dr. Ferguson holds a B.A. from Strathclyde Univer-
sity, Scotland and a Ph.D. from Bristol University,
England.

G.L. Gaile is Assistant Professor of Geography and
Urban Affairs at Northwestern University, Evanston,
Illinois. Dr. Gaile has published many articles on
urban and regional development, planning, and mathe-
matical geography. His articles have appeared or are
forthcoming in Economic Geography, Geographical Analysis, Environment and Planning, East African Geographical Review, International Geography, Regional Studies,
and the Institute of British Geographers Concepts and
Techniques in Modern Geography (CATMOG) monograph
series. His dissertation "The Spatial Reorganization
of Development around Growth Centers" won the Regional
Science Dissertation Competition in 1977.

311

Dr. Gaile holds a B.A. in economics and geograpy from the University of California at Los Angeles, and an M.A., C. Phil., and Ph.D. in geography from the University of California at Los Angeles.

William J. House is currently Senior Lecturer, Department of Economics, University of Nairobi. Publications include papers in Oxford Economic Papers, Oxford Bulletin of Economics and Statistics, Journal of Development Economics, Journal of Development Studies, World Development and Economic Development and Cultural Change. In addition, he is joint author of The Kenya Employment Problem: An Analysis of the Modern Sector Labour Market (Nairobi: Oxford University Press 1978) with Dr. Henry Rempel.

Current research interests include the functioning of the urban labor market and the role of the informal sector.

Dr. House received his Ph.D. from Brown University.

David L. Huff is a Professor of Resources and Geography at the University of Texas at Austin. He has published widely in geography, marketing, and regional economics in such journals as Journal of Regional Science, Land Economics, Journal of Marketing, Journal of Marketing Research, Annals of the Association of American Geographers, Economic Geography, and the Journal of Regional Studies. He has also authored several monographs and contributed chapters to several books.

James M. Lutz is an Assistant Professor of Political Science at West Virginia University. He has recently co-authored The United States and World Trade: Changing Patterns and Dimensions (1978). In addition he was a co-author for a monograph, Industrial Classification, Regional Market Structure and Divestiture, has co-authored articles published in or accepted by Economic Geography and Policy Analysis and Information Systems, and has contributed a chapter on Tunisia to Carl Leiden and R. Stookey (eds.), Political Parties of the Middle East (forthcoming).

Dr. Lutz received both his M.A. and Ph.D. from the University of Texas at Austin. After teaching there for a year, he joined the faculty at West Virginia University in 1976.

Wayne McKim is an Associate Professor in the Department of Geography and Environmental Planning at Towson State University, Baltimore, Maryland. He has been a Senior Lecturer in the Department of Geography at the University of Dar es Salaam from 1977 to 1979. He has

conducted research on the periodic market system in
Northeastern Ghana (Economic Geography, vol. 48, pp.
333-344, 1972) and is currently doing research on the
marketing system in Rufiji District of Tanzania.

Dr. McKim received a B.A. in history and an M.A.
in geography from Michigan State University, and a
Ph.D. from Northwestern University.

R.A. Obudho is Planning Analyst, Johnson & Johnson
Worldwide, and adjunct Lecturer of Urban Studies,
Rutgers University. Formerly he was an Instructor
of Geography, Rutgers University (1970-1973). He is
currently a member of the Board of Editors, Social Indicators Research Journal and African Studies Review
Journal.

Dr. Obudho's principal research includes the urbanization process and regional planning in developing countries, with particular emphasis on Africa.
His major publications include: co-editor of The Computer and Africa: Applications, Problems and Potential;
co-author of Urbanization, City and Regional Planning
in Metropolitan Kisumu, Kenya: Bibliographical Survey
of an East African City; author of and contributor to
Urbanization, National Development and Regional Planning in Africa; co-author of Periodic Markets, Urbanization and Regional Planning — a Case Study from
Western Kenya; author of The Nature of Kenya Urban
Hierarchy: Implication for Regional Planning Strategy;
editor and contributor to Development of Urban Systems
in Africa; and editor of and contributor to Urbanization and Development Planning in Kenya.

Dr. Obudho holds an A.A.Sc. from the State University of New York College at Cobleskill; a B.Sc. from
the State University of New York at Albany; a Diploma
in Education from the University of Nairobi; and an
M.A. and Ph.D. from Rutgers University, New Brunswick,
New Jersey.

Simeon H. Ominde is a Professor of Geography and Director, Population Studies and Research Institute, University of Nairobi. Professor Ominde has published
widely in the area of Population Geography. There are
very many textbooks, articles and papers to his credit
a list of which would fill several pages. He has
travelled widely and his international image as a
scholar is indeed incomparable.

Professor Ominde holds an M.A. (Aberdeen), a Ph.D.
(London), a Dip. Ed. (E.A. and Edinburgh), and he is
a Fellow of the Royal Geographical Society (FRGS).
In August 1978 Dr. Ominde received the first Nigerian
National Geographical Association Distinguished Award
for Contribution to the Science of Geography in Africa.

313

Henry Rempel is Associate Professor of Economics at the University of Manitoba, Winnipeg. Dr. Rempel, jointly with Dr. W.J. House, has published several articles on the operation of labor markets in Kenya. These have appeared in The Oxford Bulletin of Economics and Statistics, the Journal of Development Economics, and Economic Development and Cultural Change. He also co-authored with Valerie Collier an article in Journal of Development Studies. In addition Dr. Rempel and Dr. House co-authored the book The Kenyan Employment Problem - An Analysis of the Modern Sector Labor Market (Oxford University Press, Nairobi).

Dr. Rempel holds an M.A. degree in Economics from Ohio State University and a Ph.D. in Economics from the University of Wisconsin.

Edward W. Soja is a Professor of Urban and Regional Planning at the University of California (La.) and has written many articles and books on problems of African development. Representative of his publications on East Africa are The Geography of Modernization in Kenya (Syracuse University Press, 1968) and "Urbanization and Underdevelopment in East Africa," (in B.J.L. Berry, Urbanization and Counter-Urbanization, 1976).

Professor Soja has an M.A. (Wisconsin) and a Ph.D. (Syracuse) in geography. In the past he has taught at Northwestern University and was a visiting Professor at the Univer sity of Nairobi, the University of Ibadan and the Interdisciplinary Institute for Spatial Planning, Vienna.

D.R.F. Taylor is Professor of Geography and International Affairs at Carleton University, Ottawa, Canada. Dr. Taylor has published widely in the areas of geography, rural development, computer cartography, and regional planning. Among his major publications are: Growth Centers and Rural Development in Kenya, Thika, Kenya 1973 (with S.M. Kimani), The Computer and Africa Applications Problems and Potential (Praeger 1977); contributing editor, Development from Above or Below? A Radical Re-Appraisal of Spatial Planning in Developing Countries (Wiley 1980) with W. Stohr, and The Computer in Contemporary Cartography (Wiley 1980). Dr. Taylor has also contributed chapters to several books.

Dr. Taylor holds an M.A. and Ph.D. in geography from the University of Edinburgh and a P.G.C.E. from the University of London.

Ramesh C. Tiwari, Ph.D. from University of Reading, is
an Associate Professor of Geography at the University
of Manitoba, Winnipeg. His main interests are in
social geography and the functional structures of
central business districts of cities in developing
and developed countries. He has published on the
social agglomerations among Asians in Nairobi in the
Scottish Geographical Magazine 85 (1969) and African
Urban Notes (winter 1972), and "Some Observations on
Housing Policy and House Ownership in Nairobi" in
the Proceedings of the Regional Conference of the IGU,
Lagos, Nigeria in 1978. He is the co-author of a
forthcoming book, Nairobi: Geography of a Growing
City, to be published by Longmans of Africa, Nairobi.
He has read several papers on aspects of modernization
and urbanization in some parts of India.